Feb. 1954

b

STILLMEADOW
AND
SUGARBRIDGE

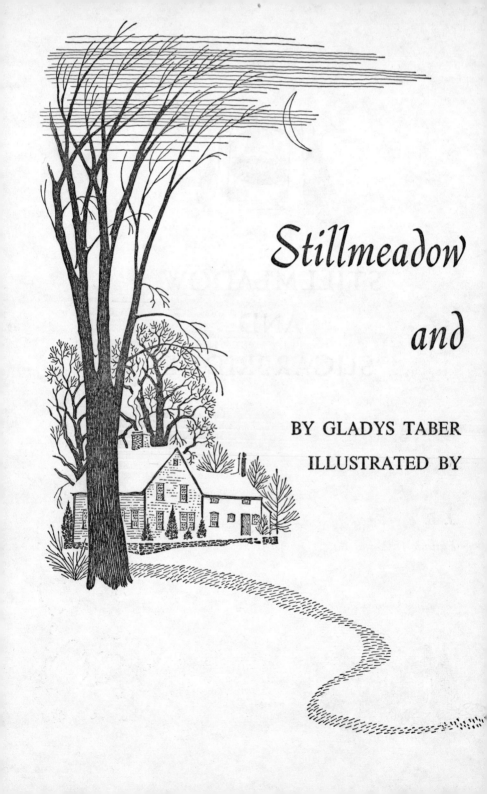

Stillmeadow

and

BY GLADYS TABER

ILLUSTRATED BY

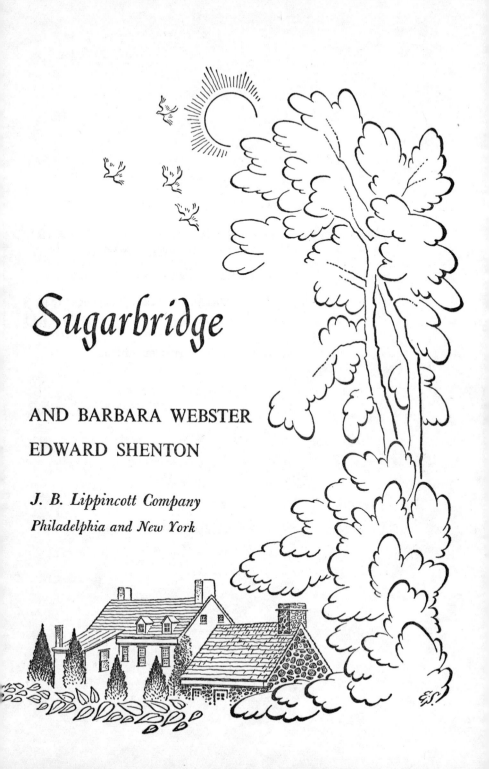

Sugarbridge

AND BARBARA WEBSTER

EDWARD SHENTON

J. B. Lippincott Company
Philadelphia and New York

CONTENTS

STILLMEADOW
AND
SUGARBRIDGE

JANUARY

DEAR GLADYS,

Do you know that wonderful figure of two-headed Janus on the doorway of Chartres Cathedral? On one side, a long-haired youth gazes eagerly ahead; on the other, a bearded old man contemplates the past. That's the way I feel in January.

When I look back, I know we have got just what we wanted out of life. It was Goethe who said, "Beware of what you wish when you are twenty; you'll have it when you are forty!" Well, we were twenty or thereabouts, and a couple of giddy art students to boot, Ed and I, when we thought that the end of all desiring was a house in the country, and enough time to work. Now we are older, and we have got our wish, but it still seems good to us. We are not wildly successful, nor will we ever become millionaires, but our life at Sugarbridge does give us the intensest personal satisfaction.

I like that pronouncement of Osbert Sitwell to the effect that a writer should see a considerable stretch of time ahead of him before he starts

upon a project, because it somewhat excuses my inability to work an
hour or so, then dash off to keep an engagement, do some chores, perhaps,
and come back to writing once more. A broken-up day is to me a lost day,
and social and business dates, no matter how delightful or important,
hang over me with a sense of doom. So I am particularly grateful for
those long intervals of country peace when we see no one, nor stir from
our studio except for an afternoon ramble over the hills. We no longer
live by the clock, slaves to time; we make our own. Even our animal
family has learned to be patient: Duke stretches out his Great Dane-ish
length beside my bed, waiting for me to get up and give him breakfast,
venturing only a few cello-like moans if I oversleep. Miaow, with his
Siamese caterwauling, is more demanding, but he, too, has been brought
to reason, since we are as stubborn as any cat. Chief, down in his stall,
has to be long-suffering, the barn is too far away for us to hear; only
his glad nickering, when we do finally appear, tells the story of his
privations. He has other lapses too to forgive us; sometimes, when we
run out of feed, he has been known to subsist for days on oatmeal, or
Shredded Wheat biscuit. Yet our own schedule is elastic, so why not
theirs? Dinner is ready when I have finished cooking it. Ed sits in a

3

small window alcove in the kitchen, looking out over the garden. From this point of vantage, he oversees my cooking, and drinks his evening cocktail. When a lilting tune comes over the radio on the wide window sill, he makes me drop what I am doing, and we dance a little, while Duke regards us with a worried air from the sidelines.

Yet we did not always live this way. Through many years we have been becoming what we are today—years of the innumerable errands that more or less conventional living brings: a maid to be fetched, a boy to be taken to school, dancing class, Sunday school, of trains to be caught, of days at the office. In those times we used to think longingly, "Oh, if we could ever be free of this round! If we could work, or not work, at will . . . !" This came to pass finally; the boy grew up, went away to college; the job was given up, the maid no longer needed. We stood on the threshold of our long-awaited dream world.

It is often all too obvious that our ideal is not anybody else's. Last summer a friend of mine, a very urban person, stopped by to see us. She stood beside our studio, which is across the road from the house, and gazed consideringly down the long lane to the barn.

"You know, I think you are very brave to live here," she said, and then I saw it through her eyes: a little house, lost in the hills, from which you could see no other habitation, at the mercy of the elements, or any chance marauders. I was amused at first, but later, thinking it over, I had to admit she was right. You are always at war with Nature in the country, to some degree, and the ordinary activities of life are made more difficult by the ever-present problems of distance and transportation. We were young when we first began to live here, and uncaring of such considerations, but in the years which have followed, a dim awareness of them has been growing in my mind. But the admission was somehow a shock.

We must have planned our house, when we did it over, with no idea that we should ever grow older. Sometimes when I must go out in the rain to reach the freezer, off from the rest of the house in a service wing with no communicating passage, or when I plod over to the studio in occasional sub-zero temperatures, I feel we may have been over-optimistic. But those are only the times when I am not on the top. For the most part, it still seems the best of all possible arrangements, all the clutter of freezing, washing, and other space-taking household work got over at a distance; the studio, deliberately telephone-less, away from it all, since quiet is a necessity. And then, so much walking does fine down the figure. I do not live to eat, I hope, but maybe, if the house were better planned, I might have to begin counting calories.

It is for us, this life; of that I am sure. And sometimes, coming back from a ride, and looking down over the brow of the hill, at the small white

Pennsylvania farmhouse, which has stood there almost two hundred years, wrapped in its blanket of pines, I am content, and know I could live nowhere else.

BARBARA

STILLMEADOW
Weather—terrible!

DEAREST BARBARA:

This is a good day to sit small and snug by the applewood fire and hope the demon winter will miss the electric wires. Sleet laced with snow, a thundering wind, no sky at all, the old house like an early whaler riding it out. You would probably be out in it in your scarlet jacket and navy ski pants, but I am content to watch the chickadees and woodpeckers and bluejays and brown creepers and the two un-named little birds as they dart in from the pines and battle over the peanut butter and suet.

When Jonquil and Teddy and Sister go out, their small cocker bodies skid over the crust, their ears fly, Sister comes right back in rolling like a snowball. The two blondes have a go at the birds and get a strong scolding from the hardy chickadees. "Chick-a-dee-DEE-DEE!"

Teddy is almost a year old, and our very youngest cocker. I wish he could stay a baby rushing about with his rubber rabbit and rubber elephant both in his mouth; his grown-up coat is in since you saw him, all the delicate fuzz is gone and he has a shining smooth coat the color of a frosted maple leaf. Jonquil, his mother, has been trying to steal the toys all afternoon and getting nowhere.

I have been writing letters, and every few minutes Teddy arrives plus rabbit and elephant and leans against me and asks do I STILL love him! Then Sister nudges him away with her compact black and white body and looks at me so earnestly. I love her too, I say. We all love everybody in the house. Maybe even the Guppy does for all I know.

When the weather settles, we must get a Mrs. Guppy to keep him company. He looks so very small and lonesome winding his way around in a canning jar.

Yesterday the men banging away in the cellar gave a horrible whack at a rotted sill and he and his bowl shot into the air and came to earth. He landed in one of the big cracks the old black oak floors are full of. Jill, who in all the years we have lived together has always risen rapidly to an emergency, scooped him out with a match folder and rushed him to a jar. She opines that fish are really a problem. But I told her it wasn't his fault, he was minding his own business in the water plant at the time.

6

We saw the New Year in the very best way. Sitting by the fire and playing our favorite records, just six of us, and talking between times and feeling somehow secure in the steadfast house and the quiet fields and woods outside. I never was much of a horn-blower or confetti-thrower even before we moved to the country, and a roast goose on the old trestle table is better than a sliver of chicken at a night club for my money.

After the New Year came in on the midnight, Jill and I had a few chores to do—dogs out, dogs in, Guppy moved to a warmer spot, the dishwasher to turn on, the heater to fill. Then a few minutes of conversation. You'll be surprised to know we decided it was a fine thing we moved to the country just when we did and that the children had grass under their young feet so much of the time. Even when the mortgage reared its ugly head, we never regretted it and now it is fine to know everything is paid for, our forty acres—although how can man own God's earth?—and the 1690 farmhouse, and the barn, even the pond, and presumably that cricket chirping endlessly on the hearth is also ours.

It seems only yesterday that we first came down this winding country road, knee-deep in ice water, leaving the real estate man to dig out his car. We had to get in through the cellar and the steps were half gone. We emerged into the coldest bleakest room in the world. And there was the fireplace with its hand-hewn stones and rusted iron fittings.

"It's our house," I said firmly, through chattering teeth.

I may tell you that those people who sail on rafts to Peru are not a bit more adventurous than we were at that time. Two women and three young children and three cocker spaniels and no well-heeled husbands to turn over their pay checks! It is still an adventure and the children are on their own, more or less, and the roof is tight and the freezer is full and the furnace is modern now.

I just know a lot of people ask you why you moved out to the country and if you don't get bored in winter. I don't think anybody could get bored in the country. For one thing you can't sit down long enough. Things happen. Pipes burst, well goes dry, heaters go off, dogs get sick, mice arrive in the back kitchen. Japanese beetles swarm on the special roses. Company drives up; in the end, all the world comes to the country for weekends. And you hope there's time to do the laundry before the next batch comes round the mailbox corner.

The house has smelled of wet cocker fur and lentil soup all day, a nice combination. I woke up to a much more violent smell and leapt to my feet and rushed out to the kitchen.

"No, the house is NOT on fire," said Jill calmly, "I only burned up the fat for the dogs' breakfast. It just flamed up."

The whole house reeked with smoke and particles of soot sifted on my breakfast tray. But the only casualty was the stove asbestos mat which now looks like a barbecue grill. And Jill had sprayed everything with the fire extinguisher which left a white chalky silt all over.

But the house was definitely not on fire!

Your stone house is not such a fire hazard, but when you think that the old clapboards of Stillmeadow were hand cut over 200 years ago and the old batten doors, painted and painted down the years, and the wide floor boards, oiled and waxed and oiled and waxed, are not exactly fireproof anywhere, you do think about fire.

But fire is everywhere. When I make a maternal visit to Connie, who has an apartment near Columbia where she teaches, I often leap up in the night and watch the great massive fire engines swish past the stop lights at the corner and wonder just who is tumbling out of bed and running for the street. City folk never know where the fire is, but we in the country listen to our siren and know. And the volunteer firemen drop their ploughs or saws or let the cows stand in the stalls waiting to be milked and fly over the roads. George, the one you met who is our neighbor and helps with the kennel and furnace, is a top fireman. He works a full fourteen-hour day but often jumps up at two in the morning and starts his old car and dashes off to fight the common valley menace, and gets at his chores at six the next morning without any thought that he is a homespun hero.

You must know George better. Although he is the son of a Lithuanian refugee from long-time ago, he is the Yankeeist of Yankees. Cheerful always, hard-working, close-mouthed, he goes his way. If he does something extra-special for us and we thank him, he blushes and looks at the ground and says, "Must help neighbors—" He has only one day off a year, and that is the day he rises early, plucks chickens, drives to the Firemen's Clambake and cooks and serves all day. For this he wears a new blue shirt and dark pants and looks handsome. Once in three years he and his wife do go to the Danbury Fair. And that is all. Whenever he comes stamping in to get the dog food for the kennel and I see his wide and shining smile, I think of all the neurotic people in the world who believe they have a hard life! He will always stop to bring in extra wood or fuss with the water pump which is making wild sounds downstairs, or get the car started on a sleety morning, or shovel a path to the gate or go for the mail.

And if we are in trouble, we simply go to the gate and scream and he materializes from the barn or the upper fields, on a swift bending lope. Quite a guy.

A few months ago, the dog warden phoned him that a stray dog had turned up and he would have to shoot her—so George now has this odd

blonde mongrel along with his old farm shepherd. Naturally, in course of time, the blonde presented him with eight mongrel puppies. Bedded in sweet warm hay in the cow barn, they grew and grew, all different shapes and colors and sizes. Now when I look out in the morning, I see George in his thin jacket and old pants and worn boots walking across the yard in that curious bent gait that farm men have. He is followed by five assorted puppies, and about ten mixed cats and kittens. On the way to the barn, he sets down his milk pail and scoops up a handful and nuzzles them. If I go out, I can hear him talking small squeaky baby talk to them.

George is in his thirties, but his face is as rosy and his eyes as bright as a teen-ager. Now and then he tells me he feels his age when he has caught cold from some really silly thing like wading in ice water half the day. I measure out two aspirin tablets and make him swallow them. He always thinks that *"medcine"* does good.

He knows every one of our ten dogs by personality. "That Blazer," he will say, "he don't eat so good if Tiki is there. I better move him. That Jerry he eats his all up and takes Hildegarde's. I gotta watch."

He feeds the dogs in the kennel in the morning and refills the heaters. Jill gives them their afternoon snack and checks again. The house dogs take their turn being kennel dogs, as we have decided five are all we can have in the house at night. The beds aren't big enough. It is a good thing

9

you aren't raising Danes. Duke is big enough for a whole house by himself. And one thing about cockers, you can have more of them. I won't argue about the Irish. When Daphne runs through the house, everything falls down.

Life with the Irish is not easy. It has color, excitement, great charm, but presents problems. For one thing, Daphne is so much smarter than we are. We have given up spelling words out in front of her, we even try not to think anything we don't want her to sense instantly.

Just let the idea pop in my mind that we might call on a neighbor and Daphne is already at the door, standing on her hind toes and firmly turning the knob with her teeth. She then unhooks the screen with a casual paw and clears the high picket fence in one shining leap, and by the time we are collected, she is in the car.

On the rare occasions when we just can't take her with us, she is perfectly aware that Jill is going to put her in the kennel. She stays just out of reach, waving her beautiful plume of a tail amiably but never letting Jill catch her. No ruse succeeds. Jill may mount to the haymow and Daphne follows with her usual curiosity. At the door she turns and bounds away. Jill calls her in the house. Daphne gets just as far as the door, draws back, gives Jill a knowing look and is off to the pond to chase frogs.

"Well we just can't go," says Jill wearily after an hour of this. We sit down and have a cup of coffee. We say hard things about the impossible Irish. Presently a very soft velvet nose nudges us. There is Daphne, sweeter than a June rose.

"You," says Jill, "why do we keep you?"

Daphne kisses her warmly.

Then we feel guilty shutting her up and as we drive away, the betrayed look on her face is hard to bear.

When she has had enough Obedience Training, she will be so much easier to handle. She hasn't had enough yet to carry the effect over into her social life.

You will be surprised at how much difference it makes in your life with Duke, giving him a course in Obedience. There is nothing to compare with it.

Connie was here for the weekend. Do you ever feel surprised at how fast your Ned has grown up? Surely it was only yesterday that I was buttoning her into her fuzzy pink bunny suit! Now she is reviewing her Anglo-Saxon and getting ready for the German Ph.D. exams.

A year in the country seems a small unit of time. Or is it that we are growing older?

I seldom stop to count back to the time when Jill and I began to dream of a house in the country where the children could spend the summers in the sun. Now and then on a Monday morning we are thankful all over that we are not packing up and rushing back to jobs, she to the Welfare Department and I to Columbia. But usually we are too busy living to look back.

Even the natives have stopped calling our place "the old Oxford Pheasant Farm" although there were times when I thought it would always be that. So I believe, on thinking it over, that we are part of the community for as long as we live.

This is a fine thought to go into a new year with.

Now I wish you all the blessings a New Year can bestow, and plenty of those fabulous guinea hens for the pot.

GLADYS

SUGARBRIDGE

DEAR GLADYS,

Yes, I've been out in the weather. No matter what it may be, I find it impossible to stay inside all day, and often I find foul just as rewarding as fair. Today I took Duke for a walk, not in the ski pants and red shirt you mention, but in rubber boots, as mud prevailed. I went only to salve Duke's wounded feelings; he was cheated of going along when Ed took Chief out earlier. Poor Duke! To follow Chief is his idea of heaven. (Not so Chief; horse regards dog as a prime nuisance, and often when he runs too close in front, Chief leans over and takes a sly equine nip at those tawny flanks.)

Now it is perfectly impossible to deceive Duke about our purpose. Try as we may, by putting on riding clothes out of his sight, by not speaking the word *ride* out loud, which he knows as well as his own name, by being in all ways as secret as can be, when he is not to be taken, he still realizes quite well what is on foot, or on horse, in this case, and begins to go through all his appealing tricks. He stands up and puts his paws on your shoulders, gazing so beseechingly out of his amber eyes that even a cold heart would melt; he takes your wrist gently between his great jaws, and attempts to lead you to the door, saying plainly, "Now, let's go!" But when he is told the sad truth, is bid farewell, and all doors which he can open are firmly bolted, then he lies down with resignation and a deep groan. This touches me so much; I think, no creature should want anything with such intensity, and not get it, if it is in your power to give. But I can only take him for a walk; although this is second best, he is glad to go, and shoots up the lane like a tawny bolt, pausing at the orchard to look back to see if I am surely coming.

It was one of those mild moist days we get in mid-winter sometimes, and we walked up the gradual ascent to where Marshall Grover's neat small house stands on the edge of our land where the woods begin. Duke was already into them, scuffling about among the leaves, but I paused a moment, and looked back into the little valley which holds our house, surrounded by the encircling hills. A day like this has a way of enhancing color, and it was a typical Pennsylvania winter scene. The distance was a deep violet blue, the hills of the next farm the tawny yellow of stubble, or bright emerald of winter rye, a red snow-fence edged a creeping road; the wild hill above our orchard was patched with the red pads of weathering honeysuckle, and across the road from it was a perfectly pink field. Pink is the only word to describe the wonderful winter florescence of bunch grass; it is as though it reaches the zenith of its growth in winter, as other plants do in summer, for never does it exhibit such color as in January or February. It is an amazing shade, partaking at once of orange, vermilion and rose, and I wonder that more landscape painters have not used it in their compositions.

Now I know that it is winter which really binds me to this countryside, for where else in these dreary months could you find a scene of such richness and variety? Other winter landscapes I have known present a monotone drabness. And I was once a painter, you know, and I still remain a mental one, and I rejoice in that sort of primeval earthiness which Pennsylvania seems to have.

Stay-at-homes reap their own harvest. Each time that we get our cold-of-the-year in February, we vow that next time we'll go away in that inclement month. But when the day comes round again, we somehow can't get off. There is always something to keep us, or perhaps we simply cannot tear ourselves away. This may be inertia, but I don't quite think so; chimney pots would not hold me, I'm sure. You always miss something if you are not on hand; even if it is only the delicate day-by-day changing of one season into another, or perhaps, a mild delicious interval like this last one. Monet painted his series of "The Haystacks" with the same instinct. He made a study of the scene at each successive hour of the day in order most fully to realize its every aspect, and I don't doubt that he got something out of the flat monotonous light of noonday, as well as the more paintable dawn and sunset. So I suppose that if we want to be intimate with a place, we have to round out the picture with February mud, and August heat. Is this sour grapes for Florida, and Maine? I hope not. No—I really don't think so.

B

STILLMEADOW

DEAR AND FAR AWAY:

Do you ever have a moment that is absolutely exquisite? Such moments are rare, they are like holding a pink pearl in your palm. Happiness, I think, is being able to live those moments when they come. I had one going out in the moonlight at bedtime, with three cockers and the Irish taking a last look-around. There was a pale winter mist over the meadows, and the sky was a clear dark wider meadow blossoming with stars. The air was quiet and cold and smelled of woodsmoke.

The front-door lantern shone on the sugar maples, the boughs were very dark, and motionless.

I held the moment in my hand.

love to Sugarbridge

SUGARBRIDGE
Twelfth Night

GLADYS DEAR,

In January I always have a salutary feeling of wanting to start afresh, with all accounts settled up, and old prejudices wiped away. I have long suspected this is due to the need for clearing away the Christmas litter, and the earnest resolution that *this* year the Christmas tree ornaments are going to be put away *right*, where you can get at them, and not, as usual, at the bottom of a pile of boxes containing miscellaneous objects saved for goodness knows what reason. This brings me to a sore subject, that of

13

our attic, in itself quite attractive (I love attics), up the last curve of our circular stairway, two low-eaved rooms looking far out over the country-side. It has, nevertheless, become a horror spot, a skeleton in the closet, a guilty family secret. I have been blushing for it ever since the days when our son Ned, a little boy then (and known as Toby, a name which he now repudiates) used to take his friends up there to browse through its cluttered confines. I would take him aside later and whisper, "If you ever take a stranger up to that attic before I have a chance to straighten it up, there's going to be trouble!"

The dusty cluttered place represents all the worst of Shenton character-istics—procrastination, confusion, haste and indecision. Now I come of a family of magpies; they never throw anything away. And since houses, even those of yesterday, have a more or less fixed capacity, once in a while something has to give—or be given. Since the articles in question are usually well past their prime, the recipiented are poor relations, or young couples just starting out in housekeeping. Ed and I, when first married, were the perfect objective for this sort of largesse. We had nothing but the confidence of youth, and a few odds and ends our immediate families had given us. At once a tide of dubious things began to flow in our direction: Uncle Eustace thought it would be wonderful if we could use an ancient shaving stand. (This collapsed immediately when we tried to use it as a typewriter table.) Cousin Delilah gave us a Boston rocker which creaked most dolorously, and other unexpected donations. We received them with thanks and optimism, thinking we might later put them to some use, or else re-give them to someone else. And I must con-fess, too, that occasionally, included among the white elephants, would be something rare and beautiful, a set of Meissen fruit knives, a 15th century ivory plaque in bas relief, which we still treasure. Thus we lost our initial dismay at this influx, and philosophically stacked the misfits in the attic. It was all right as long as the space held out but when there was added to it our own clutter, the out-of-season things and all the put-off mending, there was no place left for walking.

Over it all the years spread their detritus, making a sort of kitchen midden of Shentonalia. Time goes so fast, and has actually so much less effect upon inanimate objects than upon us. I have often mused upon the oddments up there which have outlasted the lifetime of their donors, or perhaps only their affection for us, and I am constantly coming across an absurdly small sock with a hole in its toe, dating from Ned's Toby period. This never fails to give me an uncanny swift sensation of time's passage, something like the shock you feel when an elevator which has been quite motionless in its descent, brings you to a stop with one of those sickening lurches. It is simply incredible, I think, that the years have flipped by so fleetly as to trap these little ghosts from the past.

This year, I vow, the attic shall be weeded out, and all possessions which cannot prove their usefulness shall be ruthlessly cast out on the dump. It shall be a bare and lovely place, where it might be pleasant to go and think sometimes. Of course we'll have to spare the little trundle bed Ned slept in as a child, and my sewing machine, even though I don't often use it, since it is inimical to me, and then, I must keep the rag-bag. I am old-fashioned enough to like one; you never know when you may need a piece of this and that . . . Now perhaps you can see why the attic has never been really cleaned out.

B

STILLMEADOW

The "electric" is off again. Wonder why we don't all get a canoe and head for Tahiti? What would you take for your one book? Excluding the Bible, I mean. I settle for the letters of John Keats. Jill would take Dorothy Sayer's "The Nine Tailors" and just re-read it every few days.

The world outside looks like a wedding cake in a bakery window, very much glazed, and decorated with iced twigs and branches. Even the birds skid as they try to hop around the seed bin. The most surprised bluejay just landed and one leg shot out and away.

So—we have no heat, no water (pump electric too), no lights, no radio. I am glad I didn't succumb to the charm of that white electric typewriter I saw this summer. As the furnace stops breathing, the freezer sighs into silence, the refrig defrosts itself, the house takes on a very odd silent thinking personality. Jill has the great fireplace whacking hot, the oil stove in the back kitchen booming and we are leaning hard on instant coffee—naturally the electric coffee mill is resting on its rubber paws. At this time, of course, the big heater in the back kennel goes out and Jill has to slide out to struggle with it. It is the most maddening single item we own. In warm weather it is roasting hot, when a real Northeaster blows in, it goes out. The two heaters in the front kennels, which were not expensive, boil merrily along. Jill brings a couple more cockers into the house, and shifts the biggest boys around.

And I wish I had my old rusty iron woodstove back again! We had to retire it because it so often went out in the night and all the back plumbing froze stiff. But it was fine to cook on, the baked beans, the tender turkeys, the big glazed hams I did in that stove were really something.

Yes, there is something to be said for *living it out* in this climate.

Don't you notice a kind of special warmth between the folks who stick it out? Who wants to go pick oranges and grapefruit, we ask? A winter sunset is worth all the gold in the Indies. And shoveling tons of snow is fine exercise, just as good as water skiing!

I have put all my African violets by the fire. I wish you could see my Blue Heiress—it is the purest rich color and the leaves are scalloped beautifully. Sailor Girl is sweet too, and the new Painted Girl has one tentative blossom. The white is especially lovely, the color of snowdrops in spring. When we come to see you, I hope to bring you a couple of the sweetest ones. With your green thumbs—both of them—the violets will grow bigger than horses.

Jill has been stumbling around in the darkness of the cellar—flashlight batteries all gone—and hollering up through the floor as to whether we should do pot roast or beef stew. It is pleasant to hang the old black iron kettle on the same hand-forged crane that the early people did. Fireplace cooking is a comfortable thing. The good smell of browning beef, the savory lift of onions, the nip of garlic—all heartening on a bitter winter day when the electric is gone.

By the way, do you have a garlic crusher? Most wonderful gadget in America. Must take on that Tahiti trip. We can grow garlic in Tahiti, I should think. I would really hate a life without garlic.

George has come in and promises to make it to the mailbox and bring us our mail. There is sure to be a letter from Sugarbridge, and news of how you are faring. I hope you will let Chief manage on plain hay if this storm goes that far south and not try to go to the barn with oats. Many a horse would eat hay and like it!

I am glad we gave up our hens, although gathering warm brown eggs was such fun. Hens and cows take too much waiting on. Goats too. I had a friend in Virginia once who got a couple of goats and in no time at all he found he had fifty. He was quite desperate, poor man.

My secret yearning for a seal will never be satisfied, either. I doubt whether a seal would manage in our pond, and we could never get enough raw fish to toss. But a seal is a wonderful animal!

I also would like to have sea horses. Did you know they are the only fish that sing? A small flute-like sound? There is something faery-like about them to me with their strange little faces and mermaid tails.

Jill gave me an Audubon bird call for Christmas and I can now spend any amount of time working at bird calls. I don't think any bird that flies will recognize my bird-talk, but I am making some headway with the chickadee. My Aunt Minnie, who is in the upper seventies, carries her duck call in her knitting bag and can whip it out and call ducks at any time between a purl and a knit. But I am just not the woman she is.

Aunt Minnie, I will have you know, gets her deer every Fall, and she says it is quite simple. She just goes to the place where the deer will be! Then she sits comfortably on a log, rests her thermos of tea beside her and waits. When the deer comes along she shoots him and sits there until some other hunter finds her and helps.

I am a weaker vessel by all counts, for I could never shoot anything. Everyone in my family has been a crack shot and I would like to be able to pot tomato juice cans stuck on a fence post, but to extinguish life in a wild free creature is just not my dish.

I do manage to fish, but every time I pull in a flounder when we are at the Cape, I can see a look in those two eyes that are on one side, and I have to be told all over again that a fish is a cold-blooded etc., etc.

Man is certainly the most predatory animal in the universe. Other animals kill for food, to survive. Man kills to kill. It is not a happy thought. We ought to live on roots and berries and let God's creatures live. On the other hand, a good steak adds strength to the body and zip to the spirit, so I just cannot be consistent about it.

I do hope your oil burner has stopped making those mysterious booming sounds, so unexpected and queer, and that your dishwasher is doing her bit. (A dishwasher must be feminine, nothing masculine would abide such a repetitive job.) And that Ed has time to practise the piano. Sitting in the chilly studio that day after Christmas and hearing Ed's Bach was a fine experience. If I could start over again, I would play something! But my struggles with the mandolin were not crowned with any great success. About all I ever played was "Throw Me a Rose" and "Long, Long Trail." And making music is better than getting it on the air waves, no doubt about it. I get anxious about the children today who get everything secondhand and I am rather glad Connie grew up just before the screen moved into the home. I would love to have TV for some things myself, but I think children are deprived when they do not have to invent their own amusement. It's getting to be a very passive era.

Have your seed catalogues come? And what are you planting come April?

Love from your unelectrified friend,

GLADYS

DEAR GLADYS,

A hunt passes through our land. . . . The sweet cracked note of the horn sounded suddenly near at hand, and Duke, who had been lying before the stove, jumped to his feet with a thunderous roar. He cranes his neck out the window, trembling with eagerness, and watches as several riders come trotting up the lane. Of course I had to run out and look, first being sure the door was firm. Once Duke tried to be a fox-hound, but wasn't a success. I can still remember how dextrously that huntsman whipped him out of the pack. All the neighborhood dogs are barking, and without glancing in that direction, I know that Chief is standing on his head down in the paddock, or running to-and-fro with head upflung, and tail streaming out behind him.

It is a pretty sight as the hunt makes its way over the brow of the hill behind our studio, the fine tall horses and their riders silhouetted against the sky, hounds fanning out before them. But today I can turn away from this colorful picture without a sigh. I have at times hankered after hunting. Although it would be as impossible for me as for Chief, who is quite unmanageable on a hunt; in a crowd, he can't let anyone get ahead of him, even hounds. And I, a writer, housekeeper and chief bottle-washer, dog-trainer and gardener, have no business to take on anything else. But the irrational urge persisted. I would visualize my horse sleek and clipped, whereas in actual fact, the poor dear has to grow a thick wooly winter coat, being all alone in a cold stone barn; I would see him possessing the impassive savoir faire of good hunters, never batting an eye at goats, donkeys and cows, which is far from the case.

I wasted some time in vain regrets. But now all is changed. Not long ago I happened to see in the "Times" Book Review section a picture of a Tartar horseman and his steed, which at once took possession of me. Why, that's like Chief and me, I thought, the stout round-bellied Arabian stallion, wheeling on his short delicate legs, his eye wildly rolling but intelligent under his short furry mane, his head fierily thrown back as his rider reins him in. But there is the feeling that his ferocity would be directed, not toward his master, but against a possible enemy, and that, in the tradition of the great horses of history, he would not be loath to taking a piece out of anyone who opposed him. It was this which most impressed me: their togetherness, the horse and the man. The rider sits easily upon his embroidered pad of a saddle; his small Oriental foot is thrust through a stirrup, the heel well down. (Where was it I read that the heel on a shoe came into being primarily to hold a horseman's foot

in the stirrup?) These two have the air of having had many adventures together, and of having relished them.

Well, Chief and I feel this way, too, I thought. We go over the countryside at will, and at our own pace, jumping obstacles if we are in the mood, or if it is really necessary to be on the other side of them. Since my horse's individuality is what I value, I should not try to change or polish him, I suppose, or object too much to his mental quirks. No horse should be hampered by precept which has as one of his endearing tricks the habit of always trying to include in every ride a certain little apple tree, off which he can pick a withered apple or two as we pass. I ought not even to mind that he occasionally throws me, by some inimitable twist in mid-air that I've never yet been able to analyze. For he always takes care not to trample me, and he waits, a little distance off, cropping the grass, until I get up, and remount him.

BARBARA

SUGARBRIDGE
Day's ending

DEAR GLADYS,

What a wonderful climate bed is! A refuge from all care, a place to lick one's wounds, and to plan afresh for the future. I often think that, when by the efforts of primitive man, beds got off the ground, and no longer were merely a heap of skins, a truly important discovery was made, and I am all against some modern thought which for considerations of space saving, proposes to fold them up into the walls, or to do away with them altogether, in the Japanese style. Beds have a soul, I think, in their infinite variety, from the heavily curtained bed of mediaeval times to the satin-padded ease of today's Hollywood bed, and as such, I have a sentimental attachment for them.

One of the chief delights of country life is going to bed early. Right after dinner, in fact, preferably upon a rainy or snowy night, when you can hear the gentle sound of the elements upon the roof, and rejoice that you are inside. Although sometimes in the green twilight of deep summer it is enchanting, with the birds still fluting a bedtime song, and rags of vivid sunset color still visible through the windows. When I say, go to bed, I do not mean to sleep. Not at once, that is, though it is delicious to do so intermittently. The real purpose is to read, and I do not know any more satisfactory way to accomplish the thing. To read, quite uninterrupted, fall asleep—to wake, and read again. . . . There is no more delectable way to spend an evening.

It may sound stuffy or senile to the uninitiated, yet almost every dyed-in-the-wool country dweller comes to it. Else they go back to the city, where there are movies, people, and noise. But like all pleasures, this retreat to bed can take on the aspects of a vice. It can be a dreadful social handicap. Suppose you have a guest who does *not* like to go to bed early. Then the after-dinner hours spent in mere desultory amusement drag interminably, and we exchange anguished private looks. *Can we ever go*

21

to bed? It has to be a truly enchanted evening which continues to enchant us after ten o'clock. You, being at one with us on this subject, we never have to worry about. And one of our chief attentions to each other on visits is the selection of bedtime reading matter for the guest. A lot of thought goes into this. "Do you suppose Gladys would like 'King Solomon's Ring'?" I ask, about that most wonderful of naturalists' writings.

Have you read it, by any chance?

Written by Austrian Konrad Lorenz, it at once touched a responsive chord in me, for he chose as his testing ground the Lobau, a beautiful wild tract of land outside Vienna, where I once used to go on Sunday hikes. Leafing through the book, I found Mr. Lorenz's greylag geese merging pleasantly with my memories of brown boys in *Lederhosen* and girls in brightly colored dirndls. The book holds many a delicious shared experience for any nature-lover, and strikes a happy balance between sensitiveness and over-sentimentality, the bane of many Nature writers.

I like to remember those once familiar places which he describes, snug in our quiet Pennsylvania farm-house, looking through the window at the winter orchard, asleep until spring.

Come to think of it, I'll send it to you, just in case you haven't seen it.

DEAR B:

Much thanks for "King Solomon's Ring." It is a book nearly everyone ought to read and has the same charm that the work of that other naturalist, Gustav Eckstein, has. Do you remember reading about his canaries? There is another man who writes for the "Atlantic Monthly," Richardson. His revealing studies of the birds on Cape Cod are excellent. I can recapture the hot summer days even when the sleet gnaws at our old windowpanes.

Such men widen our horizons so.

Hastily
G

FEBRUARY

DEAR BARBARA,

I know exactly what you are doing at this minute! The old stone house is very quiet and you have stopped worrying about Chief not having enough exercise this particular day. It is dusk-dark, and you are moving lightly around in the old kitchen fixing that elegant chicken dish I am so fond of, the one with tomatoes and peas and herbs and simmered. Ed has brought in a load of that fine burnable wood which is so seasoned and makes such a soft gray ash.

Duke is lying in the middle of the floor where you have to detour to get around him. A Great Dane is such a spacious dog! Even the Irish seems slight in comparison, and I can scoop up an armload of cockers and carry them around. Teddy is the only one that really seems big, if I pick him up he dangles.

Here the pines are letting the snow sift from their branches—Jill is lanterned across the yard on the way to check the heaters. Followed by leaping Irish, skipping Linda, trotting Sister, and butterfly-darting Teddy. Soup's on and 'tis soup, we unfroze the turkey bones that we put down

at Christmas and have had the kettle over the fireplace simmering most of the day.

A very lusty tenor is in the midst of "Rigoletto" via the radio. I love the rich, robust sound of opera, the swooping excitement. When you come, I shall play you my new "Lombardi" trio redoing of Caruso, Journet and Alda. It is like the full height of summertime, like gardens in the moon, and all lost and lovely things. I suppose it is purely senti-mental. I like it in its own tongue too, which means I am old-fashioned. Like Hamlet in costume, not business suit!

The trouble is the words and music belong to each other and fit.

When you have the English words, you get something like the virtuous Lucrece hopping about a bedroom singing clearly, "I refuse! I refuse!" as the misguided Tarquin leaps after her. Then try to do "Hamlet" in French and hear him striding about saying, "Mon Dieu—mon Dieu—" Probably what I really advocate is everyone knowing all the tongues there are. That would fix everything!

When "Rigoletto" winds up with the great flourish, I shall finish today with Glenn's records of Bach and the Schöne Müllerin cycle. Wonderful to have such flexible programs, to sit warm and comfortable, not squeezed in an impossible concert seat.

Have you defrosted your freezer during its ebb? Jill uses the vacuum cleaner and blows warm air in ours, but we still stand on our heads to wipe up the sliding ice. And no matter how we plan, Barbara, we always end the winter with all of one kind of thing. We have a mort of squash and lots of stewing beef. One of our neighbors came over and said she found nothing in her freezer at all but capons and they were getting a little tired of capons every day. So we bought three of them. They are as big as young turkeys, we shall have them when the children come for a weekend.

The night has closed down, very deep and very cold. The insatiable bluejays have finished every scrap of food—must get up early and fill the feeders. Also we have now three starlings—what does one do? My poor brave chickadees flutter around while the three fat pompous rusty things beak into all the best. How to remove starlings and not disturb the small ones? It's like getting obnoxious women off the club committees.

Music and good books to you both,

GLADYS

SUGARBRIDGE

GLADYS, PET,

I always begin to write to you with a slight sensation of guilt: now you are going to have to answer me! (In addition to your daily stint of fan mail.) Why can't science give us something better for communication than the cumbersome machines we now use? Even a wire recorder has its drawbacks. I suppose I mean something like telepathy; primitive peoples seem to use it, but then . . . when you stop being primitive, you have to depend on machines. Well, I only hope technocracy catches up with me some day.

In my youth, I used to be a great Rider Haggard fan. Not long ago, I re-read "SHE," just for fun. (Fun! It seems to me now the gloomiest of tales!) I was struck by the fact that SHE has a small pool of water in which she is able to watch the movements of people at a distance, a rudimentary sort of radar. Now Rider Haggard lived in Victorian times, well before its invention; I read him in 1915, or thereabouts, and that pool business, if I thought of it at all, as the most impossible magicking. Yet here, in my lifetime, radar has become almost as usual as the telephone. So I don't believe I'm asking too much when I point out the need of easier communication between people at a distance. My ideas tend to dry up when I have to pound them out with one finger.

Alas for this, but it must be told. Reading your rhapsodies about "Rigoletto," I knew I had to make a horrible confession. I hate classic opera! For years I suffered in silence: there was (and still is), to my way of thinking, something insurmountably absurd about a stout tenor bellowing out confidences which are supposed to reach the ear of only one person, however beautifully he sings them. After I reached the age of self-determination, I thankfully took my way toward orchestral and chamber music, believing that as far as opera went, there must be something left out of me. Then, quite by chance, I went to hear "The Medium" of Gian-Carlo Menotti. I wavered; this was more like what I thought opera should be. Soon, along came "The Consul." Well! There I alternately sat on the edge of my seat, or swooned away in ravishment. There, in my humble opinion, music and drama both play their parts superbly to make up a moving and integrated whole. I liked the use of modern stagecraft too; why not? Yet in spite of what Mr. Rudolf Bing has done for classic opera, it still seems dusty and artificial to me. You can play the Bach for me when I come.

No, we never, never defrost our freezer. (Look, Ma, I'm answering questions this time!) We just never do. In the past, the very paternal company we bought it from has dropped around for one thing or the other, looked inside, and said, "Oh, my! Your freezer does need defrosting." Then they would do it for us. It's as icy as the North Pole now. I hope they'll come soon.

Right this minute a fox is barking behind the studio, very loud. If you once know a fox's bark, you never can mistake that queer complaining sound for anything else. I couldn't resist putting my nose out to try to get a look at him; it was full moon, and he was so near that I could hear him scuffling about in the leaves. But then I be-thought me of rabid foxes, that bane of last year, and prudently retreated. It was then we had the scare, you remember. Foxes began to behave in a very un-foxy way; they often came right up to house doors, and a number of people were bitten, and took the Pasteur treatment. Newspapers warned that no one should go out without a club; Clinton, our handy man, had a line of them posted all the way down to the barn, in strategic places, some as big as young trees. There were various programs of extermination launched; when trapping and shooting got no results, they began to use poison. Our countryside was at once the scene of controversy. Those with small children and livestock were for it (many cows and horses were bitten, too); those who objected to seeing the balance of wild life disturbed opposed the measure. Opinion ran high; there were speeches, petitions, quarrels and bickerings; it was almost like a presidential campaign.

The game wardens laid the poison bait in a wide belt across Chester County, and as they came nearer and nearer to us, we began to get worried about Duke. He can take in a couple of townships in one of his

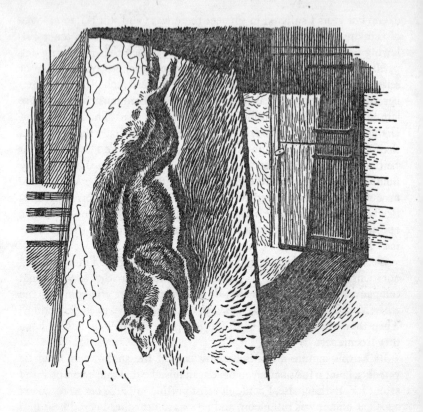

night walks, and with strychnine, you don't have time to get a dog to a vet, even if he is able to crawl home. So we sent him away to kennels, and I can still remember the Judas-feeling his reproachful eyes gave me as the door to his cage closed. Duke is strictly a home dog. Well, the fox poisoning was finally called off because of the determined opposition, but not before many valuable dogs were victims, and various famous last words said. My favorite was the remark of a witty man who said that if so much free poison were left lying around, a lot of unprincipled people would take advantage of it, and do away with their mothers-in-law.

Clinton's clubs proved their usefulness at last. A poor fox in the last stages of the disease crawled into our barnyard and collapsed. Clinton gave him the coup de grâce with a loud war whoop and a staff Hercules might have handled. I suspect that I'm always on the side of the fox—rabid or not. But something good came out of it, for Ed, who was just then illustrating Almet Jenks's "Huntsman at the Gate," had a model for the fox-men in the book practically on the studio steps.

BARBARA

Hi, for a cold bright sparkling day! Have you ever noticed the dramatic change in light which comes about this time of year? It is one of my special timemarks. One morning I look out our only eastern window: the sun is coming up like a big yellow daisy behind the little round hill up the orchard lane, outlining it in dawn primrose. Then, as I watch, a flood of ruddy light, which is different from that of yesterday, or the day before, washes over, and flows down the lane and over the intervening fields, until it mantles the western hills, lying brown and purple in shadow; it touches their tips with vivid rose, carmine, crimson. Banks of dead leaves near the house turn warm and pink; bare silvery branches, mauve; the whole scene is suddenly glowing, encarnadined. Today there is a blinding radiance, an ardent-looking warmth to the sun which makes you long to bask. If it were not for the shrewd wind, and the air like cold wine, you might imagine you were in a tropic climate. But this is only an early morning effect; after the sun is well up, you have just another clear winter day. That is, until sunset, when the whole phenomenon occurs again, and everything is once more transformed, the stubble fields a hot ochre, the wild meadows running all the gamut of ruddy tones from brown to red, madder, magenta, ruby, like the scruff of some tawny animal's neck. It always makes me happy when first I glimpse it, for I know that come snow what may, now winter is not going to last too long.

I took Chief out on an afternoon like this. It was one of those days when it is sheer heroism to ride, and everyone to whom I announced my intention began to shiver, safe by the fireside. The wind had a kind of fiery chill; it ruffled Chief's mane until it stood straight up, every hair distinct and gleaming, like a crest of pink ice. He is a very red horse. All the little streams we passed had silvery fish-scale ripples in them, so hard did the wind blow against the current. But somehow, it seemed a spring rather than a winter cold. We went down our lane, a protected wooded way, past the Grovers' house, looking snug and shut-up, a small white box beneath the huge forest trees. Once I asked him for whom he had made the swing back of the house, suspended from a giant tulip poplar; they have no children. "Oh," he said, "that's for HER." I knew he meant his wife, a short plump woman. "Yes," he went on, an unexpected twinkle in his eye, "I bought cable for that swing that'll hold up to five thousand pounds!" This is one of my most precious nuggets; pure gold, in fact, the thought of Mrs. G, all alone, swinging in quiet middle-aged satisfaction on her swing. It has character, somehow; if she lived in the city, she would only go to the movies, or watch television.

We were on a tour that day. Next we came at the foot of the hill, to the little crumbling stone house where Miss K and Mr. D live. It always looks perfectly uninhabited, the windows staring sightless, like eyes rolled up in the head, every door tight-shut, as though it had not been opened for a long time. Chief stopped, because the grass is good there; I called, but no one came, so we went on. These two elderly people have fascinated me ever since the day I got a letter from her, without any warning, saying,

"Dear Mrs. Neighbor:
"I am sending you a poem about vampires. I have always been interested in them. . . ."

"On Skull-Dome Hill the moonlight falls
In ghastly brilliance cold,
While up the hill a horseman rides
In habit gray with mould;
He's mostly seen on Hallowe'en;
Through vista, misty-blurred
I see, perched on his battered hat
A chirping little bird . . ."

The poem was quite a gem in its way, too; it had real eerie feeling. Later, I pressed her for more information about this unorthodox taste of hers. She really had done a good deal of reading, and she told me about it, her pale steel gray eyes sparkling. What a windfall for any writer, I thought to myself. Who could have invented anything like this? Are writers just lazy, loving to get such a situation handed to them on a platter? No, I decided, it's not that; we merely admire life's virtuosity. "Nowhere," I exclaimed to Ed, telling him about it, "but in Chester County could you have found a person with a hobby of vampires! But," I hastened to add, "it's quite all right. Miss K's poem has a strong moral tone. Didn't the little bird redeem the vampire knight? So I don't suspect her of indulging in black magic." But I put her on my list of special people, and she has never let me down. Other fascinating bits of information have come my way: she had an ancestor who was a French nobleman, she told me once, and on a separate occasion she showed Ed a daguerreotype of him, which seemed authentic, and in character. Miss K would like to give up the needlework by which she supports herself, and to become a writer or an artist. "But Fame," she told me portentously, "is slow coming." Don't I know it!

Sometimes it seems to me that you should know all these people who are part of my life as well as I do. As though they were a part of me. For is not man said to be the sum total of his experience? This all in line, no doubt, with my feeling for advanced communication. Have I been reading too much space fiction?

Viola is another one. She lives not so far away, as the crow flies, though Chief and I cannot always fly that way, owing to mud, or, perhaps, the spring planting. She and her mother live with a friend who owns a farm, and they are an entertaining household, something like the childhood tale of "The Cock, and the Mouse, and the Little Red Hen," since they share the work, and have the similar tastes of animals, birds and flowers. Their place is one of my most frequent stopping points; they always have something in bloom, literally every month of the year, often something rare, for Mrs. F, the friend who owns the farm, is an accomplished horticulturist with a knowing way with wild flowers, and a green house where she raises orchids.

"Aren't you going to stop in?" Viola calls to me, as she sees me passing by on the road. "She's got some things in bloom on the terrace." They each have their own gardens, and Viola, who cultivates the hill behind the house, disclaims both responsibility and credit for anything else. She is a short person, with a feminine figure; she wears blue jeans like everyone else in the country, but with the difference that she is accustomed to add a frilly blouse or a pastel sweater. And since she once had a job at a cosmetics counter, she always smells good, and her lips and nails are bright. Because I like her, I find this attractive, although I might dislike it in someone else.

So I tie Chief up, and we go into the house. As always, there is a cat sitting on every table. They have cats beyond counting, and they are all very special cats, one with six toes, and one without a tail, and one that is part Persian. They sit on tables to be safe from the dogs. The terrace opens off the dining room, and almost before we go through, and out, I can see the snowdrops; there is an attractive line of them, nodding white and graceful, green-flecked. It seems a miracle, this time of the year, we agree. "But then it's so sheltered-like here," Viola consoles me, for my snowdrops, which are only shoots under the leaves. The Lenten roses are in bud, too, she points out, all pinky maroon and rose. Later would come hardy cyclamen, andromeda, and spotted lungwort, all to be seen blooming from inside while the weather still kept them there. I am in their debt for many an unusual plant which but for them I might never have known about, boon without price to the amateur gardener.

"Come up to the woods," invited Viola, "and see the pipsissewa I found. It smells so sweet when it blooms."

I said I'd take a look at Chief first, and did, only to find him vanished. With the dismal premonition that I should have to walk over half the county to retrieve him, I was relieved to see his red brown flank gleaming on the hill behind the house. There we found him in a cornfield, happily munching at some ears dropped by the harvesters, and not in the least abashed by his lapse. So we all three went to the woods to see the pipsissewa, a dark glossy evergreen leaf, which I knew, but not by that name. It was almost sun-down then, so Chief and I said good-bye, and rode away west, full into its glory.

B

HAPPY VALENTINE DAY TO YOU:

It was lovely in the days when we made our own lacy valentines, pasting little violet-blue birds all over, and gluing hearts and roses around the edges. Something innocent and young went out of life when the modern comic valentines came in, say I. Do you think it is because we have to find everything funny since the world itself is so sad, or is it we are cynics about romance and young hearts?

I used to save my valentines and go over them again. *Guess Who* was never any real problem. Later I saved the candy boxes tied with fancy brilliant ribbon. Store candy was a real treat when I was growing up in the little town. There was a German family that had a small shop on the corner on Main Street. Mamma and Papa made the rich dark chocolates, the creamy ivory-colored fondants. Made fairy-tale apples and oranges and carrots of marzipan too. Papa also played the horn in the town band, and usually if we went in for a small box of the delicious candies, Papa's tooting could be heard in the back of the store while Mamma wiped her rosy face with a clean napkin and bustled in to measure out the treasures. Most of the time, we made our own fudge. I was allowed to make fudge on Sunday afternoon, and that was a saving grace for a day when one could play no games, go to no social gathering, or read light books. I must have made tons of fudge, and my beau ate his way valiantly through batch after batch. In summer we sat on the porch in the old swing and the creaking sound of the rusty chains was pleasant in the dreamy stillness, that Sunday quiet which is like nothing else on earth. In winter, we sat on the sofa with the buttered platter between us.

It was a great change when Father decided God wouldn't mind if

33

we took a small ride in the afternoon. Father and Mother sat in front, of course, and we sat in back, jouncing around over the rutted dirt roads. Every few miles, we stopped to fill the radiator, we carried a pail for that purpose. It was a wonderful time! We always got home in time for a bite to eat before Epworth League and the evening service at the old red Methodist church. Nevertheless, I am sure Father always felt just a twinge of guilt as he settled himself behind the big polished wheel and swung down Alton Street.

I cannot imagine our own children ever sitting quietly in the back seat while Papa and Mamma were in front. From the earliest age, Jill's son just climbed in and started the car, and we held our breath while we sped down the highway at a fearful clip. Also, the main function of parents these days seems to be to provide enough money, but to stay decently out of sight most of the time.

We have had the February thaw. A sudden soft look of the snow at the edges of the swamp. A sound of water running dark and free under the ice. A lace of tawny meadowgrasses emerges from the white cover. Against the sky over Stillmeadow, the trees have a different look, although it may be imagination on my part. The sharp lines of midwinter look softer to the eye. The gray stone fences emerge, the old giant boulders dark and wet with melted snow. The pines shake their feathery branches in the wind, bracing themselves for the utter fierceness of wind to come in March.

Lichen on the sugar maples is dark green, like very old jade. In the morning, the plump sparrows sit on the hemlock outside my window with a new and busy look about them. I wonder if they know the long winter is coming to a close?

George has been cutting wood during the mild spell. The sound of the saw is clean and quick, George and his hired man call to each other and their voices sound as if they had been sliced neatly by a good cutting knife. The dogs bark loudly when the cows come in to be milked. Small Barby, our neighbor, comes in from school walking down the slushy road, singing.

At night, a fox barks up the hill, the hunting must be good. There is a sudden sense of life, a stirring and awakening, as if every creature enjoys the sudden release from the bitter cold.

Jill cleans the kennels, burns trash, picks up fallen branches from the January storms, keeps an eye on the pond in case it should thaw. Brings me a few green branches from the pine, the hemlock and the yew, so I can fix a new arrangement for the table.

She firmly resists my suggestion that we TAKE OFF the storm windows the first mild day. Instead fills the woodshed with wood for the next round of freezing. And drives to the dump with a load of rubbish. "Road'll be impassable any minute," she says as she and Daphne take off.

The sky has such a pale glow at sunset time. The horizon is the color of a fresh-picked lemon, somewhere there is a faint splash of green, and the rest of the sky keeps its polished pewter tone. There is an austere beauty about it, cool and restrained and yet exciting. Probably we need New England winter to be really intimate with the sky.

Firmly determined to cut down the garden this year, Jill is wrestling with the catalogues. She begins by eliminating the rosy-stalked chard. Then she decides maybe just one row of it—but I am not going to have a big garden, she tells me. Just a few salad vegetables and tomatoes—and some corn—and a few parsnips. A row of potatoes—they are so good freshly dug and cooked with a mint leaf, says Jill, writing down seed potatoes, Golden Coin.

In the end, the garden is just about the same size it was last year, and will be even fuller of weeds, beetles, moles and rabbits to battle for the crop we try to raise.

Do you grow the black Mexican corn? Really blue, and very firm on the cob. A platter of that and a side dish of beefsteak tomatoes sliced thin—elegant. Lunch or supper either one.

As for flowers, never so red the rose as that on the seed catalogue in February. But we always hope this year the beetles will not be in such phalanxes. I know Ed has a fine disregard of the Jap beetle, but that would be cured if you set him to picking a dozen rose bushes of the massed ranks. But since he doesn't care for cultivated flowers, he would wish the roses to do their own fighting, I expect.

Mr. Bennett drove down the road today as he had several packages too big for the box at the corner. So your letter was delivered right at the picket gate. I am glad to hear that when Chief threw you lightly over his head, you were unbroken as to bones. And I do appreciate that it was noble of him to wait for you to climb painfully back on—but I would ask you whether he really had to toss you off in the first place?

He seems to be a very impulsive horse. Think you should carry bits of torn-up white paper in your jacket pockets and leave a trail, so Ed can follow you if necessary. It's all very well for a tracking dog to sniff a hanky and take off, but let's face it, Ed is not a trained tracking dog.

GLADYS

SUGARBRIDGE
Ash Wednesday

DEAR GLADYS,

Today, Lent begins, and I have as usual, given up smoking (easy), and being violent (hard). Ed, who experiences just the reverse—he tried to forswear smoking too—thinks me a strong character not to backslide toward a cigarette. But I doubt if I deserve any credit. I can do without almost anything, which is purely negative, yet I find it impossible to form any good habits I don't come by naturally. I *can't* be always patient, good-humored, equable.

Coming out of church, I reflected that the attitude of prayer tends to make everyone appealing—the clasped hands, the bowed head, the humble mien. Then, if ever, I can come close to loving all my fellow men, for everyone is equal here. Suddenly I see that each old lady, withered and bird-like and withdrawn from life in the way that age withdraws, is, under her bonnet, only the same small girl she was in childhood, needing help and guidance, perhaps now more than ever. The lesson that we are the same beneath our varied exteriors, all suffering similar disasters, identical hardships, is taught us first by the Christian faith, and later by life itself. Who has not had the revelation that under some proud hard front there lies a bitter private grief, a galling lack, which cries out for sympathy and assuagement? But we soon forget this, begin to envy again those seemingly impervious ones, and must have the vision offered us anew.

I re-read Dostoievski's "The Brothers Karamazov" not long ago, and found it meant something quite different to me today. I can understand the saintly Father Zossima's conviction now, that each of us is accountable

36

for the sins of all, because any one of us is capable of committing them. I am struck each time afresh with the scope of man's soul: how quickly hate can creep in, if not checked! On the other hand, though it does not take place so easily, a good deed freely done does illumine all the days around it with a great flood of love and hope. It urges on to further accomplishment, as though to show that man's powers for good or evil are limitless.

My great fault lies in finding it difficult to turn the other cheek. I come of a family which always believes itself to be right. While I go the opposite way, and question my decisions too much, if anything, still I have passionate convictions, and when these are outraged I cannot go on. That is, in the past, I could not. But a while ago, I came to a turning point. On one side, I saw myself becoming a sour crabbed old person, with no friends and no human outlets. On the other, a life of struggle, learning to be tolerant, making myself behave as though I might be wrong when I didn't think so at all. For nothing stands still, I found. One quarrel leads to another, and the second comes much more easily than the first. There again, the converse is luckily true, and though I don't have an easy time of it, for I shall perhaps always be an undisciplined person, the way no longer looks impossible. "It shall not be too hard for thee," is written somewhere in the Bible, and this is true, isn't it. To know it gives you the most amazing feeling of release, of perfect freedom; it's as though you suddenly could fly. Even if you only have it once in a while, it makes life worth living.

Don't be worried; I'm not trying to impersonate Billy Graham. It's only that I've been thinking about life, lately. Perhaps everyone does, after they live longer, and find out something about it. When I was young, I thought that everything important happened in youth, love, disappointments, tragedies, triumphs, disgrace. . . . That certainly, after forty, you sat comfortably by the chimney-side, and dozed, forgotten. That is so little the case that it would be comic, almost, if you could laugh at something which isn't amusing at all. No, the really deep moving things of life, both terrible and wonderful, come later, I'm sure, with understanding.

STILLMEADOW

DEAR BARBARA:

Yes, it takes living to find out what values life has. I think, when we are very young, we dream of everything on such an immense scale. Possibly only Alpine climbers keep a young dream forever. For them it is the highest peak of their mountain or death. I admit I do not understand this, but it seems so.

Most of us, as we grow older, gentle the wild ponies of our heart. Then you find, on the lower pastures, the small flowers that are there, and you know the richness of small busy tasks of ordinary living.

You find your way around in a few people's hearts, and you feel a deeper understanding of *all* human beings.

Mr. Bennett wanted to know how the birds were doing, and exactly how many of each we have been feeding. He is a true naturalist and the man who has done more than anyone for our county. In the right season, he talks his entire mail route into planting shrubs and bushes, and one year he had us all out feverishly trying to graft flowering crab and several other things onto worn-out trees in the fields. At his behest, Jill staggers under a load of fifty young pines to set out in the upper meadow for bird cover. Not too many years from now, a whole generation of Chinese chestnuts will enrich our landscape, all because one day Mr. Bennett delivered the mail and held out a few glossy nuts in one hand and talked about the miracle of a blightless chestnut to replace the blighted ones. In his office at home, countless little jars hold colored seeds and berries, and in his yard rows of seedlings are heeled in, waiting for planting. Comes the day when Jill is barely able to creep around after eight hours of such ladylike pursuits as kennel-painting, hoeing, pruning, dog-trimming, Irish setter bathing, taking the Obedience jumps with four successive dogs—and then Mr. Bennet points out that fifty multiflora roses would be a fine thing for her to plant.

This means work. Every spadeful involves rock removal, from small stones to great boulders. But multiflora roses are just wonderful for the wildlife, says Mr. Bennett. One day last summer Jill came in around noon almost bent double.

"You tell Mr. Bennett I can't plant fifty of anything, no matter what," she said, sinking on the sofa. She had been moving several large bushes from where they were to another place—our garden is always migratory.

Mr. Bennett's given name is George and we call him George. In our valley nearly everyone calls everyone by their first name, it is a warm and intimate life since we are so really country. But Mr. Bennett addresses us firmly as MRS. When pressed, he says in his Yankee voice, "Wal— if I call one by a first name, others might expect it—" He would not discriminate by calling us our first names and addressing some new householder on his route as Mrs. His pleasant and friendly little wife calls everyone by their given names just the same.

Mr. Bennett is a lesson in courage. He has only one leg, and wears one wooden one; and off and on suffers a great deal of pain. But he never lets it interfere with his work, and he takes his day off to go hunting and gets through any kind of cover and bags his game. He can shoot, I think, with a clear conscience since he has personally raised pheasants for the gun club to stock, has built pens, has needled the other hunters to donate days to work on stocking the woods and fields. He works actively with the group fighting the water pollution that has ruined our lovely swift streams. It is wonderful to think what one man can do, one village postman who happens to have a dream. Now and then someone invades our valley to "write him up." He thinks nothing of this, what's all the fuss about?

Long after we are gone, the tall pines will be growing, and multiflora roses blossoming, the chestnuts standing against the sky and all our part of Connecticut will be blessed with a beauty of flowering crab and black alder—just because of Mr. Bennett. It gives one to think, Barbara, about what is important in living.

I have trouble with him over the fact that I often forget to stamp my letters. I can't see why, with the postoffice running over with stamps, he doesn't stick one on and get the letter on its way, but he will never do it. He brings the letter back next day—a whole day lost— and I have to go down and get a stamp, three miles away, and start over.

39

And sometimes I find a small note, written with a stub of a pencil saying, "Mrs. Taber two cents due on a parcel addressed to you—" Once I taxed him firmly with not bringing same out and he said, "Suppose you or I died in the meantime?" I suppose in that unlikely event, both of us carried off in a twinkling, that the Government would have lost two cents!

Miss Evangeline, the postmistress, is another very special person. She raises watermelons! She has a gentle delicate face and never is flurried even when knee-deep in Christmas mail. But she can be firm too. She had the telephone taken right out of the postoffice because too many people kept calling up to ask if they had any letters that day!

We have no Special Delivery naturally, but in the early days, if we KNEW one was due, we could give her a ring and ask had it come in and then take the drive to the village. City people never really understand that we don't have any Special Delivery—I have some friends who persist in sending Specials, no matter what I say. I'll wager you have the same trouble.

Teddy is tall enough to peer in my window, and just came to lean his elbows on the outer sill and look pleadingly at me. If I don't rise and FLY to let him in—traversing the whole house in a leap, he moves to the next window and his thoughtful face again peers at me. How stupid people are who say dogs don't think! He knows if I see his face, I will wait on him, hands and both feet. He figures I am at my typewriter, he no doubt thinks I am writing to you, and he picks the window where I can't help seeing his golden head. Nobody taught him that.

I notice you always address Duke properly as Duke. Teddy's real name is Especially Me, but I call him Mister Bear, Honey Bear, Teddy, Mister Marshmallow and even, I blush to admit, Angel Pie! The truth is that he is so especially enchanting that no one name covers it. His mature coat is now in, a minted deep gold. But his eyes are the eyes of a baby still. If I get up in the night to go for a drink of water or to see if the back heater is really NOT setting the house on fire—I come back and find him with his head on my pillow, his compact self under the blanket. If I ask him to move over, he folds his paws over his stomach and his eyes look sad. He feels I ought to take some cold spot and leave him the nice warm nest.

In the end we both collapse, laughing. He gives me a warm and sandpapery kiss as I lug him out to the sofa.

Sister thinks little of this whole procedure. She settles neatly at bedtime on her corner portion of the bed, her head on her own pillow. Once in a while it comes over her in the night how much she loves me and she flings herself on my shoulder. But in a minute, she goes back to her own place. She just tells me I am very special and then feels satisfied.

Teddy is coming along with his Obedience training, although when heeling his tendency is to be in the air more than on the ground. He is really too large to be a butterfly. But he doesn't know it.

With his father being such a famous champion, the first black and tan ever to win the spaniel specialty, we feel we ought to show him in breed. Jonquil is a good daughter of Cover Charge breeding too—but when I think of giving him up to the circuit, my heart fails me. In Obedience, you go in the ring with your dog, it is a partnership. You work together. But to make a breed champion, you need to send your dog with a handler to enough shows to gather the points. Teddy would not be happy traveling in a crate. And I would be horribly lonesome. So the chances are he will be just another country dog, although I hope a Utility dog tracker.

Tracking is one thing you haven't tried with Duke, and should. It always rains or snows or is broiling hot when they have the trials. You get up at dawn, you drive a hundred miles, you stand around while the tracks are started, you are always hungry, either cold or hot, and invariably very tired. But when you see your dog on the track, and the gallery cheers, it is something not to miss.

Jill says she doesn't see how I can write such long letters. Her letters are not only infrequent but terse. Usually she writes, "We are all well. Everything is fine here. We lost Buddy but found him again." Frantic phone calls from the children ensue: What has really happened? Jill in great surprise says, "Why I wrote to you only two days ago!"

She never says in ten words what she can say in two. And conversation via paper is not to her taste. When we first had Stillmeadow, I kept the fort with the three young children. She worked in the city. I wrote her reams of happenings and comments. Now and then I had a post card. Like "All fine here. Will be out Saturday."

I think I got the letter habit when I was first away from my mother. I wrote her almost every day and she wrote as often. Her letters were witty and wise and colorful, and every other word mis-spelled. Father had a fine academic scorn of her spelling, but his letters were mostly advice on how I should behave. Mamma told me all the funny things, the little gay things, and just how the river looked at sunset flowing past the house glowing with flame. And how she felt at twilight looking at the church spire against a pale sky. Although she didn't know a rhyme from blank verse, she was a poet at heart.

After she died, I found every little verse or piece of prose I had written from kindergarten up, copied out in her delicate hand, tied up

with colored ribbons, things from the High School paper, the College magazine, bits in papers—anything at all. Cherished. Something to live up to, I thought.

The light slants over my desk—that means it is time to cream the turkey— Have you tried adding a bouillon cube to cream sauce—very helpful.

This from me, beleaguered by sniffles from going out in the thaw in a sweater, to you, not yet lost in the woods after Chief gets excited—

CONNECTICUT COUNTRYWOMAN

SUGARBRIDGE

DEAR G

Sometimes I think that if I had a whole new life to lead, I'd like nothing so much as to be a really good gardener. How easily, and with what relish they go about their appointed tasks! They are endlessly patient and persevering over failure, quietly assured of the success which always crowns their efforts in the end. But it is a demanding avocation, and all else must be given up to it. That is my downfall. However propitiously I start out, however earnestly I vow to be punctual, so surely does something unavoidable intervene so that some seed are not planted, cut worms mow down those which have been planted, and weeds sweep over all. For time is inexorable to a gardener. If you let it slip by, all excuses are in vain. You simply have to wait until next year.

One of the most maddening things I know is that calendar of gardening chores in the Sunday "Times," called "Around the Garden." I never can bear even to look at it, and read what I should have been doing during the past week. I tend to rely more and more upon Clinton for the vegetable garden, although there was a day when I thought peas tasted sweeter when I had planted them. He is by no means a meticulous gardener; he weeds only once in a while, and has never been known to dust or spray. But he always gets around to the important chores. He has that faculty of good gardeners: he never seems to work very hard, nor very long, yet he manages to have a recognizable garden, sometimes an excellent one. I think the reason for his success is that he lives in the present. When he plants beans, he just plants beans, and gives his whole attention to it. Unlike me, who thinks about finishing up some writing when I get through in the garden, or maybe about something I have to do two weeks from now. It's the penalty we pay for doing too much, thinking too much, trying to be too much, alas.

P.S. I can see Clinton, out of the studio window, beginning to spread compost over the bare brown garden. That is *such* a satisfying

43

occupation; I envy him as I sit here, and that is typical of us. We want everything. I ought to be content to sit here and do my writing. Besides, what does this mean? That soon I shall have to struggle with seeds? Again? Another year already? Please! Just last week the ground hog saw his shadow.

Yrs

B

Sugarbridge

Dear Gladys,

Off to the city in a rush this morning (due, as always, to that extra thing I *must* accomplish before departure, in this case, Ed's lunch, since he just wouldn't eat anything if I didn't) I saw Miss K and Mr. D waiting at the bus stop, as I turned onto the highway. They have quite a walk across fields from their house to the road; back through the folds of low hills you can just see its tall narrow outline, glancing secretly through the empty eyes of its windows. Mr. D was standing with his head turned carelessly aside, so that he should not seem to be soliciting a ride; Miss K, on the contrary, waved her umbrella at me, and I slowed down, and stopped for them, as I am always impelled to do. Now I *will* miss the train, I thought, with that kind of resigned despair which is rather comfortable, since it relieves you of further effort, and places the responsibility clearly across the shoulders of Fate.

"Well, can *I* use a lift today!" exclaimed Miss K, as Mr. D gallantly helped her in. He followed, a dapper old man, conventionally garbed for town in overcoat and felt hat; at him one would never give a second glance on any city street, but Miss K presented her usual odd and in-

44

teresting appearance. A long and voluminous wool coat muffled her tall figure, not quite covering her ankle-length printed calico dress, under which were visible her tiny feet in high black laced shoes, as remarkable in this day of wedgies and open sandals, as are feet that Cinderella might have envied; her gray hair was tucked up under a green wool cap. "Yes," she said, carefully placing the satchel that I knew contained her wares more exactly upright as the car got under way, "I have an important engagement with a woman I'm making a dress for."

Now Miss K's dresses have always commanded my awe and admiration; made of calico or some similar small-printed material, they are simplicity itself, being usually merely gathered around waist, neck, and cuffs. Yet they have two qualities which I consider essential about clothes; they are individual, and they are timeless. How dull it would be if she looked like just any small-town woman, I thought, my gaze resting upon her fondly. It's a curious thing, this perhaps purely mental attachment you can have for someone you don't know, and never will, but who pleases your fancy. "It would have been quite a walk from where the bus stops," Miss K said, "but it's right on your way, around the corner from the Home, there on High Street." She fixed me compellingly with a cool gray eye.

It wasn't on my way. I'd intended to let them off at the main corner, and go on down to the station, since I still intended to get into town *sometime,* but I found myself agreeing. I might as well, I said inwardly.

"Do you need anything?" Miss K pursued, gesturing toward her satchel. I said cagily, mentally bypassing the aprons and the handkerchiefs, that I might take a few pot-lifters. Red ones.

Miss K's face fell; she had no red ones, she said. But she would make me some at once. Mr. D had maintained silence as a man will, between two women. Did I ever dream a poem, Miss K asked, and began to recite.

It *did* sound a little as if it had been dreamed up, I said. But then, I wasn't talented along those lines. "Well, I'm really working on a novel," Miss K told me. "A novel laid in Roman times. The heroine is modeled upon myself. Although she is a bit younger."

We had come to Miss K's destination now, and she prepared to alight, thanking me absently, and laying upon Mr. D who got out to assist her, a myriad of admonitions and reminders as to what he was to do, and to get, in town. He got back into the car, and we watched her march away, her satchel swinging.

"A wonderful woman!" Mr. D said, sighing, and I agreed, reflecting that in Mr. D's generation the word "woman" was in better odor than it is today, when it seems most often used to distinguish between the rival capabilities of the sexes, usually to the discredit of the feminine.

45

We remain "girls" much longer in present times than we did a score of years ago; we may be designated too, if somewhat slangily, as "dames" or "dolls." There is no contemporary expression for that other word, I believe, perhaps because in the general leveling of all values, such a concentration of femininity is not the general thing.

I let Mr. D out in the center of town, and proceeded on to the station, where, with undeserved good luck, I found the train still waiting. Thankfully ensconcing myself, I got out my notebook, which always travels with me—since train-riding is most conducive to composition, I find—and wrote you this letter.

BARBARA

P.S. Ned home briefly at mid-years. After his departure, we took stock of the signs of his passing. "He still has a good deal of the human fly in him," Ed observes, as we contemplate the black finger marks on the ceiling, and we smile together with that parental commingling of pleasure at still having a child, as well as the more practical apprehension that he never will grow up. Of course I really understand this habit of his—a natural exuberance, expressed in measuring his growing length upon the walls. Yet can it be possible that he will graduate from college in another year?

MARCH

DEAR BARBARA:

The world is blowing by, and the house holds hard to its anchor.
Jerry flies by my window carrying his favorite yellow rubber rabbit. His
ears stream out level behind his eager nose. Jill braces herself against
the wind as she stuffs more peanut butter in the feeder for the insatiable
chickadees and peckers and sparrows.

The wind whips in through the broken pane in the back door, re-
minding me we must get it mended. Mr. Beech, our new weekly helper,
carried in an armful of logs for the fireplace last week and as the door
swung back, crash went a maple log through the middle pane. Did I tell
you Mr. B is writing a novel? He decided the city was not for him, and
moved to the country with his pretty young wife. He gets up at four
to work on his novel, and makes a living the rest of the day at odd jobs.
I admire him very much, as many would-be writers lack the industry
and independence. It's more usual for the little woman to support the

family while the aspiring husband types. At least I have known several families set up like this.

The day is incredibly clean-looking with the great sweeping wind, the sky looks as if it had just been hung on the line.

The last secret silver hollows of snow in the woods will go now, and any minute the pond will overflow. How I hope it doesn't carry the brown trout on down George's brook and into his barnyard. Whether they survived the winter, we do not know, we neglected to feed them hamburger balls as we were advised to do.

Reading "King Solomon's Ring," I realized our pond is not balanced correctly anyway. I like what he says about the balance of nature, and how fatal it is when man upsets it. The pond teems with its own life, but whether adding the brown trout will fit, I wonder.

In the smaller shallow upper pond lives a turtle as big as a wash tub. How he suddenly came there, we can't imagine. Where was he before we dug out that pool? Are there places deep in the swamp which have mysterious wildlife that nobody has ever seen in these parts? It is impossible to get in to see, you would sink out of sight after three steps.

I like to pretend that in the exact middle there is a small round green island where all the little folk come out at midnight under the moon.

It is good to wake in the night and hear the wind blow and cool and sweet the brave music of the peepers.

I wonder whether this same wind blows over the hills at Sugarbridge. You are beating your way to the studio and Chief must be restive in the paddock. Ed will be down the road taking the mail out of the big red mailbox. Duke will be thinking going-away thoughts, for there is something about a March wind—a special excitement for all things that are!

ESPECIALLY ME

SUGARBRIDGE

DEAR GLADYS,

You have a lot of little dogs (and the Irish!); we have a solitary big one. So life evens it up. It must be fine to have a multitude, and often we have longed for millions of Danes. But we are a one-thing family: one child, one dog, one horse, one car. More proves too distracting; I'm afraid we are delicate.

Duke does not seem especially big to us. Knee high when he came at six months, his subsequent growth has been so gradual that (perhaps on the old theory of lifting a calf each day in the hope that at length you may be able to heft a cow) he is only an ordinary-sized dog to his masters. With the consequence that the tinier varieties of canines beside him seem not really dogs.

Of course we have taken a good deal of ribbing at having an animal of his dimensions in our very small house. And truly, one of the sights of all time is Duke descending our steep narrow circular staircase. If Marcel Duchamps had even seen this, he never would have bothered with his famous "Nude," he would have painted Duke, as I have often longed to do, halfway down, his head and forelegs occupying the lower steps, at a dizzy slant, while quite out of sight, his rear quarters are negotiating the upper curve. The first night he spent with us, when we showed him that almost perpendicular ascent, he just sat down, wagging his tail apologetically. We carried him up for a week. Sometimes even now he doesn't make it. Then he turns around a couple of times and tries another take-off, like a runner coming into a jump.

Standing in front of our fireplace, staring into the flames, or sitting solemn as a stone dog on his haunches, Duke gives a baronial air to our establishment, we think. If my mother is there, one of us is likely to observe to the other (this never seems repetitive, no matter how often it comes up) that Duke recumbent has a certain archaic quality very like those amiable smiling sculptured stone lions in front of St. Mark's Cathedral in Venice, which we saw together and both loved so much.

But being an heraldic emblem is the least of Duke's concerns. Always a dog who likes to be in the center of things, he stretches himself across doorways, which in our house are small enough anyway; or blocks the narrow passage between a chair and sofa; visitors just have to get used to stepping over his extensive prone carcass. At meal times he underlies the table, like Yggdrasil, the ancient monstrous tree of Norse legend which rooted itself about the foundations of the earth. From this vantage point, he is able at will to reach out in the most promising direction for tidbits. Yet Duke is innocent of the customary canine depredations where food is concerned; any unchaperoned ham or roast is safe alone with him. But sometimes, after the table is cleared, he cannot resist running his tongue in a long yearning smear over its surface, pursuing some vanished enticing odor, and leaving a silvery snail-trail behind.

Everyone, I expect, falls in love with the species to which his special pet belongs. I know you always look first at the cockers in any dog gathering; I have become irrevocably attached to Danes. I adore their melancholy majestic air, their heavy jowls, red-lined like a pocketbook, their silky pliant coats, which you can take up in great handfuls, their enormous paws. A big dog is somehow so satisfying to hug. At the shows, I am beside myself in the Dane section, and long to take each entry home with me. The harlequins, piebald as ponies, are so striking; the brindles are beautiful, too, all black and gold, and tiger-marked; the fawns I like best of all, because that is Duke's color. But I have yet to see one with such a juicily black mask as his, or such a glowing amber coat. Some dogs gray in the mask very early, almost as soon as they are mature at three years, but Duke, although he is four now, shows only a few scattered white hairs. It seems sad to me for a dog to age, sadder much than humans. A Dane is comparatively short-lived, too. Once Ned worked out a chart, comparing canine age with human aging. He informs me that Duke is about forty, now, by his calculations. I can see that, too, for sometimes when he sits, solid and solemn beside Ed in the kitchen alcove, he looks to me just like a sober businessman in a derby hat, come home from work in the city. In his early years he had a different air; he was a young prince, carrying his tail like a sword, his ears like a pointed cap. That was a lovely time, and I could wish he had a son just like him.

As you may guess, my Duke is to me the flower of all Danes, for his loving disposition, and his personality. I wish that breeders would con-

sider a dog's soul as something to work for, as well as his conformation. Your dog, all aphorisms aside, ought to be your best friend, as well as an animal with which you win blue ribbons. This Duke is, although his eyes are too far apart (I think this gives him an intelligent look) his tail is a whisp too short, and his hind legs have too little angulation. Yet to have this great noble creature which can look fierce as a lion, but which I know is baby-gentle, for my constant slave and companion, who interprets my every mood and adjusts himself to it patiently, yet preserves his own individuality and sense of humor, is a great boon indeed, and, as you say, a trust. Duke is to me, I think, somewhere between a younger son and a passionate friend.

The face of every loved pet becomes in time almost human to its owner. The anguished remorse upon Duke's face when his delicate digestion betrays him in the house is something painful to see; he is bowed down by sorrow, he turns his great head aside, and hides his eyes. I do not need to speak any reproaches; this is a matter of conscience with him, and well he knows his fault. Except for this physical idiosyncrasy he is a perfect gentleman. But how can a dog with a sweet tooth help begging for ice cream, or an ever-loving master or mistress avoid going against their better judgment once in a while? And when Duke gazes at me imploringly with those big black-rimmed golden eyes and makes the deep-moaning musical sounds only he is capable of, I think sometimes he must burst the bonds imposed upon the animal world and break into intelligible speech.

Ed and I would not be too much surprised if he should. For "Talking Dog" is one of his pet names, and the language he speaks, "doggerel." "Calves' Brains!" says his master to him fondly, as he sits in his kitchen nook with Duke's great head on his lap. "Speak to me in Dog!" meaning dog talk, I suppose—and Duke does.

Ed swears that when I go for a ride without him, his incoherent mumblings during my absence are very near to "Where did she go?" . . . "Why didn't she take me, anyway?" . . . "When is she coming back?"

When I return after one of these absences, we usually have affecting reunions. He licks me over well, stands upright and puts his paws around my neck, pulls me about, taking one hand in that big gentle mouth; I rub his ears, pummel him about a little, take big handfuls of him. This would go on indefinitely did I not at last say firmly, "See, I'm *back*? And yes, I love *you*, too!"

There is a book by Franz Werfel published after his death which you may or may not have read; it wasn't one of his best. But I read anything he wrote with pleasure, and this one did have a memorable speculation about dogs. It was a book forecasting the future, and was purported to have taken place many thousands of years hence. In that world, as he imagined it, dogs had evolved to the stage of being a sort of sub-human species, able to communicate directly in a kind of half-coherent chatter. Every dog has his day, they tell us. Perhaps Duke is a little bit ahead of his—or I may have been born too soon.

DEAR BARBARA:

Such a nice fat mail this morning, including your good letter. As far as I am concerned, Duke is a perfect gentleman. He is a dog of great integrity, and if he looms a little large in your house, he continues to feel like a lap dog.

I must take issue with you, though, on this hugging business. A huge dog is fine to hug, but so is an armful of cocker. And a cocker is no toy, far from it, he is basically a hunting and field dog, strong and vigorous. As for the Irish, one only has to be owned by one to succumb to the impulsive lovable, super-intelligent personality.

Faith Baldwin says she never likes breeds of dogs, she only cares for individuals and this is about the way I feel. She does, however, accuse the French poodle of being a costume piece for some women. Her own dog was a blonde cocker, now buried in a special garden spot. But Faith does not like all of ours by any means. She cocks a discriminating eye as they bounce around and says firmly which character she most admires.

The moles are at it again! The yard fairly billows as we walk across it. I wonder what they do in their dark secret burrows all winter? Presumably they hibernate, but they are certainly busy the minute the ground softens with the end of winter. And as fast as we roll the humps and reseed the holes the dogs have excavated, there are more jutting up. Followed by more and deeper holes, of course.

We gave up croquet on their account. There was no level space left on the lawn. I always liked the idea of croquet, it seems such a romantic game. One thinks of delicate ladies in full sprigged gowns tapping the round hard balls through the wickets, and smartly turned-out gentlemen allowing the weaker sex to reach the post first.

And afterward tea and very thin bread and butter served in the arbor. This is pure fancy on my part, however, since a sprigged gown would have a hard time resisting four or five bouncy cockers. And their definition is, a ball is to chase!

Do you ever wonder whether Americans play enough games? Ping pong is fun, so is Badminton. Archery is a fine sport, quoits can be exciting. Bridge and Canasta and the newest variation are all right in their way, but good group games played outdoors are better. I like games that the whole family can play at once.

I am sorry also that reading aloud has gone out. Radio and T.V. are partly responsible, I think. Too easy to turn the knob. But reading aloud is an exciting shared experience.

Poetry needs a special mood, I admit. The fire just so in the fireplace, the apples just rosy enough, the popcorn buttery and crisp. Lamps gentled down. And between every poem, a little talk about it. But prose can be read any time of day, sun or rain.

We do go to bed early in the country. Long midnight sessions are not for us. Perhaps in the city the noise of the trucks rolling and the busses grinding their gears helps keep one awake, but in the country it is so still after sundown. Very early it seems a good idea to pop off to bed with a book. This reminds me of Millay—"Was it for this I uttered prayers, and sobbed and cursed and kicked the stairs, That now, domestic as a plate, I should retire at half-past eight?"

I am reading the life of Charles Dickens. I never did decide Dickens was not a good writer, so it all comes very pleasantly to me to have him re-estimated.

GLADYS

SUGARBRIDGE
A small miracle

DEAR GLADYS

For a week we had been mourning our lost Siamese kitten; we had searched everywhere for him, inquired of all the neighbors. Then one day Ed struck out in a new direction, and talked with a farmer's wife who made this provocative statement. Cats always went off in February, she told him; hers were gone, too. They got together in a barn somewhere; had had a time of it. "But don't worry," she'd said. "February is for cats. Your cat will be back the first of March." Ed had been much taken by this; he'd hardly been able to wait until he could get home to tell me.

I agreed it was an amusing bit of folklore. But I hardly thought we should see our pampered darling any more. After all, he had spent the whole of his kitten life in our warm guest bathroom, where he slept on a green cushion with his ball and a catnip mouse; he could hardly survive long outside in the rude winds of February. But I wished very much that he could, for he had engaging ways, our Mr. Miaow. He loved to nestle in the curve of a shoulder, or to creep up under our chins in bed

at night, purring like a vacuum cleaner. It was then toward the end of February, and we noted the days as they passed, hoping, or not hoping, as it came to us.

One morning soon after, I was up early; I went out to have a look at the day; it was cold and bright. Suddenly I heard a loud mewing, and down the orchard lane came Mr. Miaow, running. I rushed in and looked at the calendar; it was March first!

Ed came down in his pajamas for his first cup of coffee, and we held an awed consultation, while the prodigal wolfed down a dish of salmon. He had screamed with greed when I opened the refrigerator. No wonder, he was skin and bone. And he was certainly no longer a kitten, that was sure, I said to Ed. "Look at the way he swaggers his hips when he walks! And switches his tail, and demands more food in that deep insolent voice!" Ed pointed out that there were nicks on his satiny black ears, and a cut over one eye.

"Pussy, pussy, where have you been?"
"I've been to London to see the Queen."

We wished that Miaow could tell his story, but since he couldn't, we imagined it for him, a great rout of cats from all over, a cat convention, where all business for the year would be transacted, to the sound of yowling, caterwauling and meeowing. And they would hold high revel at night under the light of the moon, a great Cat Ball, beginning ceremoniously enough, the slick feline gentlemen bowing decorously, the ladies sinuous yet demure, but ending up in a sabbat of shrieks and wails and demoniac passions. It brought to mind a story we had long been fond of, "The King of the Cats," by Stephen Benèt, with its intriguing figure of the cat orchestra leader who conducted with his tail, and finally vanished up the chimney in a burst of flame. Cats are inevitably linked with the supernatural; it must be the noises they make, especially the Siamese.

Mr. Miaow had now finished eating, and had taken a complete bath; he curled up on the hot air register in the kitchen, the most innocent little cat you ever saw. That's what makes them such a puzzle, I thought; the combination.

Now while Miaow had been off on his travels, the barn cat had invaded us. He must have sensed that we were momentarily cat-less, and decided to move in and absorb the unoccupied milk. I found him one day standing by the kitchen door, watchful, ready to run.

"Kitty, Kitty, come here." I rubbed his ears. Shyly, unbelievingly, he brushed against me. Poor cat, I thought, looking down at his broad undistinguished tabby back. "He's had a hard life, I guess." Of course I put some milk before him, which he drank ravenously. The next day he came back, and the next, till we began to consider him a regular.

When Mr. Miaow returned, of course they had to meet. The barn cat gazed at me reproachfully. "So you had a cat all along?" With resignation, it began to retreat. Miaow followed, looking interested. The barn cat slapped him, and he fell back, his feelings hurt. But he couldn't believe it, and he went back again. This time the barn cat really socked him. I thought my one-time protégé wasn't behaving very well. "Go away!" I cried, and picked up a stone. With its sad patient look, the barn cat turned and fled. Alas, he seemed to say, that's human ingratitude for you.

As always

B

SUGARBRIDGE
Spring song

DEAR G

My February cold was a little late in coming. But I got it finally—or it got me. For one who isn't often sick, it's rather pleasant to sink into bed with voluptuous abandon, saying, Now I'm going to be an interesting invalid for a time; I don't care what happens belowstairs. Someone other than I will have to look after things for once. Après moi the burned toast! I collect all the books I've been only hoping to read so far, a lot of notebooks for stray thoughts, and resign myself to the not-unpleasant dream world of a slight temperature.

When I look over my diary for the last year, and see that I have noted the first knee-deeps came in March, I cannot believe it. March seems too early. Why, that's the month of rough winds, I think to myself, and that last determined snowstorm, of bleak slate-colored skies, and massed ominous clouds; it just can't be. Then one day, a little earlier, or maybe a little later this year, I am coming along the creek road, nothing much on my mind, letting the car drift around those high hairpin curves banked all wrong and perilous under winter ice, with the water meadow below and a steep woodsy slope grown thick with laurels above, when suddenly I hear as though from some other life, those piping, peeping, questing little voices, just a few at first, then others answering, like little children calling to each other, and I know that they have come; hylidae, knee-deeps, spring peepers, pinkle tinks, call them what you will. To me, they are the voices of spring, and might be some invisible Pan off in the woods piping to the young a premonition of what spring may mean to them, to the old a memory of other springs.

Their arrival always makes a unique day for us. The first one to hear the glad sound goes home triumphantly to announce the event. "The knee-deeps have come!" As evening falls, we go out again to listen; the chorus has deepened, swelled by other added voices; it sounds like silvery sleigh bells lightly shaken over the land. On each succeeding night, this pagan music grows in intensity, until at its height you can hardly bear its orgiastic volume; it might be all the little temple bells in the world summoning every living thing to the rites of spring.

There is a sequel to this vernal song: once in the fall, we were traveling the same road above the creek, and as we came out of shadow into the sunlight, it seemed that the whole surface of the road was alive and moving. Ed slowed the car down, and then we saw what at first we could not believe. It was a mass migration of the little greenish brown frogs, come up from the meadow en route to the woods where we later learned that they hibernate. We had to wait for quite a few moments to let the procession of tiny skipping hopping creatures pass, just as you stop while a herd of cows cross the road. But this was somehow a marvel to us, an indulgence on the part of Nature in allowing us to witness a secret gesture which not everyone is privileged to. And on some blustery day in midwinter, I like to think of the little hylidae snugly tucked away deep under the leaves in the woods above the stream.

BARBARA DEAR:

I hope your cold is just a memory now. Yes, sometimes it is a relief to GIVE IN and retire from life. Especially since you are fortunate not to weep with your cold—at least if you can read all those books, you don't. As for me, I see dimly through a drizzle and usually try to read by holding a cold washcloth on alternate eyes. This does not give me a sense of relaxation, only a fury.

With all the modern medicines, it is strange that the common-garden cold is still here, not only that, a hundred new viruses abound. Or possibly we just increase our vocabulary. We used to lump countless ailments under the word "Grippe." But I haven't heard anyone confess to a touch of grippe in a long, long time.

Jill just came in to say that after all, the by-products of our side of beef are even better than the steaks! The bones which pressure-cook and make a thick clear rich jelly for soups, and the suet, which goes to the birds, pound after creamy pound, and the chopped beef which makes Texas Hash and mushroom-stuffed meatloaf—and the sturdy stew beef which goes in the old iron pot and hangs over the fire these cold days and simmers with onions and herbs and a dollup of red wine.

Then when we celebrate something with a steak, we feel justified and very moral, not extravagant at all. Over the coals, on the grill, the sputtering comes forth and the savor of charring edges. Cuts like butter. Black outside and pink in the center.

Today came a letter from my "real pal, Hazel." If you see the Ted Key cartoons in the "Saturday Evening Post," you know Hazel, the independent and flat-footed maid who dominates all situations and manages a rather intimidated family. Hazel and I have been corresponding for some years, and I may say that Hazel is one of my dearest friends. I tell myself that Hazel is a purely imaginary person, and now and then I drop a line to Ted Key, who draws her. But I know she is real, and I venture to say she is real to Ted, too. Ted and I have always planned to meet, and since he lives in Pennsylvania, sometime when I am with you we might drive over. But I get frightened thinking of actually going to his house and not having the door flung open by Hazel herself. I feel I want to go to the kitchen and visit with her, exchange recipes—she sent me hers for lime chiffon pie once, fabulous. I shall be worried when Ted explains this is her day off!

Hazel wrote me once when Ted and I were tentatively planning lunch one day in New York. "Watch the guy when lunch is over," said Hazel firmly, "or he'll get a phone call and you'll pick up the check!"

She usually writes to me on his typewriter, warning me not to mention this when I answer or Fathead might get mad that she swiped his machine! If you haven't his "If You Like Hazel," let me know and I'll send it, wonderful for bedtime, it is so nice to go off to sleep laughing.

A great humorist, I think, is a top blessing to the world. It's all very well to write grim things, profound tragedies, but we all need a little bright sun to encourage us. I also think it's harder to be funny.

Faith Baldwin is a long-time friend of Hazel's too. Sometimes we have a three-cornered correspondence with Ted at the edge of it, just sitting there.

Maybe I should warn the boss that if and when we drop in, he had better put any help he has in residence in the cellar while I am there or I shall be furious at him for letting Hazel go!

The reality of an imaginary person (excuse me, Hazel) is a strange thing.

Have I told you about the shepherd dog that lets his mama stay just half an hour in a house while he sits in the car and then he climbs up front and blows the horn? One day she had to stay longer and she said firmly, "Now don't you blow the horn for me!" An elderly shabby man was going downstreet at the time and she heard him saying in a loud hissing whisper, "Go on, do it!"

Somehow this delighted me a whole day while I was struggling with an extra laundry.

Since you were here last, we had Steve and Olive and Mickey and Priscilla for dinner. I mentioned as we were climbing around one another in the long narrow Family room or Taproom or Keeping room or whatever it is, that I wished it could be better arranged. Steve and Mickey swallowed their dessert and jumped up. Sofas flew around, chairs were lugged, the decorating team went to work. Lamps were unhooked, dust flew. Olive and Jill went in the front room and shut the door. Pris sat in a far corner. I just hung around in whatever doorway furniture was not going through.

But oh for an expert! When they were through, the room was miles wider, and far more comfortable. It had an air. Even the oversize sofa (room enough for me and several dogs at once) seemed smaller, angled to the fireplace. The dining table (built by Jill) was in a better place. Sweating and very dusty, the boys sat down for a night cap and the girls gathered around to admire. A nice quiet evening in the country, said I as they buttoned up their shirt sleeves.

When I was growing up in the Middle West, the main thing you had to have to make a house livable was wall-to-wall carpeting. The carpets ran up the stairs too, along the halls. In March, most housewives had a "boy"—anywhere from sixteen to sixty, who helped take out all the twitchy little carpet tacks and carry the miles of carpeting to the

yard to be beaten soundly with a large wire whisk. Meanwhile the floors were unmercifully scrubbed and polished, the carpets carried back in and the hundreds of tacks hammered in.

Mama was not of this school, she liked smooth bare floors here and there with scatter rugs, which really manifested her independent spirit. We never had starched lace curtains either, and not a solitary Rogers Group decorated our piano. I used to go to the neighbors and stare thoughtfully at the Boy With The Grapes and the Rogers stand-up family group.

I grew up with antiques in a day when they were not fashionable. Oh the bird's-eye maple and golden oak and Mission furniture, where are they now? Some of course have been discovered by addicts of Peter Hunt and cut down and bleached and painted and splashed with birds and hearts and vines.

I never feel too comfortable in a completely modern décor. Possibly I feel it is too efficient.

Steve and Olive have a pair of creamy white Bristol lamps in the little red house down the road. Originally oil lamps, of course. Steve first lit the wicks, and then measured the amount of light they gave with a light meter. Then he electrified them and put in bulbs that would give the same amount. It is an experience in beauty to look at them. The round globes glow with a soft and peaceful light, the bases are translucent.

Whenever I am very tired, I like to go down and sit and just look at those exquisite lamps, they rest my spirit.

Surroundings make such a difference—more than we can realize. Recently Steve and Olive did over a house for a couple who were not getting along well at all. They hated their house, and they were in a state of great friction themselves. When the house was finished, quiet and harmonious in color, comfortable and easy in furnishings, they began to take an interest in it, and suddenly their quarrels diminished. At present writing, they are soundly ensconced.

You know how some houses seem happy when you walk in them, and some carry such an overtone of melancholy they seem cold even on a hot day? I believe everyone who lives in a place leaves an imprint on the place itself. Your house is, after all, you.

Having lived in all kinds of rented houses, in apartments, and now so long at Stillmeadow, I often wonder where the present lady of the house in these other places keeps her sofa, and does she have the table by the window or against the long wall?

The current vogue for picture windows that don't look out on anything but traffic is an odd thing to me. I do enjoy driving at dusk past such houses, looking in to see the lamp lighted and the family coming and going, but I never think their looking out and seeing auto headlights must be much inspiration!

If you have a view, then letting the outdoors in is a fine idea.

Very ancient houses, such as this, certainly do not take kindly to picture windows no matter what the view. It gives them an air of astonishment.

Do you ever worry about the income tax, I wonder? It is my opinion, after a number of years of experience, that there is something highly suspect about being a writer. Annually I get a summons to appear and bring all check stubs, all bankbooks, all deposit slips, all bills, all records of every single sums received. The communications are worded so as to make one feel a criminal, although one never knows why.

Without Jill, I should have been in jail long since because I accidentally threw away some canceled checks. But even she, a fine executive manager, has trouble tracking back four years (they are always that far behind, but they are on the track, never fear).

Having always been so honest that I would drive back ten miles if I found I had been given one nickel too many in change from the Seymour shops, I begin to feel badgered about this.

I once made one personal trip to the bureau, feeling murder was bound to be pinned on me because I didn't know enough about figures. I got charged extra on one item, but the agent disclosed that I could have taken off several hundred dollars on something I never thought of. I never knew enough to deduct anything. At that point Jill began keeping books, and each year turns over the entire financial life of poor me to a lawyer. Invariably, nevertheless, the summons comes—one can never, never establish oneself as an honorable citizen in our country, it seems. Maybe it lurks in the back of the governmental mind that nobody ought to be paid anything for writing, and maybe that is so.

Or do you think they feel writers are an easy mark, being notably in the clouds and far from the marts of business?

Jill is now burrowing in the cellar trying to find every check stub for three years ago.

Our tax system is fiendish, I think. I have moments when I wish I could just send in all I make and say, give me back whatever you feel like. Use your own judgment.

GLADYS

P.S. The peepers are singing my favorite music. George says they have to be frozen under three times before we get warm weather—is this a general belief like the woolly bear caterpillars and winter? He says they have been

frozen only once so far. Nevertheless we are turning the heaters off in the kennels hoping for the best.

SUGARBRIDGE

DEAR GLADYS,

How nice it must be to get a letter all your own from "Hazel." I think she is a frightening creature, though. But perhaps only if you were employing her. I have had maids like that, and they always made me cringe. But as a friend she would be different, and you could be heartlessly amused. Only Mr. Key has to cringe, and since he does this to so much financial advantage, no doubt it is not really so painful.

Next time you come we certainly must pay a call on her. It would be an honor, and we shall boast around among our friends no doubt that we know Hazel. Looking ahead a generation, perhaps anyone who has known *any* maid will plume herself upon the fact.

This has been a week of gaiety for the country mice. A really gay person would not think so, of course. But for us, an orgy of entertainment.

First, we went to the rehearsal of Ed's poem which Harl McDonald has set to music. This turned out to be a musical soirée as well, with a lot of musical V.I.P.'s present, and supper afterward. The instrumentalists, brasses, flute and drums, were drawn from the Philadelphia Orchestra. It was a thrill to see these faces so near which I have long stared at through opera glasses from the top balcony. We sat on the sidelines in the huge music room of Harl's big old-fashioned house, and shivered slightly as we waited for them to begin. Frances Rains sat beside us (Claude is doing the narration) but she didn't shiver; this sort of thing is an old story to her; made me realize how detached writers and illustrators are from their audience; actual contact is shattering to them. Ed confessed later he'd had terrible stage fright.

The music is so stirring it makes your hair stand on end. Perhaps words and music can never mean exactly the same thing, but in this case they are very close. The poem is about Washington and Lincoln, originally called "Artisans," and had always about it, I thought, an exhilarating atmosphere of the early days of the country. You feel this too in the musical version, "Builders of America"; the choice of instruments, drums and horns, puts me in mind of the picture of the three Minutemen, playing flute, fife and drum as they march; and there is a wonderful simple little air the flute plays as background for the narration; you can imagine an Arkansas traveler during a dull stretch taking his flute out of his pocket and tootling away the time. The choruses are really beautiful, and then there are a good many splendid crashing spots in the accompaniment (piano here) that give you a tingling up and down your spine, just as the "Star-spangled Banner" does.

Quite an achievement all around. Ed is now known among our friends as the "poor man's Leonardo." What he can do more I cannot think, except perhaps join a juggling act in a circus.

Then, in rapid succession, we went out to dinner twice, after one of these sessions took ourselves to hear Elizabeth Bowen speak, long a great admiration of mine. I am glad to be able to say she lived up to her reputation. So often, great admirations don't. She is a big handsome red-haired Irish-Englishwoman, with an aristocratic high-bridged nose.

She speaks with, of all things, rather a stammer. I thought this appealing, and, I must say, it impressed me with her courage. To me, it's bad enough to have to speak anyway, but to undertake it, knowing you are going to stammer! The truly remarkable thing was that she was quite unconcerned about it. Usually the agony of watching a person stammer is your sympathy for them: how embarrassed they must be! But when we realized that it mattered to her not at all, the occasional long waits during which she coerced her recalcitrant syllables ceased to be an obstacle to us as well. She began to talk very seriously about the situation of the writer in the world of today, and mentioned, with a kind of mild dismay, the overwhelming competition of the radio, the cinema, television, even comic books. This was done apparently without any idea that there would be those who agreed with her; merely mentioned with detachment. Yet there was still a function for the writer to fulfill, she assured us; in the face of so much entertainment and information presented so easily, on a platter, so to speak, to the audience, asking no contribution from them, the writer served to keep open the channels of imagination, since he requires the reader to use faculties which life today would otherwise allow to atrophy.

Individualism, too, was tending to die out, she said sadly. Women wore the same clothes, and looked the same, thought the same thoughts, even in England. Here, of course . . . she paused kindly. Then I considered for a moment, the fine and fertile individualism of most English women writers, herself, Virginia Woolf, shy and fey, fanciful and profound, with a gentle musing face; Edith Sitwell, fierce and inspired, with the air of an Elizabethan high priestess; Rebecca West, a keen and subtle reporter, a powerful novelist. Though these names I mention are in the very top rank, and many lesser lights make up the total of English women writers, still, in the aggregate, I think they make our own w.w. seem superficial. They have been too early inoculated with success, caught the ear of the masses at once, come to forced growth, ripening under the glare of publicity. The day of a successful American woman writer, the thousands of words written before noon, the departure for various afternoon engagements, perhaps a speaking one, or an appearance before television or radio, sleek with the brittle polish we require of our ladies, is more that of a public figure, which indeed she is, than of a thoughtful person engaged in creative work.

Miss Bowen assumed apparently that no writers had come to hear her. She said at one point, appealing especially to creative people, that she was aware there were sculptors and painters in the audience (there had been a dinner for her earlier in the evening, and she had no doubt met them there), and, she added, "Perhaps there are musicians." But not, writers! I wondered why. In England, do other writers, jealous and self-absorbed, remain away from a rival's lecture? Ed suggested that I should go up afterwards, and propound my query. But I thought I would spare Miss Bowen this. My sympathy is always with the figure momentarily in the limelight, who must endure so many casual banalities.

And so back home to country chores deferred. Struggled through same for hours, just now see daylight ahead. Will have hewed way back to desk by tomorrow. Writing you then.

Love,
Barbara

p.s. Called farmer to remind him this was the time to spread our manure. Couldn't. He'd gone to Florida for a midwinter vacation.

Stillmeadow
Can Spring be far behind?

Dear Barbara:

I shall cherish the copy of the Cantata, and the music does look, to my untutored eye, most impressive. You and Ed must have been dizzy with excitement, I should have been.

Possibly Elizabeth Bowen never goes to hear writers speak herself! But most writers love to hear other members of the lonely art, I think. I do think a writer who speaks with ease and grace is on the rare side, there is a kind of shyness about most of those I have known. I've sometimes thought many of the best writers have had to write because they could not communicate freely by tongue. In that case, the typewriter forms a slight shield.

I have been trying to make something of Edith Sitwell. Her recording, set to exquisite music, is so fascinating. But much of it might be Chinese. Connie finally copied the words out for me from her book—since I don't have Miss Sitwell's poems. Even with the words, I would not say all of it is clear as crystal! It's better just to listen to her curious vibrant voice and catch a bit here and there.

I can't tell which of the new poets are my favorites. Dylan Thomas perhaps. Christopher Fry's "The Lady's Not For Burning" is fascinating. Many of his passages blaze with genius.

Generally, I like best poetry which is simply expressed and sings in the mind. Lines like Andrew Marvell's "The grave's a fine and quiet place, But none, I think, do there embrace," seem to be so simple, and to hold so much.

I don't care to keep a dictionary beside me when I am reading a poem.

I love lines that I can put in my pocket and bring out easily. This morning, for instance, I was hanging blankets on the line and thinking of Miss Millay's "Spring rides no horses down the hill, But comes on foot, a Goose-girl still."

Then I pinned the socks up and stood looking out over the rosy-tinged swamp. "If I were to walk this way," I thought, still with Miss Millay, "Hand in hand with grief, I should mark the maple spray, Coming into leaf."

In other words, I like my poetry to live by.

It is fun to look up things—just odd things, but that is a separate sport. Connie and I had a fine hunt for the actual genesis of Lucifer one Sunday. Lucifer, we found, was first mentioned by Isaiah, who called him the Morning Star and was referring to Nebuchadnezzar. At least as far as our pile of reference books went, that was so.

I had always thought Milton invented Lucifer for "Paradise Lost"!

Having to go to town this week, I spent the night with Connie. It always seems strange as the train leaves the green countryside, the pale young mist of the trees recedes, the tall battered tenements loom in serried ranks on either side. Little tin cans of geraniums on the fire-escapes, laundry hung out of window, getting extra soot and smog on it, children racketing around in rubble in dark corners. The city is great, and dramatic, and dazzling in so many ways, but I could wish the poor women a washline hung between two appletrees and the children a brook and a sweet meadow.

My taxi driver was a strange and gloomy man. He spent the time telling me how dangerous New York has become. You can get mugged any minute, day or night, said he. Poke your nose out after dark, you're done for. His mind was so much on the hazards that I began to feel nervous. Maybe he himself was a little unhinged. And when at a red light, he drew out his record pad and wrote my destination on and said darkly, "Now you know you're safe," I really began to quiver.

Connie's apartment is gay and decorative, comfortable with books and good paintings and furnished with the best records. If she still seems like a little girl keeping a doll's house, I realize that is only my maternal feeling. I might remember tea served in acorn cups and Hollyhock ladies sitting around the table, but I am recalled to the present when Connie opens the Vin Rose and sets the table with Leeds plates.

There is a little Italian place nearby where Joe has made his famous Pizzas for over twenty years. Connie dashes out and comes back breathless with a Pizza as large as a dance floor, steaming hot and redolent of garlic and cheese and tomatoes and anchovies. Joe has a brick oven and slides the Pizzas in on a long flat shovel. He will positively never make them ahead of time, you must go and wait while he bakes them.

Connie brought an Italian salad in, and Joe, out of sheer friendliness insisted on a serving of spaghetti.

Crusty hot bread came too, and Connie staggered under the load. She has become an expert cook since she acquired her own kitchen, but she knows my weakness for a true Pizza and she served it forth with a gay "here it is, Mama."

The salad had those little wrinkled black Italian olives in it. And crisp greens, and a smooth tangy dressing.

I decided New York was not as fearsome as the taxi driver opined!

In the morning two of Connie's young Columbia marrieds brought their respective year-old little girls for a visit. Marcia is grave-eyed and has a fluff of soft silky dark hair. Liza has gray-blue eyes and a shock of red-gold hair. They staggered around in widening circles, walking being a great accomplishment. Now and then they fell back on their round little rears and looked amazed. They got up by bracing their arms and legs and upending on all fours. No knee action at all. When they collided on their journeys, they grabbed at each other, passed on. Marcia made a serious effort to sing, by sticking her round pink tongue out at one side of her mouth and making rolling noises. Her mother *said* the song was bye, baby bye low. Liza took her mother's scarf and draped it over her and then forgot it and staggered off, trailing the long silk behind her like a Princess. Their only mutual activity was to empty a jar of hard candies and hand them to each other, snatching them back as fast as they gave. Then Marcia ate a wad of cellophane and had to have it fished out of her throat. The only time they were quiet was when they wavered to the kitchen. It was so still. So still that one mother flew out. They had extracted a paint brush from a can of turpentine and were really engrossed.

Liza thinks the world is funny, already at age one. She twinkles and grins. Marcia is more of a ponderer.

I deeply admire the young couples who are getting their Ph.D.s or starting in the advertising racket, living in a matchbox apartment and raising such normal sound little children. They paint over old second-hand furniture, they budget their small salaries, they baby-sit for one another, they do their own laundry in the basement washer, they walk the streets and go to the Park twice a day for what they assume is fresh air for the babies. And they have a lot of fun! It is a kind of Young America I like to see.

When I got home, in the deep clean country, I wished I could pack a few boxes of unsullied air and mail back to them.

Two bluebirds and a grosbeak today!

And I picked a bouquet of snowdrops. They look so fragile to be blossoming so bravely against the cold dark earth. I sometimes think they are the purest of all flowers that are. Their bells are so translucent—but then, I have probably told you before about me and my snowdrops. When the tender cool little stems break in my fingers, I think the feeling alone is enough. Is frangible a good word?

They are a thoughtful flower, with their bent heads. And they would

never be noticed at a party given by the peonies! There is nothing tender or retiring about the personality of a peony. Full and rich and luxuriantly leaved, I enjoy them too, in their own day. But not as dear to me as the gentle and shy, but incredibly brave little first flowers of spring.

Much love, snowdrops in your border,

GLADYS

SUGARBRIDGE

In some ways Ed and I are like Jack Spratt and his wife, which although we do not know how Mr. and Mrs. Spratt actually got along together, is still our example of complete marital cooperation. Ed likes to go to West Chester, our nearest shopping center. I hate it. So when he began to be at home all the time, it was natural for him to take over the marketing.

This was ideal for me, for when I am working, I do not like to be distracted. And writing, I find, is a cumulative thing with me: the more I work, the more I am able to. If I begin in the morning, and nothing prevents, I roll right along through the afternoon hours, and really like, when I can (this means when some kind soul clears away the dinner dishes) to go across to the studio to utilize that still expendable time before bed. I still remember with a sigh the one time I was totally unhampered: Ed and Ned took off for Maine in the early summer, Chief was out at pasture, and even Duke was parked somewhere, so I had nothing but my work to think of. I lived the whole time in a pair of jeans, and slept on a sofa in the studio when the spirit moved me. I felt like Balzac, writing at top speed on nothing but black coffee (occasionally I cheated and nibbled bits out of the freezer). My hair strang around my face, and I do not doubt I resembled a beachcomber, but I finished half a book in six weeks and it was pure heaven, as well as a proof that I could really work hard if nothing deterred me.

Ed is completely different in his work habits, being much cleverer than I. He gets through all the mental labor he is capable of in a few hours. It's wonderful to watch him: he dashes off a complete story in an afternoon, or turns out all the sketches for a book in one morning, or writes a couple of poems any old time. Often in the morning when he's still half asleep, or when he is just dropping off at night he will mutter a couple of lines to himself, or some quip; these bits it is my duty to write down at once, for he will forget them forthwith. It is a habit I formed years ago, disliking to see this mental quicksilver lost. But when he has done his stint for the day, he needs a change, and so he goes in to West Chester to do the errands.

However convenient this is for me, I cannot resist teasing him a little, and remind him of a jingle he once contrived:

"He put on his mental plumage,
And went out to do some damage . . ."

For it refreshes him to sharpen up his wits a little on the local characters, making the round of the shops, and to garner a fine hoard of town gossip, enough for us to chew over in several days to come. He meets the other "wives" puckering their brows over long lists, and he takes care afterward to tell me how much I am envied. "Little do you realize," he sighs, "what a husband you have." His face secret and alight with anticipation of imparting the hidden nuggets of news, he carries in the large cartons of provisions. Bit by bit, to get the best effect, it all comes out, and to his obligato of West Chester fact and fable, I unpack his purchases. Although I have given him a list, it encompasses only the humdrum needs, and the articles which he has bought on his own are what I'm interested in, for they are usually on the fantastic side. Such as the day he brought home a dozen cans of rattlesnake meat. Today it is Greek olives, the dried, bitter ones, artichokes, a round loaf of Portuguese black bread. . . . I think, So these are his hidden desires. Perhaps there is a secret longing common to all males to express themselves this way once in a while. I remember hearing one woman of my acquaintance say, "I never let my husband go to market. Why he buys anything at all!"

Strange events wait for Ed, even on prosaic Gay Street, the town's main thoroughfare. Last Sunday he came back with the "New York Times," and a tale to tell.

"I saw a man carrying the most enormous horned owl in a bucket."

"Go on!" I said, breathless.

"He was crossing Church Street followed by two policemen."

"What *happened?*"

"I stopped and got out. It was a stuffed owl."

He looked so rueful I couldn't help laughing, and we fell to talking of the baby owl which he picked up on the road once, and kept until we grew weary of providing it with "fur and feathers," and passed him on to an owl fancier nearby. He did learn how to fly in our bedroom however, flapping from picture to picture on the wall, and I can still remember the curious low hooting he used to make, clinging to the window screen as night fell. For a long time after we suspected every owl which came to hoot of being *our* owl, returned to greet its foster parents. Who knows, I hazarded, but what *that* owl was ours grown up, dead, stuffed and carried in a bucket? It might be, I said, liking the sound of it. Anyway, it makes a good end to the story.

B

APRIL

When that Apprille, with his shoures . . .

MY DEAR:

Think of me having another birthday! Here it comes, a-gallop, a-gallop, and nothing I can do about it either.

When I was growing up, I could hardly wait for my birthday. We made a great to-do in our family over anybody achieving a birthday. In the morning, I found a special surprise at my place on the breakfast table. We had all my favorite dishes to eat, and usually a party for me at night besides. All day packages appeared, and everything was special. My birthday cake glittered with blue candles.

In that time, girls could only accept candy or books from boys, or flowers. Our Riverside greenhouse sported carnations, red and white, Easter lilies in season, Jerusalem cherries for Christmas. I never got *any* flowers from my beau. For books, the stationery-book store was rather limited. I never got a book either.

What I got, and hid, and cherished was a thin silver locket, entirely

taboo. I spent more time hiding that locket than I ever gave to any other activity in my teens. If Father had ever discovered and confiscated it, I think I would really have died.

I had one friend whose parents were so lax they let her accept an ivory comb and brush set from her current steady! I was a little shocked, all the while hiding my locket under my camisole!

There is a definite milestone in this birthday business. Growing older means being free—leading one's own life—being independent. And then suddenly one realizes that nobody is ever either free, independent, or leads one's own life. From there on in, birthdays lose their charm!

I never feel any older, that much I know. I hope I feel wiser and more tolerant and more full of loving kindness. But it is a frightening thing to wake on one's birthday and sit up and ask oneself, what have I done for the world this past year to make it better for me being a year older? At this point, I sink back and feel quite desperate. I add up my virtues and they make a very small line. I have tried to be cheerful day in and day out—maybe this is wearing to the family, too. Maybe I should throw an iron spider around once in a while, who knows? I have fed the birds, loved the dogs, given of my small substance to the needy, cooked my head off for visitors, washed and scrubbed and polished copper pans. Sent my monthly letter to the world via the "Ladies Home Journal" and faithfully answered every bit of mail.

Doesn't sound very much, when added up.

I don't suppose I could get any credit for loving the moon over the budding maples, for that is purely selfish.

We celebrated my birthday chiefly by driving around the back roads and stopping to pick up fallen branches for kindling. Winter strews them, his tide recedes and there they are, crisp and inviting. The lure of kindling is quite universal, I think. For when we were at the Whitneys' to get Daphne after a special operation, they were having a glass wall built next to the receiving room in the hospital. Mrs. Whitney, who looks as if she just stepped out of Bendel's window, or had just said goodbye to Fath, Dior, and Valentina, kept hopping over and snicking up a discarded piece of the framework. "I just can't resist kindling!" says she.

The Whitneys are fabulous people. Leon not only operates as a full-time surgeon and medical man in his hospital but does research for Yale, writes several books a year and has a column in a leading magazine. In his spare time he hunts coons and raises guppies, studying genetics with the latter. Mrs. Whitney runs the desk, wraps pills, answers the phone, and tries to persuade Leon to buy a new suit, which he never has time to do.

"A real loss to human medicine," said a Yale doctor to me when Leon sent me over for my arthritis. "He would have contributed something great."

Naturally I feel he does now, and when I see the rich and the poor streaming into his office with their dearly loved dogs, I think he does a pretty fine job. It's quite a story, for his son decided to be a veterinarian and told his father so. All right, I'll be one too, said Leon, and went to school again and was. We speak of them as young George and The Doc, but no disrespect to George, who is an expert if there ever was one.

The last time we took a sick dog over, Leon presented us with a pair of guppies, some medicine for me, and his newest book. I also checked over the galley proof for his next tome on distemper, which will be the volume to end all volumes on distemper.

But they had to get an auditor or accountant to balance things because Leon hates to charge people for anything!

Great personalities are rare in these days. He is one, and when he comes into the room, puts a dog on the table, and twinkles his bright eyes at you, you know it. There is never any hesitation, he knows. He gives it to you straight, whatever it is. And Mrs. Whitney runs over to the house to scramble eggs if your dog needs coddling and loves eggs!

A great breeder, Leon raises Red Bone hounds and offered Jill one for Obedience training. "He will howl all the time," he added.

Jill thought of our neighbors and decided to wait!

Leon told me when he hunts, he only kills old coons, mean old males and that he would give me enough for a fur coat. I thought a fur coat made of mean old skins would be fine! Haven't got it yet.

Leon hunts whenever he can. I daresay spending fourteen hours a day saving animals' lives wears him down until he wants to go out and shoot something as an anodyne.

He seems to be a man who never needs sleep. Otherwise how can he turn out several books a year, do research, manage a full-time busy hospital, and go in for tropical fish?

One trouble with most doctors, human or animal doctors, is they never tell you what is wrong, or what it implies. But Leon always tells you the exact picture. We can do so much, no more, he says. This is so and so and caused by such and such—that's it. I think people can face the truth better than not knowing anything.

Well, I know I can equably bear these accruing birthdays when I think of my friends! Life would be a heavy pilgrimage without the richness of friends. Every one special and heartroom enough for all of them. We all have a deep inner loneliness, I suspect, but the warmth of friends does nick the edges of it. And to be worthy of friendship is a fine goal for a life.

For that matter, to really deserve the love of a dog is a good goal. The love and loyalty of a dog, the patience with queer human decisions they cannot understand, the all-forgiving wags and licks after being abandoned—these are priceless. People have to be pretty nice to justify the way their dogs love them.

So here I go to feed mine—

GLADYS

You have an April birthday, too? I must have known this, but somehow it never struck me before as such a coincidence. April *looks* right for you, blue and gentle and spring-like, but astrologically, you know, it comes under the sign of Aries, the Ram. (Once I occupied myself with cusps and trines.) It is a fiery sign, and Aries people are said to be savage creatures. Now, I cannot think this of you, Gladys. Oh, well, you might get a little tried once in a while, but not really fierce.

Aries does not belie me. I know I have a violent temperament, but I do try to master it. Sometimes Ed looks at me while I am in a rage, and says wonderingly, "How can anyone so little (not that I am!) be so full of unruly passions!"

This year my birthday falls on Easter. My mother had her heart set on my being born on that day, and I almost was, but see how long it has taken me to actually make it! Out of all childhood birthdays, the best remembered although not happily, was that one celebrated by a party on the nearest Saturday, which was April first. You've guessed the rest; nobody came. April Fool!

In our family, we make quite a thing of doing our own birthday cards. No commercial monstrosity dare cross our threshold. The night before everyone but the birthday celebrant are busy with pen, paints, and rhyming dictionary, amid whispered consultations, and wondrous are the results. Even Duke has been known to send a print of his paw, and, down the years, the various pets of the family have found a willing amanuensis in any of us. "Happy Birthday to Ma-Ma from Kitten," I came across the other day in my manuscript chest, in Ned's baby handwriting. For we never, never throw them away, our birthday cards. We have enough of them to fill an album right now, I should guess. All of Ned's earliest ones. Trains, boats, and cars these were, strikingly composed, changing then to landscapes, till finally they became neat decorative script, and expert collegese, "Sorta late, but . . ." you turn the page to find a mammoth birthday cake, all alight, with appropriate salutations. Each one brings back its memory; that year he was snowed up in his Maine college and couldn't get out to buy anything.

Ed's are always lively and spontaneous, so gay and affectionate that it lights up a gray day to get them out and look at them.

> "Not so warm as me,
>   But as warm as fur can be,"

he once wrote to accompany a tippet he gave me. Though that has long since passed out of my hands, the verse remains, more precious still, and should I lose the scrap of paper on which it is written, the echo of its lines would remain. A birthday memory-book—it's a nice thought, isn't it?

A cloud, against the light in April is a thing I love. April clouds are small and fleecy, and seen thus, its edges bright with sun behind it, its center shadowed, it puts me in mind of an ethereal poached egg.

Stillmeadow

Hi There:

If you are there! I have been riffling through the mail daily looking for your letter. Instead I have many opportunities to join Quilting Societies, try that new shampoo for my dogs, and contribute to the Girls' Vacation Fund. Also letters from women who want to know how to break a dog from howling at the radio, to keep a daughter from marrying a man she doesn't like, to decorate a kitchen, to raise lemon thyme, or to make barbecued spare-ribs.

You, too, Aries!

You are no doubt planting. Which is more important to a country-woman than any other pursuit! Tucking those hard little pellets in the rich earth and just knowing they will grow is a wonderful experience, recommended for any kind of heartache. We can't plant as soon as you, we are constrained to wait until the maples are in bud or even in leaf. Except for radishes and onions and lettuce and peas, we have to postpone the main planting until some time after you are all set to watch for the pricking of the ground.

We never have any luck with peas, except the edible-podded ones, which are so good and so many people do not know of them. The delicate slender pods, snipped casually in pieces and cooked with a mint leaf are perfectly delicious. No shelling either.

A bouquet of dog-tooth violets in a milk glass salt shaker is a lovely thing. The tawny pale yellow pinked with brown is a contrast to the milk white. The long lance-shaped leaves are beautiful in themselves. A browny-green. A stippled effect, really.

Since it has rained today, not an April shower, but a hearty downpour, we have done the small things waiting for a long time.

Jill has sorted the spools of thread, all inextricably wound up, the way they always seem to be. Set up a new clean sewing-box. I washed and re-hung the pictures in my dressing room. Wish I had that picture of you and Ed on the boat to add to my gallery. Pictures of loved ones give me to think as I wash their glass and fish up the hangers again, and drop the box of assorted household nails and pick every nail up laboriously.

Time keeps going on, I think. But the people I love never seem to age in my eyes. When I see them, I look at them with the eyes I focused when I first knew them. This is a fine and comforting thought, they do not grow older to me.

I always hope that I do not resemble my pictures. The few times I have had to have a portrait photograph taken, have been horrid experiences both for me and the perspiring photographer. We barely lived through it. Hal Phyfe did a masterful job by discussing the real and only way to make bouillabaisse, but I know he had a hard time retouching me to look like a glamor girl.

Hal himself is a fascinating and photogenic person. But he had asked me to wear white and, in December, I had considerable difficulty finding anything white. I ended with a kind of nurse's or companion's surah silk, suitable for boating off the Bermuda beach. I could see myself determinedly herding a retired banker and wife to a shady spot on the deck of the sight-seeing yacht. It made me feel even more self-conscious, knowing that immediately after the posing, I would be bound back to the farm to get into jeans and wash the dog pan and pick the briars out of Teddy.

When a photographer tucks one finger under my chin and raises my head ju—ust a trifle—I go rigid. My smile glues itself on, and looks glued. I breathe heavily. My knees go stiff suddenly, from my perching on the thing that feels like an old-fashioned piano stool.

I try to concentrate on something noble, so as to get a nice expression on my face. Then as the shutter clicks, I realize I have shut my eyes and squinched up my mouth.

The result is not world-shaking, even when re-touched.

Whereas Faith Baldwin can be snapped at any moment, by any newsman or photographic expert. She looks poised, natural, gay and wise, charming, and exquisite. It is not just her size nine figure either, it is a camera attitude which I, alas, shall never achieve.

Steve and Olive came for tea today. They have a new fancy bird feeder, so fancy that no bird would have traffic with it. But Steve brought out a stuffed canary which he had used in a very special decorative set-up. He put the stuffed canary inside the feeder, and the birds are now rioting there. The problem of getting the birds to Sugar Hill is over. Steve and Olive now have all the kinds we have, plus a morbid hunched up large bird that nobody knows. Maybe this bird was emotionally upset by the canary.

Tonight I looked out of my door to see the moon slipping through the branches of the great sugar maples and I saw the reason our own

peanut butter feeder empties itself so fast. A very small, pointed nose sliced around the trunk of the tree, a bright dark eye peered at me. I stopped breathing. In a moment, a tiny flying squirrel snicked neatly onto a chickadee perch. The little wingspread was oyster bisque and looked softer than any silk. The body was minute, but vibrant with energy. While I stood, not breathing, my lungs constricted, the tiny nose vanished completely in a peanut butter hole. Then with a whisk, the small one flipped back to the trunk to investigate the world all over again. Satisfied, he nipped back and took a large morsel of the nice brown buttery meat. Then he ran up the trunk, disdaining his wings, just on tiptoe. Back again.

I missed the climax of the radio program I was listening to, which happened to be a Charles Dickens story. One I had not read. But no matter, I saw the delicate, shy, wild thing, and knew he was happy with my peanut butter. I felt like Our Else in Katherine Mansfield's "Doll House." "I seen the little lamp," said Else, who could never, never have that doll house. I saw the baby flying squirrel having his first great adventure.

Jill said, "No wonder it goes so fast." And we began to think we might turn into a mammoth feeding station, with peanut butter two feet deep all over the place. Suet covering every tree trunk. And the lawn nothing but left-over sunflower seeds sprouting and growing lanky and firm.

But never mind that, we know we had the experience of seeing a very small, very shy wild thing feeling that human beings might be all right.

Not death-dealing always. For the baby saw me, saw Jill when she came. And dove into the peanut butter again.

Caged birds, caged animals, as well as caged people are not according to Nature's plan. Johannes has a friend who owns a parakeet. The parakeet sulks in his cage and when urged to come out says crossly, "I'm perfectly happy as I am." When he does come out, he sits on his master's shoulder, then goes back in his cage. When they again urge him to stop sulking and come out, he says snappily, "I wish you would leave me alone for three days!"

Now this sort of thing would drive me mad. In the first place, I would worry about the bird's negative attitude, and then I would worry because life didn't look any more exciting. Then I would begin to have complexes about my relationship with the bird. It wouldn't do.

As far as the cockers are concerned, I simply speak their language. This is more comfortable. But I wouldn't want them to address me in nouns and verbs. They utter one long careful sound and it says, "Please, I would like you to open the oven and slice me off the end piece of that beef." Very simple, and not thwarting Nature. Or they make a woof which means, "I will go out now and hunt mice in the barn." Or, if you are going to town, "I am going with you!" But this is all in cocker tongue, not human. Better so, for my comfort.

April is a chancy month here. Bitter knife-cold, oven-warm. Rainy. Sunny. But always the feeling of spring, the definite excitement of things growing. Such a wonderful month, promise of richness to come, restoring faith in the good bounty of Nature.

A bouquet of violets to you, my dear,
GLADYS

SUGARBRIDGE

GLADYS:

You have never been here in the early spring, and that is a real sorrow to me. For this is a friend's mission in life, to view one's favorite flowers in bloom, and admire. In April, all my best effects are to be seen, my wild flower garden, and the first and shyest of the season's bulbs. Sometimes no one at all comes to look, during all the three weeks of its luxuriance, and then I could weep. For it is like a mirage, or that Indian trick by which a plant seems to come up, flower, and die down, in the twinkling of an eye. My garden under the pines is for forty-nine weeks of the year merely a smooth blanket of needles. No one would ever guess that in the early weeks of April, it is a riot of bloom. It's no good to tell you, here mertensia shoot up, blind greenish purple heads, bloom in bluest bluebells, changing to pink; daffodils rise to set them off, and spikes of wood hyacinths, pink and white; Jacob's ladder, palest of celestial blues, Dutchman's breeches with its white waxy bells, yellow and red primroses, hugging the flagstone walk, white violets like velvet, pansies, spring beauties . . . what are words beside the reality? Then I have made a special planting around the little white birch by Ned's private entrance (the bachelor quarters of the house, once destined for a maid) a red, white and blue of crocus and tulips, ill-fated, had I only known it, because continually walked upon. I never make allowance, when I plant, for the space people's feet take up.

Well, anyway, later the dogwoods along our little stream come out in the usual way, and above them on the bank, a great bed of jonquils all the way down to the pool; I do love a mass of them. These my mother put in when we first came here, and each year they bloom again to remind us of her diligence. I think that perhaps, this is the finest way of all to be remembered, by some growing thing.

The mail has come, and I accept the violets from Stillmeadow to Sugarbridge. All else is bills and circulars. Dale Carnegie, I think it was, said never open second-class mail. But, you know, I suspect it exists just for people like us. Some mornings, I open even that labeled: TO BOX-HOLDER. Why? To stall off that dreadful moment when I must go back to my typewriter and the blank page. Anything for a reprieve.

P.S. There *was* something else after all. A long package, overlooked, lying on the ground beside the mailbox. I knew at once it was the much-awaited shrubs for my winter garden. This is my newest project for the side garden I've just been describing, to be located in the sunny angle made by two house walls, warmed by inside heat. There I hope they will prosper, and some day climb up to look in the front windows. Can you imagine anything more enchanting then having yellow jasmine tapping at the pane in January? I can hardly wait for next winter's chill winds to come, with this in view. When, cozily ensconced in my hibernal bower of wintersweet (yellow blossoms in December), Chinese witch-hazel (cowslip flower in February), winter hazel (yellow flowers in March), you may picture me looking down upon the sleeping wild garden below, not a shoot showing above the leaves (or only the unwary) and saying to myself, If winter comes, can spring . . . ! Certainly not far off.

On second thought, it might be a very fertile idea to have a garden of the seasons, all around the house?

B

BARBARA:

Lilacs are budded! Varnished and pointed and ready to come out in showers of loveliness. I am the watcher of the lilacs now. They cannot bloom yet, but they look so hopeful.

But the real announcer of spring is the red-winged blackbird. When they flock in the maple and make a to-do, we know spring is truly with us. Here we are, we are, we are, they say. I long to ask what they have seen, where they have been, but they will never answer. They only say here we are!

Where have they journeyed from? What vast distances are tucked under their feathers? Who can know? We can only welcome them with joy and peanut butter and suet and grain and assure them this a free hostel.

Swift and clear runs my brook, imperative with spring. The swamp is greening, the rich dark mud has a fine patina of moisture in early morning, everything smells so heavenly I nearly burst my lungs trying to get it all in at once.

"What's the matter?" asks Jill. "Do you feel bad?"

"Just breathing," I say.

April is a month of beginnings, of tender colors, of swift clouds and sudden sun, of the world made new!

Pull your first radish for me!

GLADYS

GLADYS MY SWEET,

Appropriate to April, when lambs frolic, and leaves come out, *our* man-child arrived home from college, for spring vacation. With the un-wisdom of most parents, we still think of him as a baby, although he drives the long way down from Maine in record time without a mishap, thriftily carting along with him a cargo of passengers who pay the expenses of the trip, and with whom he stops over. I am amused, though (and secretly gratified) to hear him say sometimes, "*She* didn't have any money, so I took her for free." Then, immediately after I wonder, parent-wise, Did we make him *too* generous for the hurly-burly of life today? An only child, we always urged him to share.

Anyway, he came in looking lean and fit, tough as a hickory nut, hefting a duffle bag I couldn't budge. If possible, he likes to surprise us, and get home anywhere from a day to several hours before we can hope to expect him. His delighted grin at our surprise is the same we remember from babyhood, and we love to see it.

His first day home, we prepared ourselves for uninterrupted bull sessions, with intervals out for snacks. We catch up then on all the episodes he thought it better to leave out of his letters. In order, of course, to spare his parents worry which might have given them a few gray hairs. He loves to torture us, now that danger is past, and he really makes it good. "Well, of course I'd have had my license taken away if there'd been a cop around," he says, with a sidewise glance in our direction, or, "That would have got me expelled from college, if anybody had known." This youthful sadism is quite normal, a psychologist told us; they torture their parents until they get some girl they're fonder of, he told us, and then they begin on her. I suppose loved ones exist to be drawn and quartered, and our children are not the only ones who do it.

Ned let it be known soon that he has asked a girl to stay during vacation, and this at once seemed strange to us. Although we have had a constant succession of boys since the age of three, and though during teen age the house was full of girls too, they came only for parties and picnics. I know quite well that young people have changed since our day, and visit indiscriminately, but still a girl staying overnight has inevitably a sort of a serious sound, to me. I wrote to her mother, and we have been in quite a dither. She doesn't come until next week, and I foresee the time will be spent in speculation.

Do you ever muse upon the coming state of being a mother-in-law? I have, since Ned was twelve; the beings I'm very fond of I always have to consider from all angles. Of course, since this question rates No. 1 as subject for "True Confessions," I'd say, we are all primed with it: Don't offer advice unless asked for, and maybe not then; consider the young couple as a unit, not *your* son or daughter; and *never,* never live with them. . . . It's one of those serious affairs which has a half-comic connotation in most people's minds, like having the mumps, or being hen-pecked; I suppose from being joked about over the ages. But I read once in the "Golden Bough" of a pertinent taboo held by (time out to look it up).

If a son-in-law has the misfortune to come face to face with his mother-in-law, custom dictates that he hide his eyes, and run rapidly in the opposite direction. This gets neatly to the heart of the matter, and shows, I think, that there is some basic difficulty in the relationship common to all men. And no doubt this is as good a way of solving it as any. But like birth, death, and marriage, it has to be got through as best we can. Bring on your daughters-in-law!

My own mother-in-law was perfect. She must have had an instinct about it, because I'm sure she was not an introspective woman. When she came to see us, she was kind and loving and interested, but not too interested. You never felt that she, like many older people, was avid to live vicariously in the experiences of her children. She had that pleasant kind of self-sufficiency that made you guess that while she was glad to be with you for a while, she soon longed to go back to her own concerns. This she always did; she never stayed more than a day or so with us, and I never was able to learn to know her as well as I should have liked to.

This is a Gladys-day. Bright blue sky, little white fleecy clouds. Just the day for airing blankets, or putting out a big wash on the line, if the same weather prevails in Connecticut. All these domestic traits of yours, so lacking in me, are delightful. I have to become enraged in order to make any housekeeping instinct function. I have to be angry with the house for getting dirty, or angry with myself letting it happen, before I feel any urge to remedy it. Then, sustained by my fury, and muttering peevishly to myself the while, I can do the job with some satisfaction. How alike we are, and how different! Perhaps the necessary basis for such an impetuous correspondence.

I'd love to see your new puppies. Our Mr. Miaow was carted off to the hospital the other day to have a rather middle-aged operation. Ed said reflectively, thinking it over, "I wonder how much we're being charged a day for his room?"

BARBARA

DEAR BARBARA:

Indeed this worry about being a proper (your word) mother-in-law is a grave one. I fear I should be a sorry one. Every time it seems inevitable, and then does not happen, I admit I sink back with a very cosy feeling. I think it is harder, perhaps, to see your daughter promise to honor and obey, than to see your son. A son tends to go away into his own private world more completely—at least judging by Jill's son—and becomes rapidly just a very welcome guest in the house. A daughter is part and parcel of living. This probably dates back into pre-historic days when the family was a clan—or rather, when it was a Matriarchy.

I have read many books and articles and I would certainly strive to be "no let nor hindrance" to any marriage my child made, but I would always have a sneaking wonder as to whether he really fully appreciated the fact that when great music is being played, she does not like casual conversation. Or that poetry is a real, live being to her.

When Jill's daughter got married, it was fortunate that both Jill and I had said if Dorothy refused him we were going to have him as a member of the family for ourselves. This makes a good comfortable start. We were in the hazardous position of not daring to speak too well of him lest we start one of those adolescent rebellions.

When Jill's son got married, we had only seen the bride once and it took us a year to get over the surprise. It taught us that the young people today go their own way, and expect the world to go with them. This is probably more sound than when we were young and Papa had to approve and Mama had to really like the prospective marriage partner or there was no go.

I suppose every parent looks back and sees mistakes made with the children, and wishes it could all be done over.

Often I wish I could begin again. Our original idea was that Stillmeadow would be a haven for the children and that I, who had no city job, would happily supervise my one and Jill's two. I didn't rest much. But it was my fault. Why did I ever engage in the battle to make Jill's daughter eat tomatoes? Many a man has lived and died without tomatoes. I had read they were full of vitamins and things. I felt sure her teeth would fall out if she forewent her tomatoes. Now, in my wiser years, I think it would have been better for her to lose every tooth in her head than to acquire such a resentment to me. Store teeth can be bought, but affection is hard to come by.

So I think the trouble often is that parents try too hard. Children who grow up as they feel like, have a better chance in many respects. Vitamins

85

may come and go, but ease and relaxation about life go on forever, if one has it once.

I am glad to see that now the experts feel babies should be fed whenever they yell for food. I was just born too soon. Many a time I watched the creeping minute hand of the clock and prayed it to hurry so I could legitimately feed my child.

It's heartening to know that the world progresses in some ways, if not in all!

Well, now we must get out the fishing tackle and shovel up some plebeian worms, in case we might catch something when the fishing season opens.

Happy planting to you,

GLADYS

SUGARBRIDGE

DEAR GLADYS

Soon it will be opening day of the fishing season. The brook down in the meadow is stocked by the state, so it is quite an occasion. Theoretically I am amiably disposed toward fishermen; it seems a placid occupation to which I could wish someone in my family were addicted, since I dote upon eating fresh fish. But I could be fonder of fishermen if they did not park anywhere and everywhere in our fields, leaving behind them a trail of greasy lunch papers, bottles, and discarded cigarette packages. I suppose this is "human nature." Did you ever think how seldom this expression is used to describe an admirable trait? It must mean something.

Our stream is one that fishermen drool over, full of deep green pools, of swift pebbly shallows; it draws them in droves in the season. Even the tiny branch that feeds our pool is so cold the year around that the game warden offered to stock it for us. "Of course," he said, "you'd have to name your creek." And at once our minds were busy. Sugar Run, we decided. But there it rested. Friends advised us that you had to feed the fingerlings ground liver, and that was a chore. It did seem we had enough beasties dependent on us without fish. But one year the game warden came around with a left-over bucket full of exquisite iridescent rainbow

trout, all pink and blue and silver. He put them in our pool since they were of a size to take care of themselves. I spent days sitting beside the pool watching for them to flash their fins out from a protecting bank in a swirl of color across the clear waters. Then the dam developed a leak, and we had to drain the pool to work on it. Clinton netted the fish, and we lent them to a neighbor's lily pond, where I regret to report, ducks immediately gobbled them.

At the age of ten, Ned dallied with the idea of becoming a fisherman, equipped with a rod and line he'd inherited from his paternal grandfather, a pro at the sport. He was just on the outer fringes of little boyhood, and it was a time I like to remember. He had a blue jeep hat, with NED in white letters across the front, and a friend named Petey, and a kajak christened The Fast Frog. They were brown and golden boys, like little fish themselves; they laughed all day long about private jokes of their own and I used to love to watch them paddle up and down the stream together.

Once, on opening day, I got up before dawn with Ned. We really had the edge on everyone else, living so near, we thought. It was about quarter to six when we groped our way sleepily down to the meadow. There was, however, enough light to show that the banks on both sides were lined with early fishermen.

Poor little fish! They were only put in the stream two weeks ago, and were going to be caught before they had ever lived. As Ned and I trudged home, we were not too sorry that we were empty-handed. Later, Ed, briefed by us, wrote a poem called "Heil Isaak!" which was published in the "Saturday Evening Post," and no Chester County fisherman has spoken to him since.

Ned and I had bacon and eggs that morning in the kitchen as the sun came up.

The girl Ned invited home has been, and gone. *Tout passe*, as the French say. Just as he has passed so swiftly from those early fishing days to what he is now. Well, she was quite a nice little Maine flower, no siren (transitory relief known only to mothers!) silently respectful and adoring of him. They went for walks, holding each others' hands. There was something touching about seeing at a distance, across the great smooth slope of one of our hills, those two small figures walking together into the sunset. I had a dutiful letter from her after she went home, and a pretty, ladylike present. The whole episode gave me a new, and not unpleasant sensation.

DEAR BARBARA:

Our Florida friends, Fred and Mary Lou, planned to leave for home early in the morning. I insisted I WOULD be up to get breakfast for them. They insisted they would quietly steal away.

I woke up with a dreadful start, leaped out of bed, and saw it was exactly five-fifteen. But a frightening sound pealed through the house, shrill and sharp. I thought, where did they get an alarm clock like that? Then I thought no, it can't be—it is the freezer going off. By the time I dashed to the cellar door, I met Fred rushing down stairs. Air raid? he said, or fire siren?

Now we could hear it was outside, and flew to the door. Our station wagon by the gate was just quietly blowing its head off. Lights went on across the road, dogs barked wildly. Fred ran. He got the car door open, the sound ceased like magic.

So we had breakfast at five-thirty and they really did get an early start. But Mary Lou says we probably can't depend on the car to blow every morning if we want to get up!

Fred, by the way, is a map expert. He sent us one of the most marvelous maps of our village, it has everything, even the tiny lanes and the houses. You should have one, for you would like to follow your walks and rides on a map. It is called a contour map. The National Geodetic Survey does them—spell that right?

Do you remember the drawing Ed did of Alice and Margaret's house that day last summer? It is almost time for that slope to be covered with daffodils. Time for them to come home from their island off the coast of Florida. The little old house has waited with a look of melancholy. Closed houses are sad things. I can hardly wait for the lawn chairs to be out on their terrace and see Danny the Gentleman Dachshund waving his absurd long tail.

Margaret does steaks on the fireplace in the charming Keeping room. Her special sauce is heavenly, and on a warm platter waits until she lays the steak on. You have to wait five minutes while the sauce blends—and it is a long five minutes.

Alice is a person I would like to do a book about. She operates on all levels at once, if you know what I mean. Her mind doesn't leap, it jet planes. And most people with super-intelligence lack the kindness and warmth and generosity of spirit which should go with it. Rarely do you find all in one.

GLADYS

Robins have such an important look, so serious. They have absolutely no sense of humor. My winter chickadees are so merry, but the robins act as if they were just on the way to the bank for a major business deal.

None of our birds gives a fig for the dogs. I hope it doesn't embarrass the dogs, sometimes I think Daphne has an odd look on her face when all her leaping and flashing around only means the birds sit on a branch and watch. With the cockers, the yard is often full of birds pecking at lunch while the cockers make their nose-down way around.

G.

SUGARBRIDGE
Chimera

DEAR G

Once about this time of year, I was digging in the side border, trying to fool the season by putting in some bulbs which should have been planted last fall. Suddenly my trowel leaped ahead, out of my hands, down into a hole. I gazed startled into yawning black space. But that wasn't all. Right there in full view was a big gray mole! I had invaded his run, dropped in, so to speak, and caught him at home. We were both surprised, but he recovered first, and vanished forthwith. I probably couldn't have brought myself to kill him, anyway, pest as he is. But I did regret that Duke was not at hand to do it. For, over the years, I've been saving moleskins.

I can't remember when I decided to try to skin a mole for the first time, but I do recall my surprise at the ease with which it can be done. The fur is so beautiful and soft, it was, and is, a pity to let it go to waste when the little creatures are killed to limit their depredations on the lawn. At that point, I optimistically made plans for having a moleskin jacket. But I don't believe I realized then how many skins it would take to cover me. This depressing knowledge, and the fact that the finished skins keep getting mislaid, has rather caused the project to lapse. I doubt at the present moment whether I could produce any other than the one Clinton skinned for me last fall, although there have been at least five or six. This one was a mammoth mole, a very granddaddy of all moles, and I see it a-top the cupboard in the garden room every time I walk that way, still pegged out on its stretcher. If they were all as large as that, I sometimes catch myself calculating, it would only take . . . ? But no. My moleskin coat is a chimera. Still it was a nice idea to play around with in my mind, and that's what nebulous moleskin jackets are for, no doubt.

SUGARBRIDGE
lament for the pooch

DEAR G.,

Herewith a plaint meant to go in Ed's letter, but grown tired of waiting for him to mail same. Very stale now, even with up-to-the-minute additions. But I'd still like your opinion. Knowing a big expert like you, I don't see why I should suffer in silence. So here goes, and thank you kindly in advance.

It's about Duke, my problem dog. Always a psychopathic pooch, he has now had a nervous breakdown as a result of dog class. Teeth chatter like castanets as we start out, legs won't support him, he's so excited. But it's worse when we get to class. Anti-social is a mild description. Growls and lunges at the males, is unchivalrous to females. Almost bit a black poodle named Georgette in two. Her mistress and I decided Georgette was the kind of girl that drives men mad. All very well to joke, but extremely inconvenient working conditions. If he were a little dog, it might be different. But you can't laugh off a choleric Great Dane.

In extenuation I ought to say he was once badly bitten by another dog when he first started out in Obedience, as a half-grown pup. This was perfectly unprovoked, and after that he had no confidence in dogs on leashes. What's more, he would never go through the exercise during which he was bitten, if he could help it. You could just see him remembering: when our trainer would say, "Now we'll have 'Follow the Leader,'" Duke would begin to shake, and nothing would budge him. Unless you dragged him by main force and this proved too shattering for both of us.

The class was very long-suffering. They are all wonderful people, each as interested in everyone else's dog as in her own. They only blanched slightly when Duke let out a roar and announced his intention of eating up their darlings forthwith. But it was awkward, and for reasons of security, Duke and I were rapidly becoming pariahs. I couldn't get near enough to talk to the chic little girl with the boxer, because he and Duke thirsted for each other's blood, nor could I draw close to the amusing woman with the gray poodle, because while she esteemed Duke for his noble appearance, she did wish to preserve her Brigand intact. I began to tremble the way Duke did, before class. The only dog he would work next to was a phlegmatic spayed female.

Finally, when I was so low I would have tried anything, someone told me to take him to a match show; it would give him poise. False confidence bore me up; on a spring morning Duke and I set out. To throw me to the lions, for that's what it turned out to be. The day got off to a fine start, with some people I knew slightly trotting up with their white Spitz, intent upon our dogs' being friends. The next thing I remember was picking myself up out of the mud where Duke, the Spitz and I had been revolving to the tune of bloodcurdling snarls. There was a large crowd around us, and there our notoriety began. There's not much shelter at a match show; you just have to keep walking around, and Duke got into fight after fight. "There's that monster!" I heard one woman say. People came over and stared at us, where we had finally withdrawn to a secluded spot, waiting for ring time. And all the while I knew that Duke was really a mild dog, and that he was only scared to death himself.

When the Dane classes came up (there was only one other besides Duke present) I had to shout, "Gangway; everybody fall back!" and then Duke and I went into the ring with a whoosh, as though drawn by a bulldozer. Since I knew nothing about showing, nor Duke a thing about being shown, I think we can skip the rest. We came out of it with one of those meaningless ribbons you get when there is no competition in your class. I was pleased, though. As Duke and I were preparing thankfully to fall into the car, a man standing by said, grinning, "Well, the bigger the dog, the smaller the woman, is what I always say!"

Well, that wasn't the solution, obviously. Just at the point where I'd about decided Duke and I could only retire to solitary confinement, I heard of a Dane kennels nearby, and that proved to be it. When Duke beheld eighteen or more as big and bigger than himself, he was surprised into silence. The owners, a couple named Cappel and their niece Marge, have a wonderful way of making a Dane feel at home. They introduced him to all the girls, and he fell promptly for a pretty one named Golden Girl. After that he only made one attempt to show what a big bad dog he was, and when they laughed at him (they take fights much a matter of course) he began to lose his jitters. In no time at all, we were having a pretend dog show, to teach me a few ring tactics. Every night after

that, I went over and we gaited the dogs, and talked show. It was a time of intoxication with Danes, and dog people, and must have had an effect because Duke took second prize in his class at Devon, a fairly big show, and behaved much better. We only fell down once. And that wasn't his fault; the brindle behind us got out of control, and we all piled up together. Ned was standing on the sidelines with his camera, and I heard him say in a discouraged tone, "Mother's down!" I wasn't expecting it when the Judge gave us the beautiful ribbon, and the envelope with the still more beautiful money inside. We are going to consecrate one drawer of my desk to Duke's winnings, and never, never touch those crisp green bills, even when we forget to go to bank, and there's no money to pay Clinton. Well, it was a wonderful doggy day, everyone smiled on us, and we went home on top of the world. *Is there any more satisfying feeling than having your adored dog win a ribbon?* If so, I don't know what it is.

But, Queen of the Cockers, this doesn't solve my problem. Duke is still a neurotic about Obedience class.

BARBARA

DEAR BARBARA:

This sounds stuffy, but the fact is Duke needs *more* Obedience. That is all.

An individualist like Duke takes a little more training. Some dogs meet every other dog with a smile and a handclasp, some don't. But if you really keep at it, you will be amazed at the result.

The odd thing is that jumping on other dogs, not minding the exercises, generally thumbing one's muzzle at the whole thing is a phase. Keep at it, and everything irons out.

I have seen a really vicious Kerry Blue change to a nice friendly dog who only sniffs at passing Elkhounds. Nervous Shepherds eventually wave their tails and lick people's hands.

But it isn't a quickie, like a patent medicine that cures all ails in one bottle. It is a going and going, with patience and amiability, but determination.

I have seen the most neurotic dogs cured of their neuroses by a good long course of Obedience, and how proud and happy they and their owners are! Winning the Davis cup couldn't be quite as satisfying.

Just keep at it, and you will be surprised!

G

MAY

DEAREST BARBARA:

At lunch today in the garden, I felt I must make up a packet of the beauty and get it off post haste. My own letter to the world (do you feel the way I do about Emily Dickinson? Can't you see her lowering her little basket from her window for things to be put in, her shy face hidden behind the curtains? But she KNEW her poetry was immortal, I just feel it).

In my little Quiet Garden the white daffodils were out in the sun today, pure silver cups. The tulips were white, and blue-purple and pale, pale gold. The grape hyacinths made a deeply blue border, and against the white picket fence the flowering quince spread a glory of salmon pink. Underfoot, the lemon thyme sent a sweet odor. It was almost unbearable. Like Millay I felt, "O world, I cannot hold thee close enough!"

The spring flowers are such a re-affirmation of God's grace. And the

Poet's narcissus will be out soon, and the big double ones whose name I do not know. A bluebird came by!

The lilacs are my favorites, I think, the white and the amethyst are opening and the blue Lincoln and the deep purple French. The heart-shaped leaves are glossy and beautiful and the clusters of the flowerets weigh down the branches with sweetness. There is a kind of extravagance about all this at once, when our reluctant spring really decides to dazzle us.

Lilacs belong to old houses, they should lean and look in the windows.

The great purple one outside my own window brushes against the old hand-hewn clapboards with clusters of blossoms. At night the sweet exciting scent comes in, and in the early morning the light against the pane is tinged with amethyst. The white lilacs have reached the tip of the roof now, they never flower so profusely but the delicate white clusters are especially beautiful.

Some previous owner of Stillmeadow did not care for lilacs and either

cut them all down or put them in the deep shade of the maple. It reminded me of the woman who cut down all the trees in the yard because they were messy shedding their leaves! Takes all kinds. We moved the lilacs that had survived, and nourished them and now we have a proud hedge all along the white picket fence. This year you must come when the lilacs are in bloom, for you cannot imagine it seeing them only in Midsummer or Autumn.

Although the glossy heart-shaped leaves are handsome all Summer.

White lilacs and dark purple tulips in an old ironstone pitcher give the table an air of elegance.

I wish we had the musk rose, "mid-May's eldest child," which Keats so loved. But we have so much in May that we should be satisfied. Everywhere we look, we can see flowering shrubs and trees. And in the garden the tulips go, but the late narcissus is there, and the iris is regal and the climbing roses already have pink buds.

Today the postman brought me a thin package from England. It was from an Englishwoman who has read my books. She wrote, "I am sending you a copy of the Severn miniature of Keats—your Johnny Keats." I have it on my desk. The beauty and strength of the face are startling, and one instantly realizes looking at him why when he entered a room all the lamps went on.

Whatever may be said of Severn, he was, after all, the one who took the fatal voyage to Italy and tried to ease the dreadful last hours.

As near as I can tell, Keats's friends were all violently possessive, and each one wanted all of Keats's glory shed on him alone.

I feel I would have been at home in Keats's presence but Shelley would have frightened me. I am glad that one time when he was ill he was persuaded to eat "a well-peppered mutton chop" and at once felt better. Shelley paid little attention to food, but Keats enjoyed dinners with good wine, and "small busy flames crackling on the hearth." He was always, it seems to me, very close to actual life.

When I visited Hampstead Heath, I had the strangest feeling that he had lived there only yesterday. Surely he had gone out to the garden just a short while ago. I felt very much embarrassed at intruding.

The violet dusk has come, the dogs are quiet after a tally-ho kind of day. We have a small fire in the barbecue fireplace down by the pond, we shall eat supper there so we can watch the night come softly down the hill. It is cool, these May evenings, but comfortable if we wear sweaters.

We are having what a man in a lunch grill once called "Hot dogs all the way." I loved the expression, and the frankfurters were decidedly all the way, grilled and split and stuffed with chopped onion, pickle relish, and a lavish amount of chili over all. They were hard to eat out of hand, but delicious. We weakly use forks.

Do you too have trouble surrounding all decks of a three-decker sandwich? Some of them were designed for mouths like alligators' that have a real spread to them.

How good the first tiny salad greens are, crisp and savory! And fun to eat and talk "while the willow trails its delicate amber; And the dairy pails Bring home increase of milk," as Keats says.

May is the poetry of the seasons, which may be why I think of poetry so much. May is lyric, possibly January is epic.

Also in May, I see my Unicorn more often. As you know I have a Unicorn. He comes down from the wood in the moonlight and crops the lilac blossoms and the grape hyacinths. I know when he has come, for some scattered blossoms are left. He also loves violets, especially the white-gray-blue Confederate violets which we brought back from Williamsburg. Sometimes I see his silver horn in the moonlight and then I know this is a very fine thing. His feet are delicate and tread lightly on the lemon thyme when he investigates the garden. And in case you take a realistic view of this and think I am silly, let me say my Unicorn has helped me over many a thorny path, and through many a dark hour. Everyone, I think, needs a Unicorn.

This winter a fan from California wrote to ask me if my Unicorn was here in the snow! He isn't ever, in winter, I said. He goes away, where I cannot say. I never see him.

Did I tell you the very nicest compliment I ever had—some "Journal"

readers from states away came driving up and the husband said as they came into the valley, "These are the haunts of her Unicorn." I shall never forget that.

Love
G

DEAR G,

Did you ever fall into a fit of gloom in springtime? No. I'm sure you haven't. In fact, I doubt if anyone but myself would go so against the grain. Still I think I have, on the whole, a fairly buoyant nature. I have my enthusiasms; I enjoy life. But, like Humpty-Dumpty, I can have a great fall, and then let anybody try to cheer me up.

I do not believe, of course, that any human being can be really happy for long. True happiness comes, and goes as quickly, a rare fleeting thing. But content is something else again. And for a whole month, I *was* content. With me, this was a record. I went my little round, with its duties and small pleasures, exuding satisfaction. This is easy, I thought; why did I never realize before that serenity is so simple? It's just a matter of keeping on even keel. But came a day of reverses; unexpected failure, on your part or someone else's, can be shattering, if other physical and psychic factors let you down at the same time. I had a day of black demons. All the mischances, the disappointments, the disasters of my whole life swept over me in a dark wave. I couldn't throw it off, and then I didn't want to. I gloried in my sorrow. The worst of it was that the day was exquisite, full of the sights and sounds, the scents of the loveliest season. But I rebelled against spring. Why should I make a fuss about it? I asked myself morosely. It comes in quite the same way each year, and each year I'm that much older. As though it needed your applause or encouragement, I said sternly to myself. Those huzzas at each new crocus or jonquil, that concern that a sudden freeze might finish them! Spring can get along without all that. It's like one of those shy people who move in upon you with the secret strength of lions. Bah! *That* for spring, and all its enticements! On days of lesser affliction, I can be cured by going for a ride, but this time I wouldn't make the effort. Nothing seemed worth doing. My family cast me glances of mingled concern and impatience.

Remembering back to early youth, I could recall similar and more frequent attacks. Yes, they had been the same; always that complete inertia, a kind of nausea of the soul. My only consolation now was that quite by chance I knew the name and history of this malady. Several years ago, I read a most fascinating book, "The Corner That Held Them," by Sylvia Townsend Warner; it is the intimate history of a small and inglorious convent of nuns in mediaeval England. Related there is the incident of a particularly insignificant nun, to whom no one, neither the father confessor nor her sister nuns, paid any attention. But she developed an unusual sin, and become briefly the center of them all, to her great satisfaction. It was called *accidie*, described as a sort of hopeless melancholy boredom. Well, accidie (or acedia, the dictionary says: mental and moral sloth) was certainly what was the matter with me, but I could not see that it had enhanced my charm. However, since the realization of my condition set in, I began to take a slight and growing clinical interest in my symptoms. And then—well, of course spring won out. There was a day when the apple blossoms came out pink in the orchard; the two rows of trees stood, on tiptoe, ballet girls, twirling their skirts of bloom over the green green grass, and, like a distant ruby, Chief stood grazing between them. Slowly, reluctantly, I began to relent. Well, there *is* something about this time of the year.

Then Ed, coming back from a ride the following day, began to sing his spring song, and I, as the left-behind one always must, played audience. "The woods are all in blossom," he said, taking out some flowering cherry branches from his cap, "and here," he liberated a spike of pink flowers from his buttonhole which neither of us recognized.

"Mr. D is simply on fire to start picking polk," he said. "He's been out visiting his secret spots. I saw him on the hill."

I put the flowers in some water. Oh, I *did* love the country and its people! Faded, little by little, accidie was almost gone. A Vivaldi number was on the radio, a Concerto grosso. By the time it was over, I was so much myself again that I was totally oblivious of it.

B

BARBARA:

It was spring the first time I came to see you. I remember it especially because we went out to the garden and pulled rosy crisp radishes and bright scallions for dinner. Later we sat around a nice crackling fire and had good conversation. And when we went to bed, you had a new book on the bedside table—the "Semi-Attached Couple," which was delightful. And you had TURNED DOWN my bed! I felt so luxurious.

Burton flew in from Ohio for the weekend. Don't you admire people who pop into a plane so easily? He gave two morning singing lessons, clapped on his hat, took his bag in hand and was here in time for cocktails. He brought me the biography of Lloyd Douglas, written by his daughters and we read aloud the chapter on The Shape Of Sunday after dinner. Then we played Glenn Schnittkee's recording of his concert at the University of Illinois, how I love the Schöene Müellerin cycle! Since Glenn has been working with Burton, his voice has grown in power and purity, it is an experience to hear him. Glenn has a very heavy concert schedule, and Burton has reached the point of trying to persuade him to give up some of his fishing trips, this is a hard sacrifice for Glenn. He loves to fish. He can drop a line in almost anywhere and catch fish, too. He says it is very simple, all you have to do is think the way the fish think. If he were not a great singer, he would undoubtedly be very happy tramping around the rest of his life in cold dawns with his tackle over his shoulder.

It may well be that those of us who do not happen to be born with a great gift are much more ready to talk about the responsibility to the world. Burton and I, in short, can more easily abandon Glenn's fishing jaunts than he can!

Saturday morning when I woke up, I smelled the delightful smoky tang of bacon sizzling in the pan. Burton, who is an early riser, had breakfast ready. While we did the chores, he went back to Anthony Trollope; he is always reading Trollope. So far, I have not become intimate with this particular author but the people who read him are the most enthusiastic of followers.

The visiting season is open now that the weather is so kind. Johannes comes next week, anxious to get the New York smog out of his lungs. He always leaps from the train, his cocker just behind him, and assorted parcels surrounding them both. "I'll make it for lunch," he says. And we have one of his famous omelettes. The minute lunch is over, he bounces up and says happily, "I'll go to the dump."

This is our worst and most dreaded chore and so far as I know, nobody but Johannes enjoys lugging a carload of rubbish up the treacherous hill to the village dump. But when we know he is coming, we relax about all those cartons of junk. A true dump-lover is about to appear, our troubles are over.

Since the summer he spent here writing his book, he also has a real intimacy with the dogs. He helps feed them, brush them, carry fresh water, he makes little visits to the kennel to chat with those taking their turn out of the house. I must say, although Johannes is a Viennese, he takes to life on a New England farm with more ease than many native-born Americans do.

I don't mean to give you the impression that Stillmeadow guests have to work themselves to death. I read an article recently on How To Be a Good Hostess. "Never forget to lay a fresh rose on the breakfast tray," said the writer merrily. It made me wonder how many people she had entertained! I shall try to remember a garland for your tray when you come, just to prove I know how it should be done.

Gladys

Sugarbridge
May apples are out

Well do I remember your first visit to us! I'd been hearing about you for years, during which time you were becoming more and more famous for cookery and cockers. Ed's office force (he was your editor then, if

you think back) were so sorry for me, because they feared I would not
be able to entertain you properly. Poor Barbara, what *will* she do! I had
some qualms, I will admit, and leafed through a good many cookbooks
to try to find something fitting. But too much solicitude defeats its own
purpose. I finally saw it must be just something we always had.

But I was hoping you would not find our house inimical. Some people
do, for it is a decided house. I can see them being unhappy; it's too small,
too old; the ceilings are too low, the furniture uncomfortable (Ed is
against the overstuffed). Then I suffer for them myself, a pain far worse
than they are enduring.

I was still in doubt about you during that book luncheon at which we
met. You wore a black suit, I remember, and looked ladylike, sweet and
a bit severe. What a place to learn to know anyone! All the publishers
displaying their authors, the authors displaying themselves, the journalists
out to exploit both. But when we brought you home and went inside and
built a fire, and sat before it to sip something, I could feel that we were
going to be friends.

I needn't have worried. You were, and are, a fine appreciative guest,
with the necessary psychic knowledge of *when* to lend your aid. (Our
kitchen is small, and I hate to trample.) Every housekeeper needs a few
pet visitors to come and admire, and make her feel that the sometimes
boring domestic routine is not in vain. I think that this would be a
worthwhile and sufficient career for anyone who had no other demanding
talents: merely to be a guest through life, going from house to house,
tasting, savoring, approving. In my youth there used to be many of these
pleasant characters about, mostly bachelors. They came to dinner often,
always on holidays like Christmas and Thanksgiving, admired everything,

sighed for domesticity (and probably thanked Heaven they were single), took you to the theatre, brought flowers and candy, and were generally indispensable. I know today only one like this, and he is in such demand that he must be invited months in advance; I suppose the growing female population has simply gobbled them up for husbands. Apropos of this, I once read a very discerning opinion expressed by Dorothy Dix in her column, in answer to a query about the shyness and fickleness of a suitor: "Do not try to marry this man," she advised. "He is a born bachelor, and to do so will only land you in the divorce court!" I think they should be left in peace, poor things. Drones, but with a difference.

We have one cherished guest (female) who says she never offers to help in the kitchen, fearing to be in the way, but she likes to mend, and solicits any mending her hostess has on hand. What more could you ask? She is always deliriously welcome in our house, but not only because of that.

In May, I make a practice of first putting one toe into the pool—and quickly withdrawing it. The next day, I keep it there a little longer, until it is numb, let us say. The day after that, two toes, and so on. Until, sometime, early in June (this is my optimistic supposition) I shall be brave enough to immerse myself up to the waist, which is the spot most tender to the icy waters. Then, after that, it is simple. Some warm noonday, when the sun is hot, and the water clear cool green, a quick dip, and they close around the neck. Then, thirteen frantic strokes across, (in order to avoid total congelation) and I climb out upon the dam, breathless but beatified, stung all over with a thousand little icy prickles subsiding into a delicious feeling of well being. I stretch my arms, and smile: another pool-season has begun!

STILLMEADOW

GOOD MORNING:

I hope it is a good one for you! Do you ever wonder about the eternally cheery radio announcers who say so blithely, "Have a GOOD day!" "Have a WONDERFUL weekend!"

Day after day they go on the air with this glorious enthusiasm, yet they too must have sinus attacks, children with measles, lost dogs, leaky faucets, the ills common to most people.

I know some of them who get up at four in the morning, catch a milk train to the city, rush to the broadcasting station and sing out their cheery greetings. A hardy race.

When Jill and I do have to get up while it is still dark to start for a dog show, it is heartening to listen to a disc jockey comment on the weather or play the "March of the Wooden Soldiers." The watchbird in the broadcasting booth helps us hurry, "It is now seventeen and a half minutes past six o'clock," says he with fearsome accuracy.

Connie, who is always up very late at night, often hears the Milkman's Matinée. She tells me I should try it, but since I have become a country-woman, I find I just cannot stay up past a reasonable hour. I manage to make it to midnight on New Year's Eve and that is the very best I can do!

Sleep, they tell me, is just a habit, but it is quite a necessary one to me. My Mother used to pop up in the middle of the night and run the sewing maching if she couldn't sleep. She got a good many jobs done in a couple of hours while Father and I slept.

Unfortunately, Father got up before the earliest bird, and felt lonesome unless Mama got up at the same time.

If she decided to ignore him, he got out the lawn mower and noisily cut the grass under the bedroom windows. Or he would tinker with the car and roar the motor. "It's about time you got up," he would mutter when Mama gave in and came downstairs.

It used to worry Mama that Father slept with his big shiny blue re-volver under his pillow. She was always afraid he would knock some-body off by mistake. But the way Father slept, a horde of Arabs could have come in and set up tents and he would never have stirred.

I admire you for being able to take Duke for a walk at three o'clock in the morning and really see what the world is like at that unknown hour. And the way you and Ed, after wandering around half the night, pop up around five, is amazing. It makes me, snugged down in bed, seem like what a friend of mine calls "an old duddy-fuddy." (And isn't duddy-fuddy better than fuddy-duddy? I think so.)

When I do have a wakeful night, I resent it. It's too easy to worry over taxes, make futile lists of undone jobs, wonder if those letters did get mailed or just stuck in the glove compartment of the car. The only thing I do not worry about at such times is the Russian situation or the atomic blasts they keep setting off in Nevada. These I worry about in the day-time. My personal worries bloom in the quiet night hours.

It is a good thing, then, to turn on the light and read a poem or two.

My neighbor Alice Blinn always has on the bed a "propping" pillow, and a "sleeping" pillow. The propping pillow is firm and has a mind of its own. The sleeping pillow is soft and gives in easily. So I now put my own propper under my own sleeper and read a bit before I go to sleep.

"For I have moved companioned by a cloud—" One of Elinor Wylie's loveliest lines comes to mind, and I pick up her sonnets. Nice night reading.

I wasn't sure, however, what to think when a woman wrote me last

week that she always kept one of my books by her bed to put her to sleep!

On moon-filled nights in spring, the dogs often see imaginary fiends in the kennel and yard. The various voices make a crashing dissonance. Or if a fox barks near the barn, they tear into a chorus. We rush out and turn on the yard light. Whoever has been the ring-leader gets a firm talking to. Often it is Melody, often Blazer.

Cockers are not really a barking breed, but when there is something strange going on, they can out-howl a wolf pack.

Daphne, the Irish, barks with a hysterical note, accompanied by rushing back and forth. If she is in the house, she covers the entire downstairs with leaping sallies. Rugs skid, chairs tip, ashtrays crash. When it is over, she sits demurely on the sofa, smiling. There, she says plainly, I have saved you from IT.

My life with dogs has always been rewarding, although not exactly quiet! But a house with no dog at all never seems really furnished for living!

Cats too are worth every bit of trouble they may be. It is not true that a cat does not love people. A cat orders his or her own world, and a cat will never beg for love. The sharp Siamese cursing that Esmé indulged in the first time I left her was amazing. And the final reconciliation when I was forgiven and a sandpaper tongue rubbed my cheek was a fine thing.

The Abyssinian is more open with his affection, a little less conscious of his superior rank.

I once knew a cat that nearly died for love. She stretched herself before the bedroom door of her vanished friend and would not move. Her friend came back just in time to keep her from starving to death.

Esmé's true love was Tigger, the sturdy black Manx. If he dozed on the hearth, ignoring her, she would move over and slap him soundly. If he still paid no attention, she bit him. She pulled his flat face down and boxed it. By then, awake, he would give her a thwack. Then they would play together, a graceful, ritualized play, very beautiful to watch. Around supper time, he went off to find a good mouse for his lady, which she accepted with regal grace. She tossed it coyly in the air a few times, turned her back and washed herself elaborately all over. He would remove his offering.

When Tigger died, Esmé was heartbroken. She retired upstairs for a long while and had all her meals on a tray in the upper hall. She lost her zest for pouncing from behind the rail at unwary dogs. She was listless about catnip. She was a Victorian at heart, and she went into a Victorian decline. She never recovered. That big black compact boy was her world.

Tigger was a gentleman, independent, quiet, minding his own affairs, but devoted to his home. If we had been away, he often was in the swamp hunting, but he would hear the sound of our car, and come leaping like black lightning across the fields. Meet us at the gate, accept some affection, purring like an outboard. Precede us to the kitchen and sit firmly by the refrigerator door and utter a sharp demand for milk. When he was ready to go out again, he loped to the door and rolled himself over and over, uttering an entirely different sound. If we didn't come instantly, he turned double somersaults. We never knew how he thought this up, but it always brought action.

The Abyssinian is quite a different cat. Of all those that walk in the moonlight, the Aby is the gentlest, most charming, and with the most delightful sense of humor. You have to be a true cat person to adjust to the volatile Siamese, but an Aby can get along with anybody. We had hoped our gentle, gay Aladdin would comfort Esmé. Far from it, she almost killed him. We had to keep doors closed between them. If somebody left one open, a horrid low jungle growl would sound, Aladdin would dive for refuge under the radiator. The dogs would jump up and down.

It is too bad that the breeders of Abys are so preoccupied keeping them exclusive that few people can have the pleasure of their companionship. We can't very well raise kittens with so many dogs, but if we could, I should raise Abys and endow worthy people with them!

Dogs and cats can get along very well, but we have felt a mother cat with six or seven tiny kittens would be nervously overwrought when an Irish nose slanted in at her.

I never can understand not wanting to share wonderful things—can you? Like secret recipes—it seems to me nothing is really good until you share it with someone.

The same way with books. I can't wait to pass around any good book I find. Jill says I am just a frustrated lending library!

It is time to pop the asparagus in the boiling salted water and slide the chops in the broiler.

Good eating to you—do you have an asparagus bed?

G

SUGARBRIDGE

I agree. Dogs are indispensable, but . . . !

The disadvantages of Duke are such as to be almost insurmountable, or would be, to the average person. That is why, no doubt Danes could never be as popular or as widely owned a breed as cockers, for instance.

The amount of food they require, and their size are of course the draw-backs which first meet the eye. But oh! there are lots of others! Not that I am bitter about them at all. On the contrary, this is a kind of litany of loyalty to the breed, sung by me and other Dane lovers, when we meet and talk about our darlings.

"Does yours drool?" I may ask.

"Oh, yes, puddles." (This would have revolted me before I owned a Dane.) "But I've discovered," he or she may go on, "that if it gets on your clothes, it's quite easy to rub off after it dries. And as for the spots on the ceiling and walls which they make when they shake their heads—well, they wash off in warm water."

Neither of us say anything about the threadbare look the furniture has in a Dane-inhabited household. You can recognize it at once. Everything, unless renewed very often, takes on a worn and mangy air, for even the best of dogs likes to sit on something soft occasionally. Near a window looking out toward our barn stands a chair which Duke has literally reduced to a skeleton of itself. They tell me that when I go out riding and leave him behind, he climbs up in this chair, perhaps as an act of defiance, perhaps so he can better view my selfish departure. My little maid, coming upon him there once, said, "He give me such a start, sittin' up there just like a man!" I have only caught him in the act one time (and very droll he looked) but considering the condition of the chair, he must have spent many hours in it. No, we Dane owners don't mind the ordinary depredations, the books chewed up, the sofa pillows scattered to the four corners of the house. But the alarming-looking furrows on the doors are something else again. Anyone examining them (and most people do, when they come to our house, but I've got over being apologetic about this) must think that a panther or a lion had been at work there. The deep gashes run all the way down almost every door in the house, competing with the more to be prized marks of early adze and plane. When Duke was more impetuous than he is now, if he were to be shut up in a room for safekeeping when we went out, he simply tried to take down the door. And in one case, he really succeeded. Do you remember, again on that first visit of yours, we went out somewhere in the evening, and left Duke behind in the house? When we returned, the place had a curious open look, as though a lot of people had been going in and out, all the doors standing half open. Something had, certainly, and that was Duke. Confined in the garden room, he had systematically demolished the door. The upper half was panes of glass set in leads; these he had chewed loose, pushed away the glass, and jumped through. Then, when he was out, he became lonesome, and wanted to return inside, so he had opened the other doors from the outside, and spent the hours of our absence going back and forth. There was something awesome about that destruction. But my chief reaction was one of sympathy, and I recall that you joined me, good dog-lover that you are. "Poor fellow, deserted all that time!" I determined then and there I would not leave him alone so long again. And we quite often after that had a dog-sitter, a nice woman who worked for us, a special friend and admirer of his. So, you see, I am heart and soul committed to my Dane-ophilia.

It is as though, out of the great reservoir of inanimate animal life you had called forth impulses in advance of their time, which but for you would not have arisen. In some degree, it is almost an act of creation; each devoted dog-lover, is, in the animal world, a kind of Pygmalion. But it seems to me a betrayal to desert, or give away, a dog with which you have built up such a relationship.

Yet, even so, many are the trips and outings I've given up because of my D.P. (Dependent Pooch). For I have determined never to desert him for an extended period of time. Once, in his more unmanageable days, we left him at a kennels while we spent a summer in Maine. When we went to bring him home, and I saw what the time spent alone, with no one to understand him, or talk to him, had done, I wept. His coat was dull and colorless, his eyes without any spark of life. He had relapsed into being merely a beast, no more a talking dog, a Man Dog, such as we were accustomed to. It took months to bring him back to that uncannily close relationship which you can have, if you are lucky, with a dear dog. So while I have him, I'll make the most of it: there never will be another quite like him; that I'm sure of.

It is sad to be without a cat. I was reminded by your lament over departed felines to say that Mr. Miaow did not survive his operation. At one time, it seemed that he would, but he failed to rally (the operation was successful, but the patient died). I'm afraid we don't have any luck with the Siamese.

Miaow dug his grave with his sharp white teeth, I regret to say. He was the victim of all those good meals of salmon, of liver, of meat, meat, meat! Never milk or cream, or oatmeal lightly sprinkled with sugar, as the breeder counseled. Miaow let it be known early in our acquaintance that if he did not have meat twice a day, he would pack his bag and leave for more favorable climes. Now that it is too late, I am sorry I did not try harder to curb that voracious appetite. We have nothing to remember him by but the shredded arms and backs of chairs where he liked to sharpen his claws, his rubber mouse, and a small sketch I made of him once, curled up under the Christmas tree.

Then we had no cat, nor any heart for a new one. But one night, not long ago, when I was reading late in our "restless room," which has a

window opening upon a tin roof, I heard a crackling noise outside. It meant that some creature, "some long legged beastie or hobgoblins that walk in the night" was making its way across to the window. The only one awake in the stillness and the darkness, I felt my hair beginning to rise. In another minute Dracula would look in the window, I thought. A face presently did stare in at me. But it was a cat face, the large pale face of the barn cat. And didn't it have a look of quiet triumph? Ah, now you have no cat! May I not creep in? It did, for a time, but it went away again of its own accord. Still I knew that I was forgiven for the way I had treated it when Mr. Miaow was alive.

I don't somehow believe in the fabled independence and indifference of cats. They all adore me, and while I have been fond of a few, I count myself no ailurophile. I liked your Esmé, long such a pleasant fixture of your guest-room, and now when I come, I feel something lacking because she is not there to settle upon my chest along with the blankets when I go to bed.

B

DEAREST BARBARA:

One can face almost any problem if one looks long enough at the sky. The sky has arched over a world of trouble so often, and still the moon rides her course, the stars prick through, and the sun moves in blinding glory. When the heart is sad, as it must be at times, a look at the wide and infinite beauty of the sky gives peace. Although I do not know anything about the science of astronomy, I can always go out and lift my eyes and feel the vastness of God.

The birds were all over the yard today. No mocking-birds such as you have, we are too Northerly. But so many varieties. Some of them travel so far, to South America, to hot and steamy forests. Some of them stay the year round, like the little plump sparrows. I wonder whether the transients, the travelers from afar think they will be here only a little while and wing on their great journey again? Or do they forget while they are here? Who can tell?

Birds go North from here, birds go South. They have their own calendar. Spring begins when the red-winged blackbirds come, winter begins when the smooth competent juncos take over. Probably we are just a way station, a summer resort for some, a winter resort for others.

I suppose I am a sparrow, a stay-at-home bird. Travel is so alluring, but our own forty acres offers enough adventure for a lifetime.

MRS. SPARROW

SUGARBRIDGE

I am ashamed of our birds! Will they go near that beautiful bird banquet you sent us? No! I love its totem pole arrangement of avian delicacies, in little pans. It looks good enough for anybody to eat. I believe the truth is that there is so much natural food for them hereabouts, wild berries and the like, that they are surfeited. I notice that stray ears of corn the harvesters drop in the fields often lie out all winter without being touched.

It's a real sorrow to me that I cannot get our birds to come and feed nearby, and I'm frankly jealous of people like you who accomplish this so easily. Of course we have them around and about always; sparrows have nests in the wall ivy now, and perch upon and flutter about that little haw tree that grows against the back living room window. But when I put bread crumbs on the window sill, they ignore them. I must have no bird appeal!

I am a loss as a bird-watcher, too, I must confess. I have nearsighted eyes, and while even now I don't need glasses, I'm not able to see clearly very far. Do you remember our college bird walks? I was never able to see birds at a distance then. Except for cardinals, and the brighter-plumaged varieties, I have to take my bird-watching secondhand. Viola says, "Look, there's a titmouse," and if I'm quick, I do see it. But I wouldn't, by myself.

My dog-class friends, Miss May and Miss Rose who are your devoted fans, are also accomplished ornithologists, and whenever I can, I pick up little crumbs of information from them. Miss May told me an amusing story the other day of a woman who called her in great distress, saying, "There's a cardinal flinging himself against a window in my house, and I'm afraid he will kill himself, break the window, or both." May told the woman she had only to coat the outside of the window with white-wash; the bird had seen himself in the glass, and thought it was a rival come to invade his territory. The woman objected later that the cardinal merely went to another window, after she had treated the first one. May comforted her by saying that soon he would be finding himself a mate, and then these premarital jitters would cease. It's a new conception of the sub-human world; I thought nervous breakdowns were limited to us.

B

STILLMEADOW

DEAR BARBARA:

You and I spend a good deal of time waiting on animals. Nothing is more rewarding, or more time-consuming. Jill herself figures she spends ninety percent of her time measuring drops, giving pills, scouring pans, cleaning runs, trimming, training. But when we bring the Irish back from an operation and realize she is with us again for a little while, there is not gold enough in the world to measure the joy.

I suspect with people, even those who love us and whom we love, there is always a reservation. Dogs have none, they purely love. And people such as you and I do feel warm and comfortable around beings who never criticize, never get angry, never have recriminations. A dog figures you can really do no wrong, though you may be misguided now and then. For me, I would never wish to return to a house that had no wildly wagging tail at the door.

When Teddy smears the outside of all the windows, pawing to get in, I have to think a clean window is a small thing, but the love of that boy is important. What's a window, more or less?

If I ever get impatient with the dirt and disturbance, I remember Silver who ate up the middle of my best silk puff when left alone and lonesome. We lost her so young, and that puff is twice as treasured on account of the large patch appliquéd in the middle.

Yesterday we called on Cliff and Mary Louise, and Mary Louise had been giving first aid to an ailing raccoon. The coon came in the yard and held up his paws, and followed her into the house, and seemed feverish, she said. She called the warden, and tended the coon until he could get there. The coon had distemper, it seemed, but he felt a human being might help him, and he came to find one. Wild animals seem to know who will take a shot at them, and who won't.

G

STILLMEADOW

DEAR BARBARA:

Faith Baldwin and her friend Gonnie came for tea. We had it in the Quiet Garden. It was one of those hours that are golden. Watercress sandwiches and Earl Grey tea, Grandmother's old silver teapot, the last pale gold tulips—these make for a good hour.

But any hour with Faith and Gonnie has a shining quality. We talked of children, books, politics and poetry. Faith's conversation shimmers, her voice is one of the loveliest anyone ever heard, her wit is devastating, never cruel. Her heart is as wide as the Mississippi and she herself is so small and lovely, like a very special sapphire. Gonnie is also delightful. She has those clear deep brown eyes that always seem to indicate wisdom, she can prick pretensions with one swift salty word. She speaks her mind, and we always end weak with laughter. One of the very happiest times in our lives, I thought this afternoon, was when we went to Williamsburg with Faith and Gonnie. I suggested we go back. "No," said Gonnie firmly, "one can never go back. Don't you realize that, Gladys?"

When they drove away, Faith leaning out to wave a small, exquisite hand, we carried the tea things back in the house wishing the day could go on forever.

I am not reconciled to the fact that we see the people most dear to us far too seldom. Why do we get so involved in the busyness of life?

GLADYS

STILLMEADOW TO SUGARBRIDGE

Sometimes when I have a day with many small things going awry, I suddenly think as dusk lets fall her soft violet color, that it is very silly of me to mind the stresses and strains. It was *a day,* was it not? I had the free air to breathe, and the sky to look on. Why should I complain?

Then I think, were I ill, were I dying, were I imprisoned, or had I been involved in some horrid accident—at the point of catastrophe, would I not wish this day back, just as it is?

A day measured up so, comes to be a very dear day, and I wish it not over at all!

The same thing is true about passing the time away. When I hear people speak of doing things to pass the time, I shudder. For the one precious and irreplaceable gift is time, and surely we are in sorrowful state if we merely want to toss it out as fast as possible.

A day is a fine thing, and we shall never see this day again.

It is not a thing to take too easily.

G

JUNE

DEAR BARBARA:

This is the singing month in New England, and I daresay with you, too, in your green Pennsylvania hills. I quite literally do sing, as I look out at the dewy grass spread with silver webs of the night's weaving.

I sing everything from "Do not forsake me, O my darling," to "My truly truly fair." I run to the garden to see what's up caroling, a little off key, "When cockle shells turn silver bells—" I lay the thinly sliced bacon in the pan, singing, "From Greenland's icy moun—tains to India's coral stra—and—"

In short, I am happy.

I can certainly see why so many weddings are in June, it's not so much the bride not being rained on, as it's the fact that any woman would be happy facing life with her partner in June, even if she nourished secret fears that he might never learn to like cauliflower, her favorite vegetable.

Warm days, cool night. Garden growing. Sky like the lapis lazuli we

used to buy in Florence, or turquoise like the Indian jewelry held up in dark hands on the platform at Albuquerque as you go West.

"Fortunate breathers of the air are we," say I, wondering if Will Shakespeare felt the same way about June in England.

The birds are feeding their young, the cockers are like a hunt club assembled to find the rabbits. The mother rabbit just swishes her children under the storage house when the dogs whoop up, and pays no more attention. When the dogs give up and go to the front yard to badger passing cars, all the little bunnies fly out and play games.

The first swim is an event. Our pond, as you know, is very cold, fed by springs and the long brooks. Not as cold as yours, but still rather as if the ice cubes had just melted.

But comes the day I fling myself in, and life is wonderful. Early in June I may be numb and take some thawing out before I can operate again. But the cold sharp water is always easing. We have to find out whether our brown trout have survived the winter, Jill will set up the fishing tackle presently. Meanwhile I jump in and let the icy water take all the aches out of me. The edge of the pond is overgrown and green, the little polished frogs hop up and down. It is fine. From now on, the pond and I are daily intimates.

Bathing suits are my Waterloo. I do not wish a built-up glamor thing. With my poundage nothing could be sillier. Neither do I wish a pair of straps that fall off every time I take a really long stroke. I wish someone would invent a practical bathing suit for someone who has *not* lost 67 pounds in one month on a sure-fire diet. A suit to swim in, in fact. Even if not a glamor gal.

I do not want to swim corseted and confined. I want a covering for my frame. That's all. But so hard to get. Currently, Jill and I have rather unfortunate figured suits of cotton. Jill looks a bit like a telephone pole in hers. I, frankly, look like a barrel. But we swim anyhow.

I expect you are dunking in your ice water now. Your cold brook water is all right for me, I can swim in the leavings of a freezer.

We eat breakfast in the garden again—how lovely. The sun has a heavenly brilliance, and you can almost hear things growing. I like a momentary leisure in the work of country life, but it's not Jill's meat. I look up from putting a second piece of bacon on my plate and see her on her knees weeding something out from between the flagstones. Do sit down and relax, say I. Fine, says she. She sits. Another minute. I see her creeping along the edge with the pruning shears. Gardening, I decide, is a blood disease.

If we have guests, she does her best to be at ease. Her eyes slide around, however, and I see her planning to move this bush somewhere else, change the lilies of the valley, clip back the forsythia, cut back this or that. Our garden is always mobile, too. Jill decides one thing needs another exposure, it whisks out and away. I never know where anything may be from one day to the next.

But when we look back over the years, we think we would not know this place. The scraggly bushes, the tired-out iris, the odds and ends of perennials— Now, even with the help of the dogs, we manage a very satisfying planting and have a mort of flowers. One cannot, of course, have a border of tulips and grape hyacinths where the dogs run for the postman. But never mind, we have things growing and healthy all over this part of our forty acres that we garden.

One of the best things about living in the country, as you know full well, is working with things that grow. The root goes down, the green shoots come up, and one day a miracle of flowering appears and you have the feeling you have at least modestly helped Nature, for you heaved out the rocks and put the peat moss in and carried buckets of water for days.

I love my Tom Thumb roses, so tiny and so fairylike, but if we forget them for a day, they drown in encroaching weeds and the blossoms spill like faery dust all over the sward. I use the word sward advisedly, we have it if we turn our backs ten minutes.

But the joy of the edible podded peas is worth any amount of hoeing and pulling and weeding. The tender pale green pods we snip so eagerly. We cook in a wee swish of boiling water and salt, adding a large whack of margarine or butter. Add a slash of cream from a good country cow, fill the soup bowls and sit down to a feast. We pick the edible podded peas when the peas themselves are mere suggestions of peas. The pods are sugar-sweet, delicate green, and a little crisp. Elegant eating.

It is strange how vegetables go in fashions like clothes. New and better brands come out every year. We like the new carrots that have no woody centers, but some of the old leaf lettuces are best. Sometimes we change to a new fancy development and think it not as savory as the old. And of course a parsnip is always a parsnip. Nobody, as far as I know, has improved on the old sweet buttery parsnip.

We like mixed lettuces and endive. Jill says I am half rabbit the way I eat a green salad. We like the Bibb lettuce, the Oak leaf tinged with rosy red, bronze beauty, the plain leaf, the new salad bowl lettuce, the Great Lakes. We have romaine, celtus we tried and abandoned. "Tigger," as Jill said, "did not like this," perhaps our soil is not right for it.

I know of nothing more exciting than going into the garden on a sweet gay morning and pulling a basketful of crisp greens. Washing them in ice water and having a luncheon salad to taste with niblets of salami or liverwurst or left-over chicken or whatever, and a sharp shrewd dressing, laced with crushed garlic.

How is your garden—are the bunnies behaving themselves?

These are salad days,

G

SUGARBRIDGE

DEAR GLADYS:

June is, as you say, the perfect month, the icing on the cake; the month of brides, roses, and, if you are lucky, new peas (our goal, but we don't always make it). June should, therefore, contain a certain day, of which I shall tell you.

"Then if ever come perfect days. . . ." How much better I know the truth of this line now, than when I first heard Lowell's poem, sitting upon a school bench whose peculiar hardness has impressed itself equally upon my mind as it did then upon my younger bones. At that time I longed for the glad month's arrival chiefly because it would release me

from my prison. But now . . . well, it takes a store of years to realize
how good a day in June can be. I love, I luxuriate in this silky time, but
truthfully, I have never yet experienced an utterly perfect June day.
Although I go on hoping. For you see, the perfect day to me must partake
of many things.

First in the stillness of early pre-dawn, the mockingbirds must sing,
answering each other in those glorious convolutions of sound, welling up
into fountains of airy variations, while I drift in and out of sleep. I should
like the cattle to moo drowsily down in the meadow, too, it is a soothing
sound, and calls up a picture of them bright behind the eyelids, standing,
black and shiny in their Angus coats, knee-deep in the lush dewy grass
and buttercups, cropping, cropping, then pausing, dreamy-eyed, to stare
away at the distance, lost in herbivorous musing. Though I am now quite
awake, I still lie there, while a thousand imperious little impulses toward
action prick me: Gather the peas! Dust the beans! Spray the roses, the
gooseberries! See if those black raspberries along the road are ripe! Soon I
cannot restrain myself from leaping up to be at it.

The sun is already high over the orchard hill, as I look out our one
east window. But everything is yet still. Out there, the morning lies fresh
before me, fragrant as a ripe melon. Today could be the perfect day!

But it never has come yet. Can you guess why? Well, I could not
count it so without, as well, first, a ride through the cool green woods,

nor could I forego later a refreshing plunge into the pool. Then, in addition to the earlier mentioned garden duties, I'd like to get rid of some deferred chore—a closet cleaned out, a job of painting done. (I love a feeling of accomplishment.) Then Ed and I must have a good talk about something we both find stimulating, and there should be an hour or so of music, to have it really complete. And, too, I have to evolve an appetizing dinner (dinner should always be an event, I feel, not merely a restoking), and there must be some especial dish to make this day memorable, like "Summer Pudding," that most surprising and delectable confection, concocted in Bucks County out of raspberries and currants. And, of course, after dinner, a walk for us both with Duke, in the cool dusk of the evening. Last but not less indispensable, a little time for reading before I sleep. There are not enough hours from sunrise to sunset to hold all I wish to do, so greedy am I for the delights of June. You see, my perfect day glimmers always ahead, never quite to be attained.

B

DEAR BARBARA:

Well, if we could take a handful of June, and close our fingers on it, maybe we could have the perfect June Day.

Mine includes a little time before going to bed, playing Toscanini's recording of Beethoven's Ninth, plus the Schöne Müllerin by my friend Glenn.

The upper half of the Dutch door can be open, and the smooth, pure moonlight filters in, and the small night voices of the young treetoads add a tranquil obbligato to the music.

When school closes, I like to see the children flinging themselves along the roads, so released, so wildly happy. The great buses rumble to a stop at the crossroads and out bursts a tide of the young, squealing and whistling. The boys show off, making faces, throwing stones—not really hitting anybody. The girls cluster together and giggle in the senseless way of girls. As they scatter, the green June countryside is suddenly pricked with red and blue and green and yellow of sweaters and caps.

Country children have such riches. The brooks are running full, there are secret hollows in the woods, every farm has a pile of broken bits of machinery and discarded lengths of wood, just waiting to be a treasure. Before it is really warm enough, bicycles flash along the road with bathing suits dangling from the handle bars.

One wishes the city children could all be popped on a magic carpet and set down in a field of sweet clover.

G

DEAR BARBARA:

We are both literally and figuratively in clover, for Al has come to fix all the things that are out of kilter in the house. By profession a cabinet-maker, his way with a plane or chisel is wonderful to watch. He can patch a floor so you cannot tell the original board was ever broken. A sprung door fits again like the lid of a jewel case. He built an extra step at the bottom of the steep ladder stairs, and changed my whole dislike of mounting to the second floor. He is a shy man, quiet. Even his hammering somehow is softer than most men's. When he repaired the leg on the blanket chest which Jill did over for my birthday, he rubbed his hand over the mellow wood and said, "Nice."

Most of the country people are masters of all trades. George, for instance, is a dairy farmer, but he builds his own tractor out of second-hand parts, he rigs motors for his saw, and repairs the electric pump. He never has to have special material, either; he seems to poke around and with a bent nail and a piece of wire fashions whatever he needs. The pioneers must have had this same kind of ingenuity, it is a wonderful thing.

When I look back, I think the time we finally became ourselves accepted and not just "those city people who live here" was when Jill built the chicken house with the aid of a fifteen-year-old girl work-camper. Her name was Phoebe, she came from Brooklyn. But how she loved sawing a piece of siding, battling with the windows. She and Jill had so much fun, I expected them to go on building more stately mansions and they would have, except summer ended and Phoebe's parents came to take her home.

The chicken house was so elegant, it seemed a shame not to use it as a studio.

Our second work-camper was not the same thing at all. Don was not yet off to camp when she came, leggy and dark-eyed and brash; he was much in evidence. I could look up from my typewriter any minute and see our little helper leaning on a grass rake and studying her face in her compact mirror, smoothing on fresh lipstick. Set to sweep the kitchen after lunch, I would go back to the novel I was struggling with, and when I came out for a drink an hour later, there was our camper, resting on the broom handle and combing her dark curly hair. It did the poor child no good, for Don had a wary eye at that age.

Not a tear was shed when she departed, we just felt relaxed and happy, whereas the farewell to Phoebe was most tragic.

We are washing the blankets this week. June sun and a sweet wind fluff them out, although I can't get rid of a secret suspicion that they are always a little smaller every time we wash them. Our automatic washer is a temperamental creature. At the slightest overload, she tears herself from her moorings and throws water and soap all over the floor. Our nice Mr. Campo comes and puts her in place again and suggests not putting too much heavy stuff in at once.

One can't, however, cut a blanket in two, one must just accept the challenge and plunge ahead.

GLADYS

SUGARBRIDGE

Yesterday I went a-cherry-picking, all over our land. From every point of vantage I picked them; standing on a kitchen chair (very tippy) for the lower branches of the big tree by the garden fence; perched in the very tip-top of another, swaying around in the wind, and in hot competition with the birds; they eyed me in reproachful surprise. But how pretty a June landscape looks from a cherry tree; it's just the right frame for it. When I tell you that my yield was gallons, you might well wonder, and more so when I add that they were not pie cherries that I picked, but the half-wild sweet black ones we have so many of here. Every other tree in Chester County is a cherry tree, I do believe. In spring it is a sight.

> "Loveliest of trees the cherry now
> Is hung with bloom along the bough . . ."

so A. E. Housman describes it, and I do not know which is the more exquisite, that oft-quoted couplet, or the fairylike bloom. But still I am practical, and I spent some time over the years puzzling over what to do with these cherries, sweet and flavorful, but not large enough to warrant the bother of stoning. Then suddenly it had come to me. Cherry Brandy! I had a vague memory of having seen directions for that potion in a pet New Orleans cookbook which has never let me down yet. So I enlisted my mother, always a help in matters of this kind, and we were off.

When my mother comes to visit, we try over the old recipes. It's a good way to remember; there's nothing like taste and smell to evoke the past, except, perhaps, sound. I get out the family cookbooks which Mother has passed on to me, the written ones, too. (The members of our family were great ones to hand down recipes.) There are the church cookbooks, too, like all church cookbooks, with quotations from Shakespeare, and a large errata list in the back. Most important of all in Mother's eyes is Miss Parloa's Cook Book. It was published in 1850, and has quaint and amusing illustrations of kitchen equipment just over the borderline of credibility for this day and age. When my grandmother went to housekeeping, Miss Parloa's went with her, just as Miss Fanny Farmer's Boston Cook Book was my mother's bridal guide—and is similarly revered by me—so Mother swears by Miss Parloa. I suspect we have to go back a generation to find the eternal verities; anyway, Mother considers Miss Farmer rather a Johnny-Come-Lately.

We sit down on the sofa in front of the fireplace, with the cookbooks spread out around us, and Mother leafs intently through Miss Parloa's first of all, searching for some recipe she wants to copy.

"Was Grandma a good cook?" I ask, discreetly delving into family annals, in the hope of turning up some new story material. My mother came of a large and lusty Missouri family in which the girls were all beautiful and besieged by beaux, the boys handsome high-spirited and adventurous, and many are the tales attendant.

"Well, no," Mother answers absently, turning a page. "She didn't really have to be; there were so many good family servants then. I do remember hearing she had to go up to her room and look in a cookbook before she could order the meals, at first. She married at sixteen, you know. . . . H'm, there's custard soufflé. . . ."

"Oh, yummy! let's make it!" I cry. "Hadn't thought of it for years." Custard soufflé comes from my father's side, and I remembered it with gustatory pleasure, hot, delicate, heaped with whipped cream.

Mother puts back the slip of yellowed paper. "It's impossible, unless you have someone in the kitchen," she says. "It has to be watched constantly, and come to the table the very moment it is done."

We both sigh, admitting life has changed.

"Well, I like it better this way," I maintain stoutly, mounting my special hobby horse. "I've had some good maids too, but let's face it, domestic service is obsolete today. And if you insist on it, you have to make too many concessions."

But as we go on looking through the books, more and more pages, dried and brown around the edges, written in the spidery handwriting of bygone cooks, begin to flutter out, and insensibly I fall to thinking about them.

"There's Emma's chocolate potato cake," Mother says, "in a letter she wrote me after she had to leave us." I look at the crumbling piece of paper, dated St. Louis, 1915, and know we are both seeing the stout little German cook, her red elbows resting on the bread board as she rolled out her dumplings, and cookies, and those excellent pocketbook rolls. Then I begin to repent of my facile emancipation, and to remember with gratitude all that I owed in my childhood to the Lizzies, the Roses,

the Maggies that you and I once knew. They were a wonderful combination of foster-mother, teacher, and bosom friend—the good ones.
"Bessie, *what* can I *do?*" How many times I recall whimpering that plaint
during afternoons of boredom. "Tell me a story, Lena!" Or, most frequent
of all, "Agnes, can't you make cookies this afternoon?" And as for the
bad ones, (for human nature was the same then as now) we children
tormented them when we could, and enjoyed that as much. I am sorry
for this generation of servantless small fry. They don't know what they've
missed.

When Mother and I came to check up on the recipe for cherry brandy,
we found it called "Liqueur de Merise" and, couched in stately language,
calling for a gallon of whiskey for each similar measure of cherries. Ed
gave a wounded cry at the idea of such an outlay for this dubious venture. So we compromised upon making only half. Even then, he had to
turn away his eyes, when he saw me pour in the "milk of old age."

The directions were not hard to follow, and we made good progress
until we reached an ambiguous sentence which Mother and I could not
agree upon. "Mash two cupfuls of cherry seeds in a mortar, and add."
It didn't say where you got this cherry seed, whether from the cherries
you had already added, or whether they were extra. Mother was strongly
of the opinion that they must be extra; I thought it perfectly plain that
two cupfuls of seed from the original measure of cherries was meant.

We argued and debated, and got nowhere. My mother is a meticulous person, while I am slapdash, and neither of us gives ground. Ed, whose motto is "Never argue, never explain," sat and laughed at us. Finally Mother said, "Oh, well, it's your brandy; have it your way," implying that if I did, all would be lost. So we made it my way, and it turned out most excellently, yielding several good-sized bottles. It has a strong pungent tang of the cherry seed; a little thimbleful of it on a dark day is very heartening. I have been strongly urged to make more of it next year. If I can arrange some way to blindfold Ed at the moment of adding that necessary ingredient, I certainly intend to do so. And a bottle will be hidden away for your next visit.

Love,
Barbara

Stillmeadow

Dear Barbara:

Somehow cherry brandy reminds me of dim Victorian parlors and gentlemen with full whiskers accepting a small portion and sipping it elegantly. Gentlewomen possibly indulged in raspberry shrub. I once had some of this, and it tasted like pink vinegar, but perhaps it wasn't made correctly.

In the garden, the vegetables make long lines of vigorous growth. The weeds, as always, grow faster and are considerably *more* vigorous. An uprooted weed can lie flat all day and all night, and the next thing you know, it is clutching the earth again and lifting a wilted top. An uprooted necessary vegetable never has this stamina.

Jill is a thorough gardener, she plants succession crops and alternates the garden plan so the root vegetables are at one end this year and at the opposite end the next. I confine my gardening to bean-picking or gathering tomatoes or pulling scallions. I love to wander out before supper and find the very crispest lettuce, the youngest chard and the fattest white radishes for the salad. The white radish is a fine vegetable, spicier than the red, I think. Do you ever make a casserole of them in a rich cream sauce?

The roses "newly sprung in June," as Robert Burns would say, are blossoming in the Quiet Garden. I like them all, except the red ones that turn bluish as they fade, those are depressing, funereal. Perhaps the very best are the simple ramblers that cascade over the picket fences and along the gray stone walls in our valley. The whole world seems suddenly to be a bouquet as the clusters open with their pure soft color. Some peo-

ple have alternated the deeper reds and the moon-whites, some have the plain Dorothy Perkins.

You must come in June the next time so we can drive slowly along the winding roads and look at the glory of the climbing roses. In the border gardens of the ancient white houses, the bright blades of the delphinium begin to lift in the warm air. So many shades of blue—the delicate sky-blue frosted with shell-pink, the indigo blue, the deep regal purple. Pink roses and blue delphinium in a milk glass bowl are my favorite bouquet.

The children come home for weekends now, and we are all very merry. Don, at Medical School, has progressed as far as fractures, I am glad to say. We get a complete lecture course in whatever subject he is taking, and I must say I breathed a sigh of relief when we finished anatomy and parasitology. Although descriptions of how they drive silver nails in people's bones isn't very restful, it is far better than parasites. We view with more calm the approach of obstetrics, since we feel we know a little something about that, Jill having had two and me one child.

Sometimes when I look at him, six feet tall and all the thin childish bones of his face matured, jaw-line masculine and firm, cheekbones strong, I can hardly believe it. I remember the first time he went to camp, surely the thinnest leggiest timidest little boy that ever climbed into a camp suit. He had to go early before the haying aggravated his asthma, and he didn't want to go early, or go at all. We enlarged on the charms of the seashore. The fun he would have.

He sat sullenly in the back seat surrounded by mountains of duffel bags, sleeping bags, baseball gloves and bat, sweaters, camp blankets.

He refused an ice cream cone. This was a grim moment, and we almost turned back. Fortunately we just at that moment came into the cool clean breath of the sea and his wheezing stopped miraculously. We went on detailing the delights in store for him.

He did not like games. He was afraid of the water and only ventured in a shallow place with two pair of water wings under him. He had no ambition to sail or paddle. He did not want to make little things out of shells. What he wanted was to stay at home in a dark corner reading Comic books.

Mrs. Mac, the tall quiet camp headmistress, took one look at our pale strained faces and called a small boy to help Don unload his luggage. She gently herded us away from the two, we sat on the porch out of sight. We tried to explain all the things about Don, and she said, "I wouldn't worry. All I suggest is that you don't come to visit him for a week."

During the week, we decided to bring him home, hay or no hay. He was too little to be unhappy. Maybe we could air-condition his room—

and make him promise not to ride on the hay wagon with George as he did that one awful day last summer.

So we drove over on Sunday. The beach was full of boys, they darted around like waterbugs. More boys were in the water, active as a school of minnows. Suddenly one small one flipped out of the water and flew to us, breathless, dripping, waving his arms.

"Hi," he said, "say Mom, I can swim!"

We stared in disbelief.

"Yep," he said, "I'm one of those that can't sink. Mr. Mac says some people are that way, just can't sink. That's me."

We sat down quietly on the nearest bench.

"I'm busy now," he said, "gotta fix the canoe with Porky, see you later," and he sped off.

It was surely no time at all before he was himself a junior counselor at the camp, a sailing counselor, no less. He spent his time sailing with the campers all day except on his day off. We went to visit him on one of these days off, and asked Mrs. Mac where he was.

"Oh, Don," she said, "he's off sailing." She added, "It's his day off, so he took the Osprey."

Jill's daughter, Dorothy, whom you haven't met, was not so fortunate in her camp life. She decided a work camp would be fun and went to one. The theory was that the campers did the real work of the camp, and it turned out to be, in fact, so. She came home after a short time because as she said succinctly, "I can pick beans at home if I have to pick beans."

Connie was a Camp Fire girl and went to a camp with a complete nature program. I was glad she didn't elect the collecting of snakes as some girls did, beadwork is easier to live with.

Once in a while as the children gather around the applewood fire, they talk about the days when they were so young. It seems funny now, that Don was always falling downstairs, that Dorothy sat on a chair in the wheelbarrow half a day "getting away from it all" and that Connie wrote such a moving fan letter to her favorite radio star that his secretary phoned long distance and wanted her to come and meet the big shot. His horror at finding she was twelve years old, I can only imagine.

It is hard to believe in the evil in the world when you walk under a June sky in a blossoming garden. The natural wants of man are surely right and simple, a home, children, freedom to worship as one pleases, work, and enough wherewithal to be secure against debt. Not many people would ask for more. Add a little piece of land for a garden and you have a prescription for happy living.

It would seem not impossible to arrange the world to this end, rather than to spend more billions on weapons, don't you think?

I wonder if aggression is the original sin?

The lawn furniture is out and it looks inviting enough for a long leisurely afternoon meditating on all kinds of problems. We gave up the hammock after too many puppies had swung on the fringes.

But I sometimes see myself mentally, at ease in the chaise longue, looking like one of those gala colored ads in the magazines. A shell-pink sheer frock, perhaps, a rose in my hair, a French novel (why is that more elegant than an English one, I wonder) open on my lap and a tall frosty glass at my side with three spicy mint leaves pricking the bubbles.

I see this sometimes as I cross the yard in my blue jeans accompanied by a leaping horde of cockers. I am balancing a large pitcher of milk and ten dishes for their afternoon snack. Any rose in my hair would at once be nicked off by a galloping Irish. A carload of guests will be stopping at the gate, and alas, the strawberries are not hulled.

Goodbye, my fancy, I mutter as the elegant vision of my leisure vanishes.

I expect we should not like a world of nothing but June. The rose that never let a petal fall, the brook that never sank to an August trickle, the leaf forever green on the maple, and lettuce and peas and strawberries always to be picked?

Possibly in time we would have a secret longing for the rugged textures of Autumn flowers, for the harvested field, for the first cool lazy flakes of snow.

But it would take a long time. Thirty days is a very small amount for June.

Do you make a distinction between winter and summer reading? I've always understood summer reading should be lighter, as if the mind weakened a little with the bliss of summer. But I usually find myself with Fraser's "Golden Bough," which I always did mean to read and never got to, or "Delilah," or some analytical biography.

Around Christmas I may be reading the newest Agatha Christie. I just cannot be seasonal in my choice of books. A good book is lovely, lovely in the soft pale blue dusk of a June day and lovely, lovely when the sleet flails at the window panes.

For a book is its own climate.

G

SUGARBRIDGE

GLADYS, we are birds of a feather. Even in a gorgeous month like June, our thoughts turn to original sin, and how the world could better itself. And after a bout of this, for me it's soothing to have someone with whom to talk of nothing but Nature. Viola, my country neighbor, is such a person. As she has a job in nearby West Chester by day, our actual meetings are few, limited to brief visits on her way back from work, or on my part, a stopover at her place on Sunday as I take my horse out on a ramble. Our talk is almost entirely by telephone, and this gives it a certain cosmic and impersonal character. Our mailbox, too, does double duty, and harbors a succession of objects which must often make the mail man goggle in surprise, as they are indeed foreign to the U.S. postal service. She will call me to say, "I left a spray of witch hazel blossom for you in your mailbox; you'd better get down and take it out before the mail man sees it." Or it may have been a sackful of quinces, or an interchange of bird books.

During a slack moment in her work, Viola telephones me to say, "Did you see the wild geese go over this morning at seven o'clock? Canadian geese, they were; they were flying low, and I could make out their black necks." Or it might be about that whitish blight I had been complaining of on my phlox this year; she has looked it up in her garden book, and is prepared to tell me the remedy. Or it is to inform me that the large bird I saw down in the meadow was probably an osprey. The next time, she wants to ask me if I'd like a piece of *that plant?* She is going to divide it now. (This is probably some unusual wild flower she has found and cultivated, for she is an ardent botanist.)

Viola often telephones me about something she has forgotten to touch upon the last time we talked. "I wanted to tell you the way my cats go on when I bring them fresh catnip." (Viola harbors a family of fifteen.) "That old Billy with the six toes, he carried on like a drunk man; staggered around with his eyes shut. The others fought with each other, and yowled something terrible. Mom and I had to carry them in the house, at last. . . ." I counter by telling her that I've observed our dogs eating ragweed in this month. Are there animal allergics which seek instinctively to cure themselves this way? We cogitate upon the matter, with suitable pauses. Something else may occur to her, or not. "Well, I guess that's all. . . ."

Knowing Viola has been an inestimable advantage to me in another way. Since she comes of a farming family which has lived around here since Revolutionary times, she can always produce a cousin in any spot in the county and tune in the local grapevine toward some bit of information I need. If I hear that some man I don't know has sworn to shoot Duke if he comes around again, Viola can find out for me what sort of person he is, if what he claims is true about Duke's depredations, and how I can best handle it. Or if I want to check up on some folksy

story going the rounds, Viola can always track it down for me, usually adding to its savor.

I never cease to marvel at the stability of the early families in Chester County. My own has been in this country eleven generations, and though we had a finger in many a pie, we have gathered no plums. But here it was apparently a Pennsylvania custom to disembark, and stay not a few generations, but all of them, up till now. Reading over the old histories of the county, which I love to do, "Futhey and Cope" and others less well known, I come across the same names in the lists of early arrivals, bond servants, artisans, gentlemen, as are prominent in our townships today, to be spoken of in the newspaper, or listed upon tax records. It is no uncommon thing for farms to be still in the hands of the same family to which the patent was granted by William Penn. Their attics of course are treasure houses of ancient letters, and historical relics, and Chester County, as a result, has a pleasantly colonial atmosphere, much like your little Connecticut towns. But it also has less desirable consequences: reactionary politics not matched anywhere but in the South; a rural school system so inadequate that it still uses a number of one-room school houses, and then, a general stodginess and stuffiness more amusing to read sometimes about than to live with. Yet in the lingering old strains there is often an amazing vitality and inflexibility of purpose. Viola's mother, although well over seventy, is a rugged woman who cares for several cows, because she likes cows, and mentally has a ferocious single-ness of code untouched by the quibbling of today. She, like Viola her-self, has come to possess for me the restful qualities of Nature herself. And often, I do think half consciously of Viola as a green hill, or a tall sheltering tree, so little do personal idiosyncrasies or pettinesses mar our interchange of ideas. But sometimes I suspect that the rest of our neigh-bors, those on our party lines at least, have come to consider us as that comic but pestiferous bugbear, the country gossip, who is always on the horn just when someone else wants it.

P.S. Duke's little friend, Golden Girl, is with us on a sort of lend-lease arrangement, that is, after two litters of pups, which the Cappels get, she is ours. Duke is moderately pleased, but I look upon it as

"Little Orphant Annie's come to our house to stay . . ."

Not that she tells us tales of goblins, but that she is a goblin-dog herself, so shy and scary that someone has had to soothe her every time the dish-washer goes on, or pursue her into the underbrush to which she has fled, panicked by the most ordinary noises. I spent the first two days after her arrival, just luring her out of hiding with pieces of buttered toast, which was a novelty to her. She bays like a banshee at Clinton, and this hurts his feelings terribly, for he is the friend of all dogs. Of course the two, Duke and Golden Girl, look wonderful together, chasing about on the lawn, and most impressive in the station wagon. Over what goes on in the house, let us draw a veil. But Ed and Clinton have built them a commodious run behind the house, a dog motel. Still, Heaven forbid we ever have a flock of Danes approximating your more convenient cockers! Even one extra makes the cooking increase appallingly. Duke, for all his size, has a delicate digestion, and has to have his meat just so, an egg, wholewheat bread. . . . If only I could compromise on a prepared food in the carefree manner that so many people do! But no, I seem always to have to take the hard way. Now it has got to be a habit. With a small family, a small house, I should have an easy life, yet to hear me complain. . . ! On the other hand, can you imagine me in the im-personally ordered life of a communistic country, where housing, food and clothes are on a dead level? Heavens preserve us!

BARBARA

DEAR BARBARA:

Viola sounds exactly right. Such a countrywoman has a fresh honest observation of life. My favorite people are those who lack pretense, who are simple and direct in all things.

A group of people at a party seem to sort themselves out so rapidly, the small artifices, the struggle to seem a little smarter than everyone else, the sharp witticisms practised, these belong to one type. But there are always a few who have the quality of the countrypeople, whether they live in the canyoned city or not. You can feel it at once, you put your glass down and talk softly, almost at random. Neither you nor they are self-conscious, you are being yourselves.

Most true countrypeople, I think, live so close to the seasons and the eternal forces of Nature that they can't bother to be superficial.

And the eye that has seen the wild dark beauty in the gaze of a fox is never going to be impressed by a diamond clip.

I'd like to share a bouquet of yellow roses with you. They are in the dark blue Staffordshire sugar bowl—the one that has only one handle. When we first moved here, the bush was a present from a man who was "pointing up the stone"—a strange phrase, if there ever was one. So we call them Mr. Clark's roses.

They are furiously prickery and the petals fall almost as soon as I pick them, but the small green leaves and the little open pale gold cups are beautiful. They are old-fashioned too, nobody has improved them, so I can always think of forgotten gardens where delicate ladies walked in little satin shoes.

Good talk by the pond while the hamburgers sizzle. There seems to be something extra relaxing about taking a swim and sitting on the terrace, maybe partly because we let the guests do their own. Beginning in June, we have the house full all summer long. But we found long ago that as long as people aren't company, we can manage. We used to get up at dawn to do our necessary chores while the guests rested, then try to entertain them all day, sit up late at night, lie uneasily down for a few hours and tally-ho again. After two or three days of this, my eyes were glazed.

Now, as you know, we set up the bar for breakfast and everybody decides on eggs coddled, scrambled or whatever. Lunch is in the Quiet Garden; people carry trays. When things pile up, we give everyone a chore.

Johannes always makes all the salads when he is here, and goes to the dump, and lets dogs in and out. Burton makes a special spaghetti and has a new shrimp dish that is out of this world. And when the Shentons come, Ed takes out his drawing pad and we expect an interpretive portrait of Jonquil to frame. And you load the dishwasher, make beds, and carry trays.

When I visit you, I am shamelessly lazy. Sometime when I am there, I shall either clean house or wax some furniture, or weed the garden. I don't mean to be a nuisance guest at all.

It is certainly an art to be a perfect guest!

We have one guest, who comes all too seldom, who always makes me feel rested and very happy. She is an Englishwoman—really Welsh, I guess, and her name is Fiona. We play records to each other, we read and discuss books, she is comfortable curled up with a book while I stack the dog pans. I wish sometime you would be here when she is.

Can you remember the days when we did not have radio weather reports every hour? In some ways, it was better. We enjoyed the sun when it shone, and went our heedless way on picnics. Now we hover. If rain is predicted, we rush out and cover the chaise longue, move things in. Fly with laundry. Then maybe the report is wrong and the sky is blue as willowware platters the rest of the day.

Suppose the radio predicted our personal fortunes in the same way! Who could iron with a calm mind on Monday knowing that on Tuesday she would come down with a virus! Of course, you could get ready—do odd jobs rapidly. But on the whole, the future is better as a closed book of which we take a page at a time.

GLADYS

SUGARBRIDGE

DEAR GLADYS

Your notion of a forecasting by radio of a future virus attack sent me off into a familiar speculation: does mind influence body, or vice versa? Does a mental idea cause you to become sick, or is it a bodily illness which casts its shadow over the mind? No doubt, a bit of both is true. In any case, *mens sana in corpore sano.*

This is what originally brought up the question: I have an old misery. It's been with me most of my life, and recurs from time to time when least expected. I dread its onset like the plague for now well I know its scope and consequences: a curiously deceptive dull ache beginning like nothing much, but after a time becoming intolerable. A short sharp pain I can bear with the best, but a long-drawn-out one dismembers me, and my heart goes out to that first Chinaman who had water dropped on his head indefinitely. I like the idea of pain ennobling and refining one. But I regret to say I notice no such effects in myself. This particular anguish only reduces me to a hollow shell, with no remaining will power. Yet there is a counter-reaction which I consider interesting: after a wakeful pain-ridden night, I find that I am so thankful to be alive next morning that I am all at once borne up by a secret reserve of strength I didn't know I possessed, compounded of shame at my craven yielding of the night before, and a kind of stubbornness which undertakes to deny that I feel shattered, that I look pale and corpselike. It amounts to a kind of over-drive, I suppose. Anyway, it gets me through the coming twelve hours. I ask Ed, "Do I look frightful?" And he always can be depended to answer, kindly, "No, of course not. You look perfectly all right." Forgive all this distressing discussion of symptoms. I do it only to make my point later.

Now, while studying art one winter in Vienna, I had my old man of the sea with me most of the time. I don't know why; I was young, in good spirits, had just come from a healthy outdoors summer spent in Italy. I loved this beautiful and historic city, its romantic life, and charming people. Yet like a somber thread woven into a bright fabric, my malady is indissociable from my pleasanter memories, and when at the lilt of a Viennese waltz, a ball in the glittering Hof Saal springs to mind, or the wonderful Viennese coffee with its inevitable accompaniment of snowy drifts of whipped cream, or weekend hikes in the pretty mountain scenery, there also returns to me the actual sensation of those interminable nights while I lay sleepless, listening for the recurrent squeal of the tram to Bratislava outside the pension window, and welcoming at last the early morning clatter of the maids returning from the milk shop (no delivery there) with their clinking bottles.

In later years, I've been comparatively free from my ailment—only when I worry, get too thin, or go too hard, it returns like a warning finger. And I find, oddly enough, that when it does, it comes linked to memories or mentions of Vienna; something I've read in the newspaper has recalled some phase of life there, or suddenly, as often happens, a whole vista I once knew well, a clipped, privet-bordered walk in the Prater, or one of the bridges over the Danube canal, near which I lived, will flash before my inner eye, as clear as though I were gazing at it in reality. I like to think back on Vienna; it was a happy time, a fragrant memory, embodying somehow all of youth, and it is not true to say that every time I entertain it I am overwhelmed by my malady. Yet it happens often enough to make me wonder. Does the approach of an attack, yet unannounced but dimly sensed, send my mind back to the setting with which I connect it, and those attendant circumstances which have impressed it so indelibly upon me: the difficulties of communicating symptoms in a foreign tongue which were difficult enough in my own, the commiserating looks I received (Poor Fräulein, she looks healthy, but *leider* is not), the loneliness of being sick in a strange land.

Or, more incomprehensibly still, would the remembrance of things past induce in me the symptoms I connected them with? Now, I'm not *that* psychosomatic, I know, yet there is a slight tinge of this influence in my illness. If I were wavering somewhere on the borderline of succumbing, perhaps putting my mind back in those surroundings might be enough.

Are the waves of the brain drawn like tides of the ocean by some psychic moon, as yet unexplored? An interesting thought.

Always

B

STILLMEADOW

BARBARA DEAR:

Your ailment sounds so grim—and as for being connected with the past, isn't almost everything? I do think we are all of one piece—today's pain is the same one we suffered long ago, only time has flowed along.

I am reminded of a girl I overheard at my dentist's office saying loudly, "Well, Doctor, I think I am just psychosomatic!"

Far be it from me to say that my fiendish attack of a special new virus last summer was not just an accident. Still one can wonder whether at times the soul is a little tired, the flags of the spirit lower a bit. I don't know.

Jill has been cleaning the fruit cellar shelves. This is a strange job, for no matter how often we do it, we always find one jar of tomato chutney labeled 1944. Where has it been all these years? Is it still good? Better not risk it, says Jill, '44 is quite a time ago. We try to keep emergency shelves for quick meals for unexpected company and for us when we get in late and bone-weary from a dog show. But a secret life of its own moves in those shelves. We suddenly discover that we have five cans of pineapple juice, four bottles of Karo corn syrup, and dozens of tins of Christmas fruit peels, citron, lemon, mixed. We are currently taking a week to eat odds and ends which takes some ingenuity. Jill brings up a jar of frozen sweet peppers. Shall we stuff them with corn beef hash or meat balls and gravy? she asks doubtfully.

After supper in June, we like to ride along the little country roads and watch the evening lights in the old white houses beside the valley road. Along this road marched the French troops under Rochambeau in the Revolution. Benedict Arnold spurred his white charger from New Haven to Ridgefield to save the day against the British there—and I wonder whether he took any short cuts—he must have forded the river at Sandy Hook just as George Washington did. In Woodbury the great houses flared with candlelight as the balls for the French officers went on, and in the Bull house, a captive Britisher cut with his diamond on a window, "O beautiful Concordance!" How I wish I knew what Concordance thought of him. Did she smile when he finally was let out? Or did she hide behind the shutters and only peek?

Sometimes as we ride, I can almost see the long lines of the French, hear their high light voices—French seems a nasal tongue, unlike the guttural of the German.

They slept under the same stars, and the impartial moon shone on captor and captive then, as it does now.

GLADYS

SUGARBRIDGE

Every summer, I must learn my lesson all over again, and it is Nature which teaches me. Now I like to see things neat and orderly, but she has other ideas. I prefer to see the lawn mowed, the vegetable garden weed-free, the flower beds trim. For the first part of the season, I may succeed well enough. I spray the poison ivy which is near enough to be dangerous; I keep down the rank growth across the bank of our little stream, pull up the honeysuckle, that super-pest of this countryside, and plant in its place something which is easier of control. I dig up bushels of wild garlic from the lawn although I know it will be back next year in equal quantities.

But along about this time, something happens. It may be a prolonged heavy rain, followed by a hot spell. Or a few days' absence on a trip. Or perhaps only the temporary disappearance of the handyman. Anyway, with a whoop and a halloo, deep summer is upon you. A wave of vegetation sweeps over everything. In a twinkling, grass and weeds grow up in the gravel drive, poison ivy impudently snakes its vined tongue up the very front steps, the creek bank is a jungle, and *what* has happened to the garden? Weeds tall as trees wave a united front there, the raspberries have come through the fence into the flower border. The hop vine, innocently planted and encouraged to twine over the fence, but now the arch-villain of the garden, is triumphantly rampant over the currants and gooseberries in an impenetrable tent of horrid prickly growth. (Although the year before I spent one whole day in painful hand-to-hand struggle with it, emerging victorious if lacerated, like St.

George over the dragon.) As I go by now, it reaches out a long hairy tentacle to grasp me.

The worst of it all is that midsummer languor has descended, and I have no longer the enthusiasm I could muster earlier in the season. Things have got beyond me. I admit it; I am beaten. So I take refuge in philosophy, always the shelter of defeat.

There is no doubt of it, I muse, the raspberries, taking their own choice of location in the garden, from their original planting along the fence, do produce an amazingly luscious and profuse crop, lasting far beyond the life span allotted to raspberries. We have friends, a young couple who have recently moved to the country, and who garden with great system and enthusiasm. On a tour of their garden once, I noticed their neat row of raspberry canes, carefully pruned and tied up. Could they use some extra plants, I asked; soon I was going to have to thin out my patch. They refused politely; as I could see, they said, they had room for only one row, and there they had planted the proper number of plants, properly spaced. But they did wish, they added, that theirs would produce more; raspberries were their favorite fruit. I thought of my quarts and quarts, put away in the freezer, and remembered then my former efforts at control. I suppose you just have to take your choice between Nature and neatness.

And the weeds in the garden, I began to believe, kept the soil friable, besides doing their part to shade the tenderer plants. And as for the grass in the drive, I expect that will always be with us, in summer time.

P.S. Rain again today. And we only one week advanced beyond three solid weeks of it. But rain, I've been thinking, is to plants as love is to men. They never have enough of it. In that last wet spell, I expected everything to die, drowned out. But no; even flowers which are not especially fond of dampness perked up, and grew amazingly. Seed earlier planted, whose germination I had long ceased to hope for, sprouted and came up.

Does anyone ever have enough love and attention? I myself have not yet discovered a person who could not accept a bit more. Just to realize that should make life simpler for the whole world. It might well be the cure for every evil. Yet, knowing this so well, I often fail to act upon it. The flash of intuition fades, and leaves me in the dark. Until next time.

B

SUGARBRIDGE
June Evening

DEAR G.,

Here is a letter of Viola's that I thought would interest you.

"Mrs. Shenton:

"If either or both of you would like to come over some evening, and sketch 'Peter,' you are welcome to do so. I keep him in my room until I go to bed . . . it's always being used as a nursery for something or other, mostly cats and dogs until now . . . and at times we allow him the freedom of the room to strengthen his wings. Since he eats as often as he can coax us to feed him, it's necessary to follow him closely with a Kleenex. He's learned to come to the sound of our voice, follows our feet if he's on the floor and in the mornings, tries to alight on my shoes while I tie my shoestrings. For some reason, Mom's white hair fascinates him and he flies at her head every time he is on the wing. He holds lengthy conversations with us, and probably understands us as well as we do him. He really isn't good at flying and won't be until he gets his long tail. He preens his feathers and seems to go to the oil-bag at the base of his tail as he does it. I'm sure you'll love him, if you have time to observe him.

"Come and get your Petunias anyway
Viola."

I had been once before to see Viola's brown thrasher, which she had rescued as a nestling from a cat, and raised in a cage. He had grown to be quite a large handsome bird by that time, I thought, with his speckled breast, and bright brown back. But he was still a baby, she assured me, because he wouldn't peck at his food, and had no tail feathers. Taking him on her finger, she put birdseed mixed with hard-boiled egg into his gaping yellow bill, and he promptly opened it for more. She took water in a spoon and gave him a drink, with that universal vicarious pleasure maternal beings have. He closed his eyes when he swallowed, and I could see she closed hers too.

But lately she had been urging us to come and look at him while we could. "I won't have him too much longer," she said. "There's a law against caging wild birds. As soon as he can peck, I'll let him go."

Viola told me that she worried about Peter's first flight, since their place which he was familiar with was dangerous with cats. We considered the advisability of starting him out from our rather woodsy location, empty of felines; Viola deliberated the advantages and disadvantages for Peter, just as any careful mother would. Finally the moment suitable for his release arrived, and she brought him over in a shrouded cage. Peter did not travel well, she informed us, as she unloaded the cage. He'd dashed himself against the bars, lost two of his newly acquired tail feathers, and bashed a deep cut in the side of his head.

We set the cage around on our back terrace, on our long table. Peter was still flinging himself against the cage, although Viola talked to him soothingly. Here I was called to the telephone, and to my deep regret, summoned urgently to the city. So I witnessed his first flight from our bedroom window, where I was hastily dressing. He rose straight and true to the top of a cedar tree to one side of the terrace, and perched on a little branch, while Viola encouraged him from below. "Didn't he fly beautiful!" she said. "But," she added dolefully, "I guess we'll never see him again."

I knew what she meant, and I felt culpable, since I had agreed to stay around the first day, and see that Peter came to no harm. This had been a trust, a rare favor, the privilege of guiding her chick out into the big world, and here I was, letting her down. Ed would go back to his work, and soon be dead to the world, leaving Peter to the mercies of heavens knows what, certainly of Duke, a dedicated bird watcher, but much too prone to pursue anything that hopped or fluttered. I left with a heavy heart.

When I returned, late in the afternoon, Ed told me that Viola had come back several times. "I couldn't see a thing of the bird," he said. "But she found him, up in a maple tree, and they had a long conversation. He wouldn't come down, though."

The episode was a ruined thing, I thought sadly, and went about making what I could of the rest of the day. But I had a surprise. In the evening, as I came out the front door, I heard the brown thrasher's "Peet,

peet," from a tree nearby. There he was, sitting on a low branch, looking at me. I called to him, and he flew down. It gave me a curious thrill, to see this wild thing I scarcely knew obedient to my voice, and I understood then what an enchantment birds can cast over people. Enticing him to my finger, I carried him around to the terrace, his delicate claws cool and firm on my hand. It *was* fun to cram food into that voracious yellow maw! Then, with a full mouth, he suddenly shot up into an adjacent tree.

When it was time for dinner, Peter came, too. Hopping about on the stones of the terrace, he explored the dried-up carapace of a beetle, discarded it, pulled about a withered ivy leaf in triumph, found a fallen gooseberry, charmed us by playing croquet with it. "Well, perhaps that was all our place needed," Ed observed. "A tame bird."

Earlier I had called Viola to give her the glad news. "Why, how'd you do it?" she'd cried, admiration—or was it envy in her voice? She arrived now to see the miracle, and she and her fledgling had a touching reunion, both talking at once. "Oh, Peter, you *are* beat up!" she reproached him. "You've lost more feathers." The bird preened himself, showing off his new accomplishments as a child likes to astonish his parents, after an absence.

"He followed me about from tree to tree," I told her, "while I was weeding this afternoon."

Viola sighed. "That's what I would have loved," she said. "If it hadn't been for the cats. Well, I'm glad he's getting on so well here." When, later, she took her departure, with a lingering backward look at the bird, I understood at last how she was feeling. Doesn't everyone envy, while at the same time being grateful, to the outsider who initiates chick or child into life? For it is almost always an outsider who does, and can.

JULY

HALLOO THE SUGARBRIDGE:

Nice to sit down after a very hot day and visit with my dear far-away neighbor. And next weekend you will come driving down the winding country roads, and fall out of the dusty car. You will look cool in your casual cotton.

We shall go right to the pond as soon as you unpack your bathing suits. On the terrace the ice bucket will be frosty and fresh mint leaves will be ready for your glasses, and we shall stay ourselves with cheese and crackers and smoked tid-bits so we won't have to rush dinner.

Meeting dear friends after an absence has a strangeness about it. I always feel shy at first and cannot think of the right words. When I speak to Jill about this, she says, "Never mind, you talk your head off inside of half an hour."

Is it the consciousness of the time that has passed, the unshared things that must have happened, or is it just the self getting oriented again? In

any case, I was never any good at seeing someone between trains for an hour, I could never plunge in and really exchange thoughts, ideas, emotions.

I admire Faith Baldwin for the way she can pop in after a long separation, sit down, give her hair a soft pat, and begin "You know I don't quite agree with you that there is only one true love for any woman." Or, "Don't you think if the churches did unite on the basis of simple faith in God and brotherhood, the world might be saved?"

I think it is because she reacts so instantaneously and identifies so completely with a place, with people, that she manages this.

When you pack, tuck in something for Ed to read aloud after our dinner. I feel reading aloud is an art which we have almost lost sight of, and it is a great pity. Nothing is much better than to sit quietly and share the experience of a good book.

The quick lanterns of the fireflies make a pattern of flickering gold tonight in the meadow, the sky is deep with stars. After a hot day, a summer night is dramatic and wonderful. The cool breath from the heart

of the woods slides so softly over the lawn, the world is very still as if
the heat of the day had tired it. One feels suddenly the urge to stay up
all night, following the moonlit country roads to the pale edge of the
horizon. Surely, if we did that, we should find something strange and
wonderful!

Small busy feuds develop among the cockers when the weather is too
hot. Linda suddenly decides that Sister is in the house more than she is.
They cannot fight until they have first crossed necks, and we wait until
the neck-crossing is over before we move to separate them. Melody gets
annoyed with Hildegarde, who is mild as milk, and they begin the ritual.
Tiki then jumps up and down with excitement, he loves things to be going on. In the end, there may be a general mix-up with Daphne just nip-
ping anybody she can find.

Jonquil never gets mad at anybody. She is really what cockers are supposed to be, "the kennel angel." Her idea of fun is a party so she can sit
on a number of laps and make friends and influence as many people
as possible. She doesn't need Dale Carnegie.

As for her son, Especially Me—I wish you had seen him with the
electrician. Both were on the floor, both heads bent, both peering down
the hole to the cellar where the new wire was to come. Teddy's golden
head took up most of the space, he sniffed with joy. Then he picked up
the screwdriver and made off with it and played lovely games all over
the house while Mr. Leopold dug up another screwdriver and finished
putting in the floor plate. "Going to train him to be my helper," he said.

This afternoon Jill brought in a huge basket of beans to freeze. Seems
the hotter the day, the more vegetables just have to be taken care of. And
I sometimes wonder whether we aren't just a little bit too intimidated
by all the articles on rushing things from garden to freezer. We simply
fly. No waiting until the cool of the evening, no sitting down to snap
the beans. The kitchen is like a factory going full blast on an emergency
order.

The vegetables must be surprised. One minute they are minding their
own business in the garden, the next they are whisking around and the
next they are in the freezer.

> with love,
> GLADYS

SUGARBRIDGE

DEAR GLADYS,

Oh, the frustration and anti-climax of not coming, when we were
ready for departure! I hope you realized our regret through that hurried

long distance call. We know you detest talking on the phone, so we always try to make it brief. Aside from the disappointment of not seeing you, there is also the necessity of forcing my one-track mind back into its regular channel. There is in me an unanalyzed quality which is offended at the nonfulfillment of some planned-for event. Even a dentist appointment. With Ed at the beck and call of publishers, I should be used to the upheavals: and a job is a job.

But I must face it. The silent house, unnaturally neat, yawns back at us. Everything has been put away, the vases emptied of flowers, the refrigerator is bare of food; our bags stand ready and packed, now await unpacking. WE ARE NOT GOING. Outside, the flower borders have been cut sharply back; nothing will bloom for at least a week. The dogs have gone to kennels; the barn is empty, too; Chief is turned out in a neighbor's pasture.

The utter emptiness strikes me, the sense of being a stranger here where yesterday it was my home, where life seemed fragrant and full. How enticing the pool, I thought then; no place else could you find such a small gem, so clear and green, so pleasantly fringed with ferns! The two Danes, golden-brown as ripe wheat, ran through the tall grasses, and cooled their paws in the stream which fed it, ducking now and then for frogs. The terraced tiers of the back garden were bright with my favorite flowers; over the picket fence the tall canes of ripe raspberries were hanging. Nothing enhances like imminent departure. Haven't you ever looked out the window of a moving train and caught sight of some peaceful little hamlet, drowsing in the evening hush, and thought nostalgically, "What a lovely spot! Oh, to stop there, and see what it would be like to live in one of those little white houses! For a day, or a year—or forever." And what a comedown it would probably be if we did.

So now I wander lonely as a cloud over the lawn, and into the garden. What shall I do? Where to begin? What is the use, anyway? I am completely disorganized. Only yesterday life was too crowded. In the flurry of departure, pleasures were deferred, friends went unvisited, engagements put off. This gave a certain heightened sense of living. "Wait until we come back," I said. Now I have no heart for these once urgent matters.

Besides, I am not even supposed to be here. I cringe away from a passing car, and dodge behind a tree. What will people say, I wonder, remembering other times like this (we've done it before). I can imagine them saying, Those temperamental Shentons, you never know what they're going to do! Clinton arrives, stares at me as though he were seeing a ghost, greets me gloomily. He had thought to have a peaceful time, doing as he pleased.

Now my life is beginning to close down on me again. With the clack

of the lawnmower in my ears I think, Well, I might as well put those sheets in the washer. Yet today these familiar jobs, to which I am ordinarily resigned, can, indeed do with my eyes shut, seem impossible. Even the extra ones, which I hold out to myself as a reward for finishing up the duller round, like tying up the little tree which has been growing beyond itself on the terrace—even these seem not worth the doing.

I say to myself, I won't! Not today. If we've had to put off our trip, and with all the troubles of departure, I'm faced now with picking up the pieces, I'll make today an out-of-the-ordinary one at least. I'll refuse to do anything useful; I'll treat myself like the guest I expected to be—your guest. While it won't be so gay, here, at least it will be different. I carry one of the deck chairs from the front porch back to the terrace; this is unprotected from the elements, and it is usually too much trouble to have to take the perishable chairs in; when I sun myself there, I sit on the bare stones, or a pad, and the ants crawl over me unobstructed. But not today. I do everything in style, just as though I were you, a ministering hostess, set the chair at its laziest length, place it so that my legs will be in the sun to brown, while my head is shaded by our little terrace tree's branches. I sit down, and contemplate my newly manicured hands, going completely to waste.

It *is* pleasant. I feel a different person, and have no shame, as I normally would, at wasting these fruitful morning hours. So, let joy be unconfined!

I'll invite myself to an unhurried dip in the pool. "And what would you fancy for lunch, Milady?"

I might even lie in the hammock, I reflect. We have a hammock, bought by me, and hung in a copse of pines at the side of the house, through which the occupant may look down, and catch a glimmer of the pool below. I like the idea of the hammock, as a sort of emblem of leisure. In the six years we have had it, I may have sat there five times. While I am picking and freezing the vegetables, or dusting the roses, I often think about how nice it would be to lie in the hammock, there in the cool shade. Sometime. Perhaps until now I never realized how little I have used it. Well, it exists for a moment like this.

Yes, this has been a day of stark laziness, an utterly unusual day. And the most unusual thing about it is that I feel no remorse. I am plainly not back yet in the routine of life at home. Later, more seriously, I muse. It's the sense of being on an even keel, of normality, which helps us to continue on in our lives, no matter how dull or how monotonous. The good feeling that every morning the sun will come up, and we will rise and make the coffee, strong and fragrant, and that for this moment of leisure and release while we drink it, life will seem good, and possible.

It takes quite a bit of doing to tear me from my round, a rooted plant, and a corresponding time to become stable again. But once re-attached, I stand firm. Go away? Leave the garden to the rabbits, desert the dogs? I simply cannot. Besides, the marigold seedlings must be transplanted, if the autumn flower beds are to have any variety. And it's cool at home, and hot on the road. It will have to be something really alluring to tempt me into another hegira.

But you know this is all sour grapes. Ask us again, and with better luck, we'll be there!

B

STILLMEADOW

Dear Barbara:

Your not coming was like expecting a Christmas present and unwrapping the package to find it is the new bags for the vacuum cleaner! The house, I sadly reflected, was so clean and ready, and the broilers marinating in the barbecue sauce—and the bouquets in your bedroom looked sad and lonely.

But we shall expect you as soon as you can manage it.

If I did not live in this part of New England and you in the far-off rolling Pennsylvania hills, we should now freeze our bean co-operatively. One day we would pick mine, the next day, yours. Perched on stools at the counter, we would snip and snip, and discuss Keats and Katherine Mansfield and Edna St. Vincent Millay and Thoreau—with no regard to consistency. Talk about religion and what man has done to the good earth. Discuss new draperies, and re-painting.

Nevertheless, our beans go down, the tender delicate younglings which are the only good beans. The Yankee in me rises to great triumph as the produce of the garden is picked, blanched, packed away. Come the dark days, how wonderful a dish of baby green beans dressed with rosemary! Beans are so bountiful, we are often freezing them after dark, and then we can turn on the radio and listen to the uproar in the world. The strikes, the Communist agitations, the uprisings and the cold and not so cold wars—and all the time we know all we can do is to make up little packages to send around, give all the money we can save, and pray for the world. We may help a neighbor in trouble, and that is not much, but added up, neighborliness is the hope of the world.

Jill and I have a perpetual argument. I cannot resist giving just a little to anything, from girls' vacation funds to leper missions. Jill says I should lump my gifts and give a sizable amount to one or two that would count, not just helpless dribbles. I secretly part with a few dollars to help some Negro in the far South who needs a new trial—and when she balances the books, I am caught out. I adopted a foster son in Italy and that went very well up to the time Jill and I got him a goat. After that, he vanished from his orphanage, and I decided maybe I should turn his stipend to education in Korea. Does one think of it, even an extra helping of good robust country ham seems almost immoral. The only justification country-folk like you and me have, is that we do work for what we have, actually, physically, with blisters on the palm and sunburn on the back of the neck. But it would be a fine, fine thing if we could pack half our garden stuff and earmark it for Europe. I keep thinking some genius will arise to plan shipping of our own surplus. Americans are not as greedy as the other part of the world thinks, we only lack means to share.

Living in the country, with no bus, no streetcars, no train service, as we do, we seem very isolated and secure. The hills make a firm background for our meadows, the country road winds quietly to the small village. Summer nights are incredibly quiet, the sky so serene, the moon so glowing.

But we are part of the whole scheme, just the same. We are not alone, we inherit all the disasters that go on. There are no ivory towers any more. When I see the rosy face of our little neighbor as she jumps past our gate, I feel every child in the world should have what she has, which boils down to security. I see around her, shadowy but real, all the thin starving children in the world, the rags, the shoeless feet. And I send my

prayers for an end to this, for leaders wise enough to add two and two and not get sixteen. Or zero.

The exquisite beauty of a summer night gives the soul such a feeling of peace, as if Heaven were right in the palm of the hand. But I do not think true nature lovers, like us, ever ignore the shadows at the rim of the green valley. I do not.

Wasn't it Walter Pater who said compassion was the most important thing in life—meaning to feel with—he was writing about suffering, I think. Maybe you have Pater, my copy is gone. I believe he said as long as men have compassion, the world is well. I quote him badly, but I remember the feeling.

Connie is with us, teaching herself German for her Ph.D. orals. She got a little worried about the horse being out of focus, but that was what the text said! The horse was out of focus.

When I look at her, I am thoroughly surprised that I could be her mother. My mind is pedestrian beside hers, I have difficulty understanding Dylan Thomas and Edith Sitwell. I only speak one language, she speaks French like a Parisian, Spanish like a Castilian, has some Japanese and a bit or two of Russian, is thinking of Arabic. I think it is a wonderful experience when your daughter grows up and becomes a friend. There were times when Connie felt I was just too old-fashioned and difficult for any use at all. Now we find so much in common, and she is gentle with my curious feeling about Keats and Shelley.

The point at which your child becomes an adult person is a marvelous and miraculous thing. One day you are battling over everything, you feel the scornful lift of the eyelid, the dreadful arrogance of adolescence. Suddenly it changes. You find yourself at ease, talking together as two who have a basic love for each other. It is an experience as lovely as the first white tulip in spring. You argue about music, you reason about politics, but the stress and strain is gone, there is a comradeship, new and strange and fine. It is something most mothers must experience, but nobody has written about it.

There is nothing much more fun than to dress for some special event, and have your daughter study you, advise against the earrings, add a pin of her own, and lend you a dash of her special perfume. It makes me purr like a cat.

My own mother was such a person that even in adolescence, I felt she was perfect. Her wise brown eyes saw through all my pretenses, a quick soft word from her set me on my feet at any rocketing time, and our relationship was certainly far from typical. Her sense of humor and her deep understanding made the way easy for everyone around her. But we do not see such people more than once, and most parents and children have a hard time growing up together.

The summers I had Connie and Jill's son and daughter to raise had a quality of nightmare quite often. The simplest household tasks they were always going to do pretty soon, and in the end, I did them. I got tired. I got cross. When the girls forgot to let the dogs out in their runs one day and the entire kennel was a shambles, I made them scrub the floors. They got on their bicycles and ran away. It was too bad I was so busy, I never realized they had gone! After some miles of pedaling, they got very hungry and came back for a meal. Then Don decided he wanted to subsist exclusively on bananas and jelly sandwiches, and the smoke of that battle rose all summer over our peaceful meadows. He would not make his bed, he had no idea of ever washing his face. No amount of encouragement on my part could get the three of them mobilized until all the housework was done. Then they felt aggrieved because breakfast was not ready for them.

There were times when I wept into my pillow and GAVE UP.

Once in a while as Connie and I are reading some special bit aloud or enjoying together some of our favorite music, I think of those days and say to myself, lawk a mercy on us, can this be I?

Good swimming to you

G

Robbed of my visit, I have been thinking about you, and Stillmeadow. Do you know how I picture you sometimes? As a little girl playing with her doll house. I like this picture. I hope it amuses you, too. Everything at Stillmeadow is dainty, decorated, quaint; colored glass glows against the window panes, beautiful old quilts cover the beds, the hangings colonial, pleasingly odd. Its small and ancient rooms have been made comfortable by such tender thought, and each ornament placed just so only after due consideration.

And you, though you are, we all know, a nationally famous authority on cooking and all that goes with it, I somehow feel, that when you are seated at your table, set with the treasured collection of milk white, the dear little jam pot, the cranberry glass, the charming pitcher and sugar bowl, that you are really at play with acorn tea cups, and that if the zestful food upon the pretty plates were only mud pies you would not mind much. I find this both appealing and attractive. How rare it is to come upon anyone who is—after childhood.

Your mother must have been a lovely person, and I wish I might have known her. You do your best writing about her, and I'm sure that what you felt for her must have made her happy, since it is what each parent hopes for from his child.

They were an enviable generation, our mothers. The last before the indiscriminate use of the automobile, comic books, radio, television, progressive education, and the Oedipus complex. I'm sure it's not easy to be a parent in any age, but I do think they had a simpler path than we do. As children, we always minded the first time, and never, never talked back.

We live in an age of self-doubt of ourselves as parents. "Moms" have come under a lot of fire in this generation. We haven't the confidence that mothers of fifty years ago regarded as their natural right. And since you had a mother who seemed to you all the things a mother should be, you probably question yourself even more severely. You have to remember that you are you, anno domini 1952, and that Connie is Connie, with life today being a very different kettle of fish.

When we first visited Stillmeadow, it seemed so off the beaten track, so pleasingly secluded. We still are undecided about what appears to us the twisting, turning way over from Southbury, through the pretty farmland. And that lane past your house might be about to plunge into primeval hinterland, edged on both sides by deep woods. But this has happened to me before, visiting an unfamiliar spot in the country somewhere. I at once begin to envy its true rural quality, its apparent isolation, since this is the avowed intention of most country dwellers today. This is really *country!* I sigh. It's not this way at my house: trucks pass by, the telephone rings, people come. . . . But once I chanced to think, it was not always so in our neighborhood before I learned to know it so well, each road and lane leading to it, each bush and tree, every house marking the way, so that in time there ceased to be any element of strangeness, even in its wilder scenery. Yet when we came here first, it seemed an unknown land, all this dear familiar valley, and to the charm of novelty was added the pleasant ease of anonymity; you feel the same sensation in a foreign country. It is like being invisible; you know no one, no one knows you; you are free as a cloud. But this feeling cannot last.

You may not remember it, but you made almost this identical remark on your initial visit to Sugarbridge. We had taken our cooling drinks out to the back terrace, for it was a warm day, and you glanced around meditatively, I can recall. "H'm-m yes, it's lovely here," you said. "It seems so far off from everything, too. Much more so than at my place. But how," you asked, "do you ever get out of here in wintertime?"

I was astonished that anyone could think *we* were off in the sticks. "No trouble at all," I answered. "The State road is right down there at the end of our lane. And a neighbor beyond us always plows *that* out with his tractor." We, I thought, are *here,* while you are *there.* Yet to you, these directions are reversed. You know that the woods I think impenetrable are not, and that right over there is Woodbury; that, going this way there is a short cut; and that by train, bus or car, you can be in New York in an hour or so. Where is here; how far is near? Wherever you are becomes here, and near, to you, at least, even if it be on the Arctic Circle.

This is sometimes hard to remember, however true we know it is. But today, it is important that we try to do so. You feel this too. Another's home, another's inner life, hidden behind those defensive exteriors we all grow, hardened by dictates of custom, imposed by age or ailment, is *here,* too, and should be to everybody.

Sometimes, I wonder where the line ought to be drawn. If we could get inside of others, those whom we do not at the moment understand, the nation our nation is hostile to, the person we are on the outs with, we would comprehend their viewpoint, and could probably reach a compromise. But to be able to do this getting inside presupposes a kind of omnipotence not granted to earth beings, totally transcending conditions here below. For if we finite creatures did not have certain rigid bounds enclosing our identities, centering our will power upon ourselves, we should lack the necessary driving force to steer our way through life. There is a metaphysical gravity at work with us as well as a physical one, I think, keeping our feet upon the ground. From birth, each of us is conditioned to seek out the best environment for our own growth and expansion. Did you ever consider the purely human connotation of the word "good"? To you, to me, it means whatever is conducive to our individual well-being. But what is "good" in the cosmic sense, in the meaning which Spinoza might recognize? Certainly nothing which could concern little you, infinitesimal me.

This it is which stands between perfect mutual comprehension of individuals, or in the larger sense, of nations. If we did not have this blindness, there would be anarchy, chaos. The temporary loss of it plunges men into the suicide's last maniacal tailspin when he no longer cares what happens. We cannot do without the quality, this gravity of the spirit; it was implanted, built up for a purpose. And, keeping it in control, and using our meager knowledge of homo sapiens, together with our equally sparse store of tolerance and altruism, so painfully garnered over the centuries, we may only hope to do the best we can.

Barbara

Stillmeadow

Dear Barbara:

I have just had a long discussion with Mr. B who works one day a week for us, cutting kindling, raking the yard, hoeing, moving plants. Mr. B is writing a novel, he has been working on it for six years. I may have told you about him, he does handyman jobs to live while he works on his book.

He asked me what I thought was really great writing. I sat down on the bench by the delphinium and he leaned on the rake.

I finally managed to say that much writing was excellent, but to be truly great I felt a writer must see life whole. "To see life steadily and see it whole," as Matthew Arnold said, is the attitude which makes for greatness. I see life as a whole orange, the bitter rind is there, the necessary sharp seeds, the sweet running juice, the stable pulp. Many books written with power and passion, especially in our day, deal only with the bitter rind. Books such as Styron's "Lie Down In Darkness," for instance. Doomed and desperate people falling inevitably into a hopeless night. When I read such books, I admire the sharp analysis of character, the sense of pity for the lost ones. But I invariably close such a book, and sigh, and then look at the world as I see it. To be great, a book must also include the people who in their simple, possibly dull way, make an effort to live according to some dream.

On the other hand, a great writer faces the grim tragedy that life can

157

be, and never allows himself to sink into a saccharine state about the universe.

Life is struggle, life is dark storm and some starlit skies. To be great, one must communicate the whole reality, not a single section. Every man walks alone, every heart has its own suffering, but, except for the degenerate and criminal, every man has a hope.

It is the business of the writer, it seems to me, to illuminate life in such a way that when the reader puts down a book, he feels his spirit strengthened. It is a solemn responsibility to portray human beings so as to give the reader compassion, understanding, a sense of the value of life.

This has nothing to do, of course, with the events of the book, nor the ending. It is purely the way the writer views his world. For instance, "Cry, the Beloved Country" has more stature than dozens of "theme" books, for the author views his own people with the same clear compassionate eye as the natives. Both caught in a pattern, both struggling. And better still, both growing in comprehension as the tragic story reaches its foredoomed end.

In the "Forsyte Saga," poor Soames Forsyte causes more catastrophe than a dozen men usually could manage, and yet Galsworthy makes us feel sympathy for his struggles, we recognize the little bit of Soames in us all, and we understand.

"Wuthering Heights," one of my favorite books, paints a scene of almost unrelieved passion, but the strange lonely genius of Emily Brontë included in it the housekeeper, the natural, simple woman who might just live around the corner from us.

One always gets back to Shakespeare. In the midst of his tragic drama, we find Mercutio, say and gallant and quite normal, the serving people with their little humors, the kind and gentle Friar, the foolish, foppish Rosencrantz and Guildenstern. (I never like versions of "Hamlet" that leave them out.) And Juliet's simple scheming nurse surely makes us believe more in Juliet's great passion.

Do you find most novels of marriage unsatisfactory?

Most of them seem unreal to me, either the men are weak and hopeless creatures or the women predatory devourers of man. "But all men and women are not like that," I usually say as I close one of these.

Probably my favorite writer of today is Mr. Marquand. From the polished perfection of "The Late George Apley" to the last devasting study of the banker, one feels the true artist at work. However, most of Mr. Marquand's women play, I feel, a destructive part. I wish he could do one woman with the great feeling and understanding which he lavished on George Apley. And when I read "The Second Happiest Day" by John Phillips Marquand Junior, I laid the book down with a sigh. "He does not like women any better than his father does," I said sadly to Jill.

It is nonsense to say literature is in a decline, as some do say. Look at "Delilah," at "A Bell for Adano," at "Guard of Honor," at "The Caine Mutiny." Books that enrich us immeasurably.

In my own writing, not to be thought of in the same breath, it is true, I always try to completely realize a person before I so much as have him speak a single sentence about the weather. Even for a short story, I like to know all the detail about the childhood (which may not have a thing to do with the story) about the family, about just where he—or she—went to school, down to what kind of music he likes, if any. In a short story of twenty-three pages, I am so at home with the people that I am always lonely at the ending.

For writing, too, I try to make it as simple as possible. Never two words if one can carry the meaning. I have a horrid temptation to put down poetic phrases—as you may have noticed.

But "beautiful writing" is false. I often throw away a whole sheaf of pages because they suddenly sound too dressed up. Words themselves are so terribly intoxicating that it is hard not to use them, just for the sound and texture they have. Sometimes I fall by the wayside and I am ashamed. The discipline involved in saying, "It was an early April morning," and not going on about the wonderful excitement of spring is a tough one.

I feel just as my friend the singer, Glenn, feels about his singing. He says, "I hear the note I want, I feel it, and then when it comes out it is never quite as good as I felt it should be."

Sometimes I have moments of wishing I could have been anything other than a writer. Words are a difficult medium because they are so common, they are around all day. But I was done for when I was born. One of my childhood friends told me recently that whenever the subject of the future came up I always said with complete candor, "I am going to be a writer!"

But am I really? Certainly twenty-seven books and tons of magazine stories don't mean one is a writer. Nor living by the typewriter either. One is only a writer if at some time one communicates something so vital to another via the printed page that the reader draws a long deep breath and says, "yes, it is so."

Possibly the Social Security man was right when he asked me what I was. This was when I timidly went for my card after becoming a part of the "Ladies' Home Journal" staff. I whispered softly, "I am a writer." It seemed so bold, so—so conceited to say so, right out loud.

He gave me a look. "Housewife," he said, and wrote it down.

Housewife I certainly am. And I will settle for that!

DEAR G,

This is a letter of bits—bits of July. Up early this morning, and down to look at the pool after last night's rain. It was fresh and sparkling, yet opaque, a cloudy gem. Men should have something which perks them up as moisture does the scenery. But on the dam lay the muskrat, dead. He, and perhaps others of his family, have been my neighbors there this year. At first it gave me a queer feeling (and maybe it did him, too) but we got used to each other, and now I am sorry to see that something has done him in. Probably Duke. I put him aside for Clinton to give honorable burial. At the same moment, I caught sight of a giant Cecropia moth down on the road, spasmodically fluttering its wings; it didn't move when I touched it, and I saw it was being devoured by a wasp, clamped on to its abdomen. I knocked the assassin off, but the damage was done, and I bore the beautiful creature (Do you have them? They are such ruddy vivid velvety things) to the studio, to expire in peace, and later be given to a little girl of my acquaintance who collects butterflies.

When I returned to the house, Ed came laughing in from out of doors too. "There are three fat little birds just hatched out in the nest over the garage spotlight. It was a wise choice on the part of the mother bird; I suppose the light acted as an incubator. Anyway, they're all asleep, hanging over the edge, their eyes tight shut, their mouths open. Go and look."

I did, but by that time they were awake, and their eyes were open, their mouths shut, no prospect of food being immediately in the offing.

Why do I bother telling you all these unimportant facts? Well, they are, and they aren't. Because such trivialities are the stuff of which summer is made, I suppose.

Have you ever lain down in the summer garden, your head pillowed upon the grass? To a recumbent person, everything looks huge; you have stepped into a new world of Lilliput, spikes of grass seem as tall as palm trees, over a safari of ants, toiling by; the flower stalks stretch miles up in the sky, like jungle growth. It is a tight, warm, engrossing world, this, and by and by the affairs of men fade away; it gets to be all-important that the little golden honey-bee makes it into the Canterbury bell where he is having trouble forcing an entry; the ants have come upon a dead beetle, and are dragging it away, bit by bit. The sun beats down, hot and purifying; you can almost hear the plants grow.

I notice that often a horde of tiny white butterflies alight on the blossoming lavendar; is it instinct, or only coincidence that so many times brings about these pleasing color combinations?

In the cool of last afternoon, Miss K and Mr. D, dressed in their best, walked down to present us with two bunches of extra-special poke.

You must have pokeweed, too, with its crimson berries in the fall, so loved by the birds. But perhaps you do not use its young shoots, as we do, best cut in early spring, from under rocks, or banks of leaves, blanched and tender. It's known around here as "poor man's asparagus," and may be prepared in much the same way. Although Miss K tells me, and she should really be the authority, that she cooks it with a highly seasoned peppery sort of sausage. It might be worth trying.

It was crisp and rosy, well-washed in their creek, and wrapped spotlessly in waxed paper. I do not wonder that they have built up a custom in this unusual delicacy, for they take pride in giving only the best, a well-nigh abandoned trait in this country. Presents like this touch me (I remember too the Valentine handkerchief Miss K made me, a wonderful confection, pink, crocheted around with all the colors of the rainbow). And these gifts are valuable because they come from the heart.

The first red leaf has fallen from the gum tree! This is the earliest sign of autumn, as premature, in July, as a gray hair in a young head. Until it flutters to the ground, this harbinger of change is indistinguishable from the flowers of the trumpet vine, which blossom gaily all over the huge gum. But when I come upon this leaf, slender and scarlet, lying under the tree, I pick it up, and lay it upon Ed's desk. When he sees it, he sighs and shakes his head (this is part of the ritual, too).

"Fall's coming," he says lugubriously. "It won't be long before the snow is flying."

The thought goes across my mind in silence, a premonition that in another way, in the calendar of the mind, it is an indication. We will not always be here, with Ned; nor will the Danes chase groundhogs in the fields forever, nor Chief kick up his heels in the orchard. Like all else, we will pass, and others come after us. How will they change things, these other inhabitants? For new tenants always do. What we love, they may detest. But they cannot change the way the house sits on the gentle rise above the little rushing stream, with the higher hill behind. And I hardly think they will wish, although they may, to cut down the majestic sycamore which guards the house front, nor the tall copse of pines at the side.

I'm enclosing a copy of a letter from Viola.

LETTER FROM VIOLA:

"Have you ever been near to a possum? Because it made the kitchen more cluttered than usual, I used to put the warm milk in a pan on the little bridge outside for the cats. I discontinued that, though, when nearly every evening when I put Frances [her collie] out before going to bed, I had to chase a possum or keep her from nearing a skunk that had come to sample the milk the cats didn't drink.

"I thought I had seen the last of them, but last night I met the possum again at the garbage pile down below the maples. I always carry a big five-cell flashlight, so I spotted him before I got very close. He just froze in position, as I touched the tip of his tail lightly with my cane. He whirled quickly, and seemed to hiss. Surprised that he would fight, I stamped my feet and yelled at him. He took off rapidly for about ten feet, then went into the fascinating slow-motion stunt I'd seen him do when retreating from the milk pan on the bridge. He lifts each leg slowly and puts it down just as slowly. The best description I can give of his movements is to say that they remind me of the slowed-down motion of a fast traveling trotter on a movie screen. He lifts each leg high up, as if to avoid making a noise, but there definitely was a rustling in the leaves as he retreated. Why he freezes instead of retreating, I can't understand. Because he can move fast—I saw him do it! Although I have heard of a case where one was rescued from dogs in a park in town, and the owners of the dogs raced back home and got a pan of water, returned and carefully covered 'the poor injured thing' with leaves, and were peeved when their husbands laughed at them and told them it would be gone in the morning, I've yet to see one play 'possum.' And they sure are ugly! If they grew as big as Frances, I wouldn't venture outside at night.

VIOLA

STILLMEADOW

DEAR BARBARA:

I would love to have seen Viola's possum. How carefully she observed everything about him! I'd like to meet her when I come down next time.

162

We had a chance last week to hold a baby fox in our arms, this was very exciting. Dr. George Whitney found him, lying in a little nest of leaves, starving quietly to death. The parents had been killed, obviously. George brought the baby home and is keeping him for a house pet. He calls him Johnny. Johnny is a grave-eyed quiet little fellow with the softest red-gold fur and the most pointed ears. When you pick him up, he leans against you, with as much trust as if humans had always been his kind. If he is happy, he makes a kind of purring sound.

He plays with a puppy his own size, and the two have no idea they should be enemies, they sleep together, eat together, and have a fine time. In the evening when George studies, he has Johnny beside him.

I fear as Johnny grows older, he can never run free. There will always be murder in a gun waiting for him, and he will know no better than to run toward it. But meanwhile he has a happy life with that gentlest of men, young Doc.

G

SUGARBRIDGE

DEAR G

Frog-fishing time has come—not for me, you may be relieved to hear —but for Duke. Although we have come upon ancient frog gigs buried in our garden, miniature iron pitch-forks which bygone hands have gigged with. This is his favorite summer's occupation. There is a little silt pool, before the pool proper, and that is his fishing grounds. He spends a good part of the day just barking at the frogs, of which there is always a bumper crop, but quite often, too, when conditions look favorable, he slides his forepaws down into the water, while his hindquarters remain on the bank, and suddenly he plunges his whole head under, takes a big gulp, hoping a frog will be included. Sometimes there is, and then, unutterably delighted, he carries it around in his mouth, taking it out now and then to play with it. I try to rescue them, or to reason with him; Duke himself is sorry, and perplexed when the poor frogs wear out to limp little bits. Most of the time he is content with his mouthful of water, to stand there endlessly, with his paws in the waters, his jowls flapping, his forehead corrugated with concentration. Duke has the soul of a good fisherman.

Two Great Danes *is* a great lot, at times. There is just so much of them. No doubt of it, a loss for everything we gain. Sometimes Duke, now that Golden Girl's newness has worn off, gives me a long look which says, I am *your* dog, and this Golden Girl is not going to come between us. While it's certainly more normal for him to have a companion of his own kind, I do miss our former closeness. He was always with me, and we understood each other so well. G.G. is an insecure dog, and needs to be made much of. She's come out a lot since we had her, but do I show Duke a bit of attention, she is at once upon us. The relationship which humans are able to set up with animals is to me the reason for having pets, and Duke and I really have had it. But it fades away, I think, if you let it lapse. However, you pay a terrific penalty emotionally when you lose this dog-friend, and perhaps I am unconsciously trying to save myself something there. The physical hardships of our increased menage I don't mind so much—in order to feed two monsters as cheaply as one, I am forced to cope with tripe, a horrifying sight in the rough. (Looks just like a chenille rug, an odoriferous one.) Poor Ed! It makes his gorge rise to see me cutting it up in the kitchen before breakfast. But Golden is a rather sweet dog, and is going to be good at Obedience training. It is such a joy to work a dog that doesn't want to take a piece out of the nearest neighbor. She has a beautiful head, but the saddest eyes, the eyes of an old courtesan.

B

STILLMEADOW

DEAR BARBARA:

So far as I know, none of our dogs has ever caught a frog. But I can hear the popping sounds all day as the poor things leap back into the water as the Irish lunges at them. When I go down to swim, one very green, very wise frog sits by the stone steps and waits for me, and he knows nobody is going to disturb him. He blinks a watery eye and just watches. He is the first frog I have ever known personally and we have nice little visits.

We eat all our suppers by the pond these hot days. I expect we are the only New Englanders with a barbecue built by a Western cowboy! Smiley Burnette designed it himself and got up at six every morning of their last visit to be sure to finish it.

Smiley is such a big man that when he stands in the doorway at Stillmeadow, the whole house just has to stretch, that's all there is to it! Dallas says he once sat down in a strange chair to make a phone call and the chair just melted away under him.

When they come, Smiley likes to cook. His buttermilk pancakes are well worth getting up for. His remoulade sauce for shrimp, his spiced leg of lamb, his lobster casserole—they are gourmet dishes. On tour, he carries a complete kitchen with him, packed in various suitcases and bags. He even turns out cakes with the aid of an electric broiler!

Show people, he says, get so tired of restaurant and hotel cooking. He takes turns, when he is on tour, feeding various members of the troupe. One time the Autry show was housed in an old armory where there wasn't an electric socket to be seen anywhere. Smiley told the acrobats he had planned to give them dinner—Louisiana shrimp, but would have to wait.

The acrobats poked around and found a shower back of the stage. It was lighted by a bulb in the ceiling. Quick as a flash they made a human pyramid of themselves, took out the bulb, screwed a plug in, leaped down and said in unison, "Shrimp!"

Our barbecue is especially nice, I think, because he himself personally mixed the cement and laid up every brick. Somehow it makes me realize we are always neighbors, even when a whole continent stretches between our houses.

AUGUST

SUGARBRIDGE
August, early

DEAR GLADYS

This morning as we sat at breakfast on the terrace, chairs pleasantly damp and cool from last night's rain, our own mockingbird singing incidental music and the trumpet vine nodding to us in a sunburst of bloom from the top of the gum tree, we cast a contemplative and, in the direction of Stillmeadow, a nostalgic glance back over our finally-realized trip. We never have enough time together. I remember, too late, all the many items stored up to tell which we didn't get around to . . . special things, just for you and me. (For ages I've been wanting to ask you if you had ever thought of combining sweet peas and evening primroses. They make a fetching arrangement, the bright yellow of the primrose sets off the pastel variety of the sweet peas. They bloom at the same time, and I came upon the combination by chance. . . . And then, there was the affair of the wrens: that bunch of twigs which I'd been dumping out of my clothes-pin bag turned out to be that tiniest of birds' nests, and,

168

stupid that I was, I only tumbled to it when, after a fourth try on the part of the mother bird, I found five open little mouths gaping at me among the clothes pins.

But it was a visit to remember, a satisfying combination of good talk and good food, of swimming and *looking*. It's as though, in so short a time, we had to steep ourselves in Stillmeadow. The very essence of it all is your bright face at the gate, with Jill's tall figure looming behind, and a rout of cockers in between.

Nothing was ever so grateful as the waters of your pool after that hot trip.

"Sleep after toil, port after stormy seas,
Ease after war, death after life doth greatly please . . ."

I wish I could remember the rest of that; Spenser, I think. Anyway, a quotation which always makes me reflect, Life might be insipid without its vicissitudes. They make pleasures seem like heaven.

How very nice your young folk are, and didn't they wait on us hand and foot, with cooking on Smiley Burnette's incredible out-door oven, a kind of Taj Mahal of fireplaces—and passing and asking our pleasure, during that lazy delectable supper by the pool! It must be a great relief to come to a point in the relationship where you are rid of the twin bugbears, parental insistence and youthful rebellion, and can be just people together. I think Don and Anne and Connie are very agreeable people indeed.

Our child, when we visited him on his boat, served us up a most professional breakfast which he cooked himself standing in (and almost filling) the neat galley of the "Onward III." I still have a picture of him before the stove, intent upon broiling bacon, the sunlight streaming down from an open hatch upon brown muscular shoulders. He remarked too that he had become a great hand with a vacuum cleaner. Not the usual lore garnered from a summer on a boat, but acceptable none the less. I could use a good indigenous housemaid at Sugarbridge.

Coming home, with visions of Connecticut still bright against our eyelids (the last glimpse of Stillmeadow, remaining longest, the small perfect house in its perfect setting and you waving at the door), I always catch myself wondering if our rural Pennsylvania scenes which we have loved so much will hold up against these remembered beauties. For I admire the green black water of the Pomperaug, its deep gorges, their slopes dark with tall pines marching up them, only the tips touched with sunlight; I have become almost fatally fond of the neat little clapboard houses, framed by their picket fences, nestling among the hills, and of the rough pastures, full of gray boulders and black cedars. What a dilemma if I should have left my heart behind here!

All through the dull built-up parts of New York, my mind is busy with ideas and resolutions taken in these foreign scenes:

1) I will try wallpaper on at least one room in our house, like that dainty colonial paper, puce and gray, which I always admire so much on the walls of your little front room. (This is only dreaming, as I well know, the thick stone walls of our house will never hold paper, since according to ancient custom, there is no air space between stone and plaster.)

2) I will see to it that lots of delightful little bibelots are strewn over our house, as at yours, many colored bottles and bits of glass arranged in windows. (This is also a pipe dream, since Great Danes have a way of knocking over any bric-a-brac within reach, and almost everything *is* within reach of huge questing noses, or whipping tails.) No, I may as well resign myself to Sugarbridge's being a masculine house, with its thick whitewashed walls, its small square monastic rooms, and console myself with a mental image of the cozy femininity of Stillmeadow.

3) I will take steps about the shabbier places around the house (the

spot in the kitchen which has been waiting to be repainted). I will buy the new curtains needed, the glasses we have been out of for months. I will buy quantities of ashtrays, which we never have.

(All this is possible, and I hope I do it).

Once out of the heat and noise of Philadelphia, a spell begins to weave itself. The suburbs fly past, and then we are in the open country. Pennsylvania, I think, is like slipping into a cool green pool. It is late afternoon, and the setting sun is making that rich green magic with lush fields it does nowhere else. The far-off hills are blue, and everything about the landscape seems to smile. Nearer home now, I look at the landscape with a possessive and critical eye. It *is* overgrown; the rains this summer have encouraged a jungle of weed and vine; the joe-pye plant and goldenrod look pretty together, though. Winding our familiar way around the curves of our own road we come to our lane and turn in. The barnyard and paddock are high in weeds with no horse at home to keep them down, but the lawn has been cut, and looks greener than any I saw in New England. Our house, beneath its sheltering trees, seems shut up, asleep, and oh, how it does need painting! But home has always a humble readiness, a welcome, an awaiting for you, with a willingness to concede its faults which disarms whatever criticism you may have. And then it is yours. It is pleasant now to get out, and stretch, and unload.

Then, when the doors and windows are opened, and air blowing through, the car unpacked, clothes off and shorts on, a drink made, things begin to be wonderful, and just as they always were. The garden behind the house is in riotous bloom; the evening light slides thick and golden green down the slope of the back lawn to the tall pines at its base, and through them to the green glimmer of the pool. Far fields are forgotten and we are again sunk deep in the peace of home. All that is needed is for you to come to see us soon.

STILLMEADOW

DEAR BARBARA:

It seemed preternaturally quiet after you drove away. How I hate that moment when the car vanishes down the road! The last wave is like the flutter of a birdwing.

I am never any good at partings. To me, they seem to come so much more often than meetings, although that doesn't seem likely to be true!

Possibly the ghost of all past partings hangs in the air, and there is such a sense of how short life really is. In any case, I am dispirited and the family always expects it.

"Now, Mama, you'll see them again," Connie always says.

When she went to Europe for the summer, she prepared me in advance with all sorts of comforting statements about how near Europe really is, how short the time, and so on. I felt very adequate as we made our way to the "Queen Mary," lying in such regal vastness at the pier. We climbed hundreds of stairs, wandered down dozens of wide corridors, finally found her stateroom. Everyone was popping in and out, flowers and baskets of fruit that would never be eaten, books and magazines seemed to fill the very air. Suddenly Connie looked very small and young to me on that illimitable ship. The ocean was a large vast stretch of water, I knew it.

And in the midst of all the excitement, I sat down on the corner of the bed and burst into tears. Somebody gave me a futile aspirin and a glass of water. Somebody else produced extra tissues. I certainly added nothing to that gala departure!

Oddly enough, tears were not considered decent by my parents. If Mama had any crying to do, she did it in the sewing room with the door closed. In times of dire stress Father's bright blue eyes might mist over, whereupon he pulled out his big handkerchief and blew his nose lustily and said he was getting a cold.

The small hurts of my childhood, I was expected to bear quietly since tears never helped anything. We had no crying scenes in our house. If a really major catastrophe occurred, such as my beau taking another girl on a date, I went in the bathroom and cried myself out with the aid of a muffling bath towel.

Mama really lived by the Walpole lines, " 'Tisn't life that matters, 'Tis the courage you bring to it." (These may have been the only good lines he ever wrote, if so, they are worth it.)

But since I have grown up, I think my fibre is weakening. Never do I cry to know the richness of being comforted, however. Sometimes I almost envy the women who can make a happy bargain with life by simply weeping.

As for Jill, if a tragedy occurs, she goes quietly out to the barn and does her crying there.

When I read the articles by psychologists saying how healthy it is to quarrel, air everything, have it out, clear the air, weep and storm, I am really dazed. I cannot even have a maid in the house who explodes, the air darkens for me and I feel quite wretched.

I find words spoken in anger stay with me always, as if they were carved on some black stone. Maybe for people like me, it is better to let the harsh words churn up inside, at least the ear then has only pleasant ones to remember in the still of the night.

GLADYS

STILLMEADOW

DEAR BARBARA:

I succumbed to the prevalent virus, and have been amazed at the queer state of mind one has with a really looping temperature. Thoughts are far off, hazy and scattered, like little wandering lamb clouds in a big sky. One cannot plan anything, converse intelligently or finish a good book.

There is a dreadful loneliness about being the only ailing one in a world filled with brisk and healthy people, I find. Only the doctor's curious gaze seems to relate you to actuality, for a moment as you discuss your temperature you feel almost part of the scheme of things.

But even your illness makes you humble, for you see so many in the doctor's office who are obviously much more in need of him than you are. Who are you, just with a curious fever that will not quiet down? You feel like apologizing to the doctor as he sticks the penicillin needle in your aching arm.

Do you remember when we never heard of a virus? Did people have them then? Were they all Grippe or, later on, flu? I came on an early diary from our valley not long ago, written in a slanting pale handwriting. Most of it seemed to concern deaths, and nearly everybody died of inflammation of the bowels. Young and old, rich and poor, they died of this ailment. Was it always appendicitis? I wonder.

At least in our curiously warped way of progress we have gone beyond blood-letting and moved on to antibiotics, although we move from war to war.

I like the term the colored people use in Virginia for almost any illness. "I got the misery," they say. It covers everything. And how true, when one is ill, one definitely has "the misery."

Does it ever seem to you Americans are too health-conscious? We take vitamins for energy, take endless pills, brush our teeth with paste that will keep our mouths healthy, nourish our skin with fancy hormone creams. We even eat according to the foods advertised to provide that extra lift.

All the advertising seems geared to making us bouncy and avoiding

173

that tired feeling. Maybe if we forgot it all for a while and just went on living, we should come off better.

We are dieting again, at least between weekends. All the books and articles to the contrary, I would not feel justified in offering a diet dinner to any of our guests. We manage fairly well when we are alone, but I was discouraged today when I figured out that at the rate I am losing, I will be just right by the time I am a hundred and seventy-three.

One should lose four pounds a week steadily and then glow about buying a new wardrobe in a size nine.

This is fine for Monday to Friday. Comes Friday night, the weekenders arrive. They may come at nine at night, after a long drive. No, they didn't stop for dinner, they wanted to get here. We have had one plain, rather tight veal chop, the spinach and some greens around five-thirty when we were ravening with hunger. So we get out the fixings for a late hot snack. Some women could do this and not take just a nibble of the mushroom sauce, a spoonful of the lobster thermidor, but alas, I am not one of them. The next day the scale confirms my awful weakness.

The rest of the weekend goes in a pleasant bout of good meals, vegetables simmered in butter, meat accompanied by a good herb sauce. The desserts I can ignore, but a newly dug potato cooked with a mint leaf and served with parsley butter is my undoing.

Comes Monday I get weighed and Monday is bluer than blue. We begin again, but without much enthusiasm for nobody wants to start a race over as soon as the first lap is done.

It doesn't help any when we are planning the menus either and Jill turns to "Gourmet" and reads about the things simmered in wine, cups of cream poured over, three egg yolks beaten into the sauce.

Not for us, she says, suppose I just broil a hamburger?

I read a long article this week saying that overweight was due to emotional frustration. This sounded impressive and I read part of it to Jill. She gave me a cold look. "You don't act frustrated," said she, "and you never have. You just act like somebody who naturally loves to cook. Do they say anything about that?"

This closed the discussion.

Yes, Barbara, communion between people and animals is a special thing. With Honey, for fourteen years, it never lapsed. Most dogs, however, are eminently sensible. They have the will to live and live as happily as possible, they adjust to the futile actions of their humans. They can die of grief, but prefer not to. Honey might have died if I had gone down the road and not come back at all, but she was not a practical dog. George always cheered me on my return from a brief trip for the "Journal"

by saying, "that Honey now, she sure grieved herself sick. She wouldn't
eat at all."

The countryside has a haze of heat over it. It makes everything look
like a stage setting with a gauze curtain hung down to give the audience
a special illusion. The sky is unbelievably serene. Days are so hot I
begin to wonder if we should give in and put air conditioning in the
bedrooms. Air conditioning seems dampish and unreal to me, more like
a theatre. I like the idea of direct air through open windows, but I am
beginning to wonder whether enduring all the heat is worth while.

Any day we know we shall wake up and the first cold air will come in,
it makes it seem hotter now to anticipate this, and we move languidly
about doing those things we know we should do before the crisp days
set in and the killing frost lays a cold hand on the garden.

We need no thermometer, we can look at the old hand-hewn stone of
the hearth. If it is dark with moisture we know it is a very hot day, will
be hotter. If it is relatively dry, we know the day will be bearable.

Light shimmers on the surface of the pond as I go down to swim, it
has a special quality, evanescent. One or two rains and my friendly pond
will turn as cold as a lost lover, I try to pretend this is not so, and stay a
little longer swimming quietly.

George's truck lumbers down the road past me, loaded with the last
cutting of hay, I smell the sweet clean scent of crushed stalks. George
waves and grins. I feel humble. He never has time off for a dip in cool
dark water, why should I be blessed so?

But as George says, "I work mostly with my head" and that seems to
level things out. As indeed I think it does!

G

p.s. We have had a short trip to the Cape where I spent all the time fishing.

DEAR GLADYS:

Now that summer is on the wane, it is the time to view it retrospectively and I can bring up something I've been wanting to write about for some time. It's an article by Cyril Connolly, editor of the English magazine "Horizon," published in the Sunday New York "Times," how long ago I'd hesitate to say, so fleetingly does one season, and then a year, impinge upon its successor. But the content was timeless, so I can pass it on without feeling that I offer a stale thought.

It was about gardening, no great surprise to you, I trow. Small gardens, specifically. And much, much more about a number of subjects which was quite penetrating. The English, Mr. Connolly said, are a race of gardeners. The French are not. Nor, he thinks, are the Americans. (Of course! New York, Hollywood, radio, television, automobiles, skyscrapers.) Gardening, he said, makes the mind dull, but is infinitely satisfying to the soul. He writes with that British combination of keenness and restrained humor, that dead pan smiting of the nail on the head which can be so telling. The history of horticulture in England was touched upon, the Elizabethan importation of exotic plants, as the horizon of travel widened, the moist equable climate making this possible. Where, he remarked, that of America was too harsh, too given to extremes of hot and cold; more or less the same with France.

Even English writers are dedicated gardeners, he claimed, but few if any, French littérateurs. It appears that Victor Hugo and Anatole France scratched around a little, but not enough to amount to anything. The French taste in gardens runs to the formal, Versailles or Fontainbleau type of thing, anyway. And all the really fine gardens on the Riviera have been created by non-French estate owners. Then, too, the French have not used Nature in their writing as the English have—Hardy, of course, and Wordsworth—have not identified it with themselves, made it an integral part of their work. They are urban writers. Americans are, too.

My gorge rising at all of this, I took it to Ed. And—well—you can think of lots of exceptions. We did, one morning at breakfast, and had a fine time airing our literary views. Wish you'd been here. Gontran de Poncins, of course, did that marvelously atmospheric, absolutely tied-to-the-land book called "Home Is the Hunter," which perfectly refutes Mr. Connolly, about an old servitor who has so completely identified himself with a certain château of his vassalage, with every casserole in the kitchen, every piece of furniture in the salon, each fish in the lake, each rabbit of the woods that he has ceased to have any individuality of his own. And, of course, "Le Lys dans la Vallée" of Balzac stems right out of the country about which it is written, and is quite indissociable from it.

Certainly, as well, we agreed, there are a whole flock of English writers who have no roots in the soil: Henry Green, Christopher Isherwood, Evelyn Waugh, Aldous Huxley, as brittle and sophisticated as any Frenchman ever was. But these are the exceptions. And, in the main, you do think of the French novelists, Flaubert, Proust, Sartre, as cerebral, treating of the city streets, the illicit love affair, the revelation of character through passion or crime. So I'll give him that point.

I'm not quite sure whether he is entirely right about American literature. True, we have no Hardy—yet. And we do have a number of regional writers, some of them good, Marjorie Rawlings, Eudora Welty. But no single one towers. I suspect that is because of popular taste here, which is not true in England. In this country, Nature writing has only a small audience.

Mr. Connolly observed that he would like to hear something of small gardens in the more temperate section of the United States. Were there any authors there who wrote of Nature? All the time, my ego was screaming, Why doesn't he know about *us*? And there is E. B. White, and Henry Beston, who write of Maine, and that Pearson who does the Nature column in the "Times."

Well, I never heard of Mr. Connolly's garden, either. Before reading his article, that is. He spoke of the planting at first entirely by botanical names, and most impressive it sounded. Just like an arboretum, at the very least. Until he explained that all the rare growths were only six inches high as yet, and so far had shown no leaf.

A little bit of lightness on the subject of gardening is as welcome to the mind, as desirable in the soil.

Ah, well . . .

BARBARA

STILLMEADOW

How I wished we were all down at the pond today—for we took a swim, the first since several days of icy rain, and the water had a clear cold feeling but summer's warmth was still there somewhere. You would have loved it, swimming toward the opposite shore which is all silver and dusty purple pink. Queen Anne's lace and what I think is white yarrow cover the whole slope, and the joe-pye weed stands by the water's edge. As I swam across and turned, thinking the long thoughts of the end of summer, I saw a cardinal flower right by the barbecue. Tall and redder than red, and all by itself.

We have planned and planned on how to move cardinal flowers in, and been told they were SO difficult—and here one came, a voluntary blessing. I can't tell you the pure blissful feeling I had. Then I swam in and called Jill to come and began to worry about the grass being too tall and its needing this and that and she said, "If I work on it, who knows?" in her dark voice.

It is well over eighty during the day now, a direct and baking heat, and yet there is a feeling of Autumn. Is it the color of the giant zinnias or the squash and corn thick in the garden or the sound of the cicadas? I think it is the quality of the light. And everything is so vitally green and yet maybe there is a faint tinge of paleness at the edge of a leaf here and there—or do I dream it?

Anyhow the heart knows.

Jonquil got her first leg on the CDX degree at Danbury Saturday. When Jill went in the ring with her, I said, "This is not worth the awful heartbeat and suffocating feeling. We shall give this up and let all the dogs be wild as foxes." But when Jonnie won her blue ribbon, I wouldn't have traded it for a mink stole. Jonnie looked smug, too, and whisked around greeting all her gallery quite like an actress at her first big show.

We all came home and had a pick-up supper, Fred and Edna, Frances Peirce, who judged, Hazel and a few others. The best fun of a dog show is the aftermath, the talking-it-over. And how we do talk!

We all ate too much corn. I had the fried chicken ready to serve cold, the salad ready to mix, and the corn pot bubbled merrily. With corn, I think it is not only the ear you are eating, but the knowledge that corn is so very transient. You know you won't have it long—freshly picked and silked and rushed to the boiling water.

Fred and Jill being judges, spent a lot of time going over scores. They agree on most things, they differ sharply on some. Sometimes Fred carries his precision work as a Pratt Whitney engineer a little too firmly into the ring, but he always has his heart on the dog's getting through. Over the corn he and Jill had a fine discussion of somebody's shepherd who did or did not have a second command.

In my childhood we ate corn that was just plain field corn. It could be days old—or at any rate, old enough to know better. We thought it was fine. On picnics we used to carry a basket of ears as big as elephants and boil them interminably or char them to a cinder in the picnic fire.

Now we feel no corn is fit to eat unless it is picked five minutes before it is cooked. Possibly we are too effete.

The best of August comes now, the gladioli. We drive over to Mr. Sears' house, and go down into the cellar where he keeps the glads. They are in pails all over the whole cellar, a mass of glory. It is cool and damp there, and you can hardly bear the beauty of the brilliant glads. They have a new one called Phantom Delight—a dusky pink with fluted edges. And the icy whites—and the rich ruby reds—I ask for a dozen and Mrs. Sears gives me, as usual, an armload. She adds a large and regal eggplant. Feeding soul and body at once. This is what I love about the country, Barbara, and I think you do too. Where in the city would anyone give you triple and quadruple of anything just because you liked it?

We went to the Fireman's Benefit Clambake Sunday, down by the Pomperaug under the shade of the great sugar maples. I wished for you again because this is a kind of folk festival which must be a descendant of early times. The firemen do it all, and I may say, the men seem able to serve faster and better than women. You eat all the raw clams you want, then steamed clams with broth, chicken, yams, potatoes, sweet corn, sliced ripe juicy tomatoes, crisp cucumber sticks, rolls, coffee, watermelon. And all the foamy beer you feel like on the side.

After stuffing, everyone either sits in the shade, wades in the dark, sweetly running stream, plays softball, or throws horseshoes.

What I like best is to see a commuting New York lawyer standing at bat and the coal and feed man pitching and a good dirt farmer running like a pheasant to a base. The school principal umpires, the young boys shout, the lawyer wipes the sweat from his face and grins. The first Selectman who runs a filling station wears a white cap and manages the steaming clams. He keeps an eye on the game. It is the core of America to me.

G

SUGARBRIDGE
August, the last hot days

I know what you mean about the cardinal flower. Those rare, delicious surprises Nature sometimes prepares for us! So often they come just at the moment when we are in despair over her harshness, stupidity or insensibility. This spring I was waging a losing battle against some of these less desirable aspects: the far bank of the little stream in front of our house grows up each year in a tangle of vines and brambles in spite of all we can do. There are spring bulbs planted there and this year I determined to get ahead of the brambles before they could make an impenetrable mat over the tender sprouting shoots of jonquils and narcissus. It is a difficult tedious and thankless job; no one but me will undertake it, and I don't blame them, for the wretched undergrowth comes up immediately, and overwhelms all. I had been working all the morning, and was feeling tired and despondent; in spite of the mountains of debris I had amassed, I'd made little impression on the heart of the growth, and my arms were scratched and I was sure I had caught a bad case of poison ivy (I had, and it took months to cure). Then, as I walked along the bank, preparatory to crossing the stream, I suddenly came upon an enchanting little glade of lilies of the valley, never seen there before, standing pure and waxlike and upright, amid the poison ivy and honeysuckle. There was something fairy-like about it, almost magical. It was as though Nature had said to me, "Here, take this, and stop complaining."

And then there was the blossoming of the Christmas rose, the day Miaow died. I'd had the plant for several years, and counted it one of my failures, for though planted in an appropriately sheltered spot beside the guest-room door, it had never showed sign of bud nor blossom. That day last May, I came out the door beside which it grows, feeling sadly depressed.

Miaow had had a personality of his own, and his dainty black head and creamy coat had been an amusing foil for Duke's Great Dane-ish fawn hulk, and great dark mask, as big as the cat's whole body. They had been amiable enemies, rarely coming to blows as they competed each night for the most advantageous place under the dinner table, or before the fire. Sighing, I remembered his way of patting your cheek with a velvet paw in moments of affection. His rubber mouse, off which Duke had chewed the tail, and the round green cat-cushion I'd made him, were all that was left, now to be put away as souvenirs. I walked out the door dispiritedly, unseeing in my dark thoughts. I don't know what made me turn around, but as I did, I saw the Christmas rose. It was blooming; three large flowers, gold-centered, were opening their creamy petals. I stopped in wonder; it was like an omen, a triumphant affirmation of life reborn.

You say summer is ending—yes, with a taste of peaches in the mouth. Why is it that the very last of summer is always the best? Perhaps we prize these later translucent days of warm sun, fragrant as ripe fruit, because they seem to be wrested from the cold hand of winter. One more . . . and perhaps still one more. . . . Each bouquet of flowers picked, is snatched from the coming frost, each big red tomato. Now is the time that Ed likes the garden. He will go to any amount of trouble to garner the sparse remaining vegetables, carefully picking off the few

stalks of okra, and collecting tenderly a handful of beans. In the summer, however, when the garden teems with plenty (of weeds, too) he refuses to go near it. Its treasures are too common then; a glut breeds contempt. Males can be aesthetic; females must consider canning. I myself often ponder the irrevocability of frost: one day the vegetable bin is overflowing with squashes, and I wonder if the family will stand for it another time at dinner; the next morning, the vines are shriveled and lifeless, and the squashes within the house are something to save as long as possible, to make last; there will be no more until next summer.

Yesterday Ed asked me, "Where have our mockingbirds gone?" And I know then, with a pang, that I have not heard them either. We realize now, too, what has unconsciously run through our early morning dreaming; the dawn bird chorus has been thinning, thinning, out to nothing. . . . This is the first time I have set a date to the songbirds' departure; it seems too soon, much too soon. The air is all at once very empty, without the golden rush of notes the mockingbird trilled, or the carol of the wood thrush. There is only the chirping note of the song sparrow, or the white throat, drowned out by the plucked metallic shrilling of the bluejay. And no birds sing. . . .

All the feeling of this time of year is expressed in that ecstatic long-drawn-out note of the white throat, a trill of four notes, to be exact; it's as though he were trying to put the last drop of sweetness, the last rays of hot sun, the last of all summer's beauty into his song, a farewell to the season which must soon go.

One of the most delicious fragrances is that of bean blossoms. I don't know why it should be a surprise that a vegetable bloom should smell sweet, merely because we eat, in many cases, the mature fruit. I wonder if Shakespeare knew this, when he named one of his fairies in "Midsummer Night's Dream" Peasblossom? I might never have found out the source of that faint, elusive but tantalizing scent, for sniffing it this August morning, I knew in that half-unconscious way my mind works that I had noticed it many times before. Yet this once, I paused and asked myself: What *is* that special smell? A tree, perhaps? But there was nothing like that in sight, and, bending lower to pick the beans the way we like them, tender, and so young they have just dropped the blossom, I knew that I had traced my runaway bouquet to those racemes of waxy flowers on the humble bean vines. If I was acquainted with a perfume-maker, I should present him with this priceless nugget of information. After all, in the middle ages, they made a scent from strawberries, especially for royalty. Yet in those days, having less to choose from, they were not very demanding. In this time of ours, of "Tabu" and "My Sin," "Sacred" and "Profane," the advertising on a perfume made from bean blossom might present some difficulties.

B

STILLMEADOW
In a glass, darkly . . .

There is never anything static at Sugarbridge. Once in a while at Stillmeadow, the day is level. But the deep solid walls of Sugarbridge are really built to contain great doings, the man with too many chickens to freeze, the horse running away, Duke courting a far-off lady, the gas-line violating the sweet and hilly countryside.

In fact, the first time I met Ed, he was so preoccupied over getting nails for Sugarbridge that he was not much interested in my literary output. It was wartime and nails were just impossible and nails had to be GOT. I felt the importance of nails myself.

My quarrel with August is that it does not behave itself as the books have it. Where is this hammock-time? We get out our chaise longue for guests, we have yet to loll in it ourself. We might, except for the after-weekend laundry and clean-ups. So peaceful in the country, say the city folk, and it is for them.

But I am a very poor guest, I had rather have people than visit, except with you. I am always over-conscious of the work involved and the change of routine and the wrenched schedules, and I get miserable. So I hardly ever visit at all. I was frightened the first time I came to Sugarbridge, I went through all the washing I would cause, the cooking, the chatting. The taking to the train and back. But the minute I walked across the lawn to the white stone house, I felt at home. You in your blue jeans and soft shirt, Duke, slobbering slightly, and the prospect of helping pick the lettuce and peas for supper made me feel pleased and comfortable. And I admired you so because you could talk while cooking. This I am unable to do. I cook with a silent concentration, and the guests who recite recipes to me as I mix may find almost anything in their dinner. Whereas you can discuss religion or the political situation or eczema in dogs and at the same time measure with fidelity.

The cicadas sing loud in the trees at night. They have a sound as if they were daring Autumn to come. Surely it never will. The exquisite silence of an August night is only made audible by that grace note. It is a gift to carry in the heart in January when the night cracks with bitter cold.

The zinnias are bigger than the moon and such terrific colors. I should like to approach the end of my life with such drama and brave color.

I like to think of my favorite poem of Faith Baldwin's. And repeat it aloud to the white moon over the house, and the flowers breathing so sweetly under it:

> "I have come back to quiet ways; to things
> Of silent wonder, instinct with delight;
> To dusk, that closes in like darling wings—
> To primrose dawns and lamplit, hearth-warm night;
> To mending bag, to laughter, and old books,
> To loud-voiced clock and table laid for tea
> And that brown urchin of a dog who looks
> From sandwich plate to mistress, wistfully—"

And as I gather Jonquil in my arms and urge Sister from the inconvenience of the mole, I walk to the house.

> "Thus, Lord, my spirit keep—in humbleness,
> In still simplicity of gentle days,
> This house, the love with it, lean to bless
> And hold our feet upon the homely ways."

SUGARBRIDGE
August tale

DEAR GLADYS

About this time I begin to get worried about Mr. D and Miss K. Sunk in the deep, unthinking slough of summer, I suddenly recall I have not seen them for a long time. The poke season is some weeks past. In fact, my last glimpse of Mr. D, he was struggling up a long green hill with a huge canvas bag over his shoulder, a tiny figure, his face bright red from

the heat, puffing hard on a big cigar. Though he was going my way, I knew better than to offer him a lift; he was off to his secret picking grounds. Miss K whom I am accustomed to pick up from time to time on the highway, carrying a basket of the fresh-washed pinky poke shoots, dressed in her summer best of printed cotton and white shoes, a colored handkerchief wound round her head.

Even though they are hardy, they are aging fast, I think, as I saddle my horse preparatory to riding down the lane on which we both live; I should have gone sooner. Although what can be done for two old people who live precariously but with their pride, it is sometimes hard to see. Earlier, I tried giving Miss K jobs of mending. But although she is able to perform awesome feats of vari-colored crocheting on handkerchiefs and pot holders, the mending came back to me done in huge gobbling stitches, as uncertain as though it had been sewed by a child. Miss K informed me with asperity that she was an artist, she had never learned to mend. So I have limited myself to buying a few pot lifters now and then; they are crocheted, too, and you can singe yourself if your finger happens to be over one of the holes, but I must say they are very pretty. But occasionally some oddment which we cannot use and which our Baucis and Philemon can, finds its way down there, an oil drum for their kerosene, a few sticks of wood. . . . Thinking of this, for the tip of their chimney comes into sight as I descend the steep hill at the bottom of which the house stands, I recall the constant blue curl of wood smoke which issues from it in winter time, and the quantity of wood necessary to keep it going, for they have no other method of heating.

But before I am well down, I catch sight of the outlines of a mammoth woodpile. It is mostly faggots, and really most resembles the brush piled about a martyr about to be burned at the stake. When I reach a spot level with the front stoop, I see that both of them are there, the light from a hole in the roof illumining their faces dimly; the house is surrounded by a green gloom of trees. Mr. D is smoking, as usual, and she is seated in a rocking chair, sewing. (For a large woman, she has amazingly small and delicate hands.)

After the preliminary greetings, during which I compliment them upon the rustic beauty of their surroundings, and Miss K replies gloomily that she wishes the landlady would repair the roof, Mr. D comes down and pats Chief on the neck. "Fine horse you got there," he says. This is also according to ritual. Miss K, this time, stops rocking and looks up.

"Seems to me that's a very small horse," she says critically. "Hardly looks to be bigger than a pony."

I explain that Chief is a Morgan, a breed which rarely grows beyond fifteen hands.

"Well, you should have seen the tall old horse *I* used to ride," she said. For a moment, her eyes measured Chief scornfully, as though comparing him with that vanished steed. "Although," she added, reverting to melancholy, "he was pretty used up when I got him."

Mr. D has been stroking my horse's glossy neck consolingly. "Beautiful horse," he murmurs. Standing so close, I can catch the aroma of tobacco which always surrounds him. It is as though he had been cured in the smoke of the weed, his face thin and birdlike, his eyes quick and bright.

This seems the time to broach the really important matter I want to talk about. "Mr. D," I began tentatively, "I heard that you used to find truffles around here some place."

His sharp old face lit up. "Why, yes," he said, pleased. "I did used to dig some when I was younger. Under oak trees, you mostly find them." A reminiscent look came into his eyes.

"Would you show me, sometime, where to find them?"

"Why, yes," he said, "I could show you. I don't doubt we'd find a few, still. But it's a far way from here." His expression had altered, become secretive, closed up.

"We could go in my car," I offer eagerly. The idea of pursuing truffles, sans pig, with Mr. D, here in Chester County was one which had been tickling the fancy of Ed and me, ever since he brought home this tidbit of news gleaned in a town shop.

"Yes, we could go in your car," said Mr. D dreamily. I realized that his thoughts had already strayed away from the truffles, and I realized that we very probably would never go, since we are busy, and he is

186

aging. "But I did bring all those sticks in from the woods this summer," he stated with pride. "Even if I am eighty-five years old."

"But I'm not a goin' to let him chop it up himself," Miss K said firmly. "We have a man coming to chop it."

"Yes, a man is coming to chop it," repeated Mr. D, as though he liked the sound of the words. He put his thumbs in the armholes of his vest, and stood there proudly; he had on his town suit, and his black and white shoes, and he looked very natty. The prospect of the big woodpile seemed to give him great pleasure, and I could understand that.

I took my leave soon after. Miss K had showed me a few rows of lettuce she was able to grow under the deep shade. "It's good for what ails me," she said cryptically. I thought as I rode back up the hill that as fall came to the trees and plants, a few more months had been added to their span. They were all right, they would go on this way, until one day, like the leaves, they would simply dry up and blow away. But I knew then that my concern for them was prompted by a deeper kinship than mere acquaintance. In their circumstances, *I* would live as they had chosen to, in a little, ruined house by a stream, with nothing inside it; or outside, nothing but the freedom of the woods. *I* would live by selling water cress, or walnuts, where the alternatives were the burden of charity, or living with relatives; the restrictions of some menial job. They are fighting a losing battle with our economic system, with death and old age, as all must, but they are facing this grim trio alone, and bare-handed, without science's latest discoveries to help out, the sleeping pills, the painkillers which most people rely upon today, without the comforts provided by our industries that have come to be regarded as necessities, without, indeed, much more than people had in the very earliest days of our country. I like to think that Nature makes compensations for those who have known so much of hardship and pain, and the leaving of this world shall be made easier than for others who have more to regret. Perhaps in that moment which we all must face for ourselves, naked and alone as we came in, the aspect of that dread presence will smile upon them, and show itself as friend. In the words of one of Miss K's poems (which she writes from time to time, and bestows upon me),

> "However rough the year is,
> With hard luck as our guide,
> We never know what fear is,
> Who take Fate in our stride."

Dear B

After a very hot burning-glass day, the faint coolness comes from the woods with a smell of leaf mold and hidden fern. The evening is very gentle, the birds quiet down and the cockers dig a last desultory hole in the lawn and then go to sleep beside it. The cats yawn and stretch their graceful bodies and get a mouse look in their inscrutable eyes. George is milking. Fireflies spangle the twilight meadow. The nicotiana sends a flood tide of fragrance from the Quiet Garden. Jill pokes around the vegetables, finding another whole bushel of squash.

The end of summer means the Lions' Auction, for the Ambulance Fund. Early yesterday morning, Len Gendler drove up, and we rushed the dogs in the back kitchen—it is always a crisis when the big gate must be opened—and assembled *things*. The lovely spinning wheels—which we have no space for—the teacart we cannot use because of the up and down levels in the house—the extra toaster—everything went. Len smiled his beautiful slanting smile as I gave up five flower containers and said, "The Lions thank you, Southbury thanks you." Well, I thought, to keep anything you aren't using every day is a sin now. A sin. Still, small pieces of the past go out with these things, especially perhaps the croquet set which we no longer use on the pitted lawn. (Moles and the dogs have ended our croquet.)

Len is another "character" in these parts. He is a young New York lawyer who prefers to rise with dawn, commute two hours, work all day, commute back, to have his family in the country. He also finds time to be on all the civic projects, help on every project, supervise the Lions' Auction, be active in the town, moderate the caucus, and play baseball at the Firemen's picnic. City folk such as Len never seem to have any difficulty becoming natives in this stern and rock-bound land. Others come weekending, or for the summer, and walk with a superior air—what can you expect of these natives, they say. It makes me think that it is nearly always what is in your own eyes that composes a countryside.

In the soft deep nights, George's wild cow makes her mournful wail. Now and then he has a heifer who cannot accommodate herself to coming in the barn, being fenced in the pasture. I know one or two people just like that, and it usually results for them as it does for the cow. George just leaves her shut up and Jill, tossing in the night, wonders when in the world that cow will hush. George says as soon as she has her calf, she will quiet and settle there again, how very human!

How swiftly I gave up my dancing days when I had a small round demanding baby in that lacy bassinet. I never drew a comfortable breath if I did go out and leave a hired girl with her, I just knew the house would be set on fire, or the girl would drop a flat iron on my darling's head—although what she would be doing with a flat iron, I never thought. Then there were all the fears as a colic coming on, a button bitten off and caught in the stemlike throat—I could really get in a frenzy to be home. Now when the thoroughly adequate and grown-up child appears for the weekend, I often think with amazement—she did grow up all right!

As August comes to her slow and dreaming end, the air has a special smell, the smell of ripening, the smell of drying hay, the smell of the piny woods in the cool of the evening. The strange rusty smell of marigolds and the pricking odor of zinnias, and so exciting to breathe it all in!

I do not, ever, like ends. I like beginnings and rich plump middles, but ends are always sad. Of all the ends in this old unquiet world, though, the end of summer is one of the best. For the first small throb of color in the swamp maples in September is a fine thing to behold. And the first nip of the air on a golden morning is heavenly to feel after the languor of summer's heat.

It reminds me to get all the blankets washed clean and sweet and blowing on the sunny line, to keep the smell of summer in them. It reminds Jill to consider the tulips how they grow and decide on more whites and more blues for the Autumn planting. It reminds the cockers to dig up all the rest of the yard for moles fast, fast, before the ground is stiff and resistant. It reminds the Irish to cast a weather nose to the air and mark where the pheasant will soon rise. And it reminds our farmer, George, to bale the hay in a hurry while the good hot sun rides in a pure sky.

To each his own.

G

SUGARBRIDGE
"All the long August afternoon"

Now that the heat is over, and we are shivering in the cool of early morning and evening, it is hard to believe it ever was so hot; that we had, at the peak, that moment of panic and despair which man can still feel when he comes to grips with the elements. 98 degrees is high for our temperate climate, and a drop of only a few degrees at dark is even more unusual for a countryside known for its cool nights. Duly recorded in the annals of the weather bureau as the hottest summer in fifty years, it is there for future generations to note.

The town lay silent, stunned by the heat. The streets were empty of people, houses blank and closed up. The paved streets threw back the fieriness of the skies in waves that were almost visible. Coming in for something indispensable, we saw it was really worse here, and turned back toward home with relief. Why is it that feeling better off than someone else is such a comfort?

Entering our house, we gave thanks for our primitive air conditioning, by which our heater fan throws up cool air from the cellar into a house closed up by day. Yet there seems something monstrously unnatural in a life behind closed doors for us who in summer are accustomed to living all our waking hours outside, and to eating three meals daily upon an open terrace. It is a little as though we had suddenly become natives of a tropic land.

The pool is our other life-saver. There is something miraculous in the way it preserves a mean temperature of fifty degrees the year around, and it is a truly astonishing sensation to sit on the dam, half in and half out, numb to the waist, with the upper half of you bathed in torrid breezes. The pool was originally a small natural body of water, spring-fed, a tri-angular emerald, which we have deepened, dammed up and edged with a band of cement on one side. Nature has landscaped the other banks with an enchanting arrangement of rocks and ferns, not to be improved upon. Right here I may as well say that it is far from the popular version of a place to swim; it has no diving board, no float, no deck chairs arranged attractively around its edge. The truth is that in normal weathers I disport myself there quite alone, except for the company of

Two muskrats (they have a hole in the far bank, and I have often glimpsed them swimming furrily toward it)

Three mammoth frogs

Two yellow and black turtles

One garter snake

A thousand tadpoles

Assorted water bugs, with whom I get along very nicely. They, and I, like the company, and the cold water, which most people don't. But at the height of the heat wave, the pool came into its own. People began to inquire eagerly if it was as cold as ever; they put in a questioning toe or finger, and sometimes returned in bathing suits. Even Ed took the plunge, although he usually darkly prophesies heart failure as a result. I made him admit the shock of its icy waters and the lovely resulting chill on getting out, often lasting as long as an hour afterwards, was wonderful in this weather. Although at any time it feels very fine to me. But men have a tendency to alibi by saying that women, with their greater proportion of adipose tissue, can more readily enjoy cold water.

Sweet are the uses of obesity! I am not fat, I think, but I'd endure, or even welcome a few extra pounds if it meant the difference between plunging into those clear green depths on a hot day, and merely sweltering on the bank.

The walls in our house began to ooze damp, after two steady weeks of high temperatures. This is a regular phenomenon with old houses in which there is no air space between stone and plaster, when the outside air becomes much warmer than that inside. This no longer bothers me. Our house and I are like two acquaintances of long standing who need not make pretenses with each other. It used to be that at the first freckle of discoloration, I at once made arrangements for the walls to be scrubbed. I now know this to be of little use. The same thing will happen again, and perhaps yet again, before the summer is over.

Though the heat has been so intense as to be almost unbearable, there is something wonderful about it, too, as there is about anything elemental and uncontrolled. At high noon, the sky is a superb bright blue, banked with high-piled white clouds, dazzling and so solid-looking; the sun blazing down, incandescent. I go out for a moment and stand in its full glare, just to see how hot it is. But at once I feel glad that it is not I who must ride the tractor which I hear chugging away on the hill behind, unprotected from its rays hour after hour, as are the two hardy young farmers who work our land. Clinton mowing the lawn, encourages himself with a song, and a sudden bellow, as he finishes some difficult bit, or perhaps a revivalist yelp which is very startling unless you are used to it. "I likes to see that evenin' sun go down," he will chant. Or, more vociferously, "Yeah, *Man!*" Listening, we agree with him.

Late this afternoon, fresh from the pool, and feeling in such cool glow that I could brave anything, I went to the garden to pick beans. It was like going from one climate to another. A warm steamy vapor rose from the ground, as in the jungle. I was barefoot, between my toes I could feel its mysterious life-giving force, like something tangible. No wonder those colossal weeds, thick as tree trunks, had sprung up where last week no weeds grew. I couldn't resist pulling up a few of them, since the ground was soft from a recent rain; there are few occupations so satisfying as weeding; the results are so apparent. But it is not the best way to stay cool, I soon found. I went in and took a bath before dinner. We have modified our diet to suit the weather, and eat such things as jellied pot roast, cold and succulent, tartar beef steak, raw ground beef mixed with everything you have a taste for, mustard, Worcestershire sauce, chopped onion, parsley, very appetizing when nothing else is. Crisp, crackly things, cool cucumbery salads. Only one hot dish, a popover, maybe, to make the rest seem cooler.

192

This is the time, I thought, to put up the screen in the window at the head of my bed. In an old house, there are always some windows which you never open. Our bedroom, typical of farmhouses, is low-ceilinged, square, with four windows, two at the foot of our twin beds, two at the head. Ed never has his open, considering, perhaps rightly, that it can only contribute to having a stiff neck. But I, when summer comes on apace, refuse to think about such a practical drawback, or that, once up, we often cannot get it down, and that I may be letting myself in for rain in the face for the rest of the season. For this open window is one of my chief summer pleasures, which I cannot forego. There is something delicately sensuous, on a hot night, about sleeping so close to a window; you feel any breath of air which may be going. There is an enormous sycamore tree directly in front of the house, and all night long little breezes steal in and out of its branches, as though it whispered to me in its own language. Sometimes in the dimness of earliest morning light, I raise myself in bed, and look out at it, stretching wide its great pale arms, and then I have an uncanny feeling it really is mysteriously trying to communicate something to me. This, in its own way, is part of all that summer means, heat, and growth, languor, delight, and discomfort.

P.S. Ed caught a baby groundhog. It was no bigger than a mouse. When he tried to do a drawing of it, cradled in his hand, it bit him twice. He says being an illustrator is not only becoming increasingly dangerous, but also more humiliating.

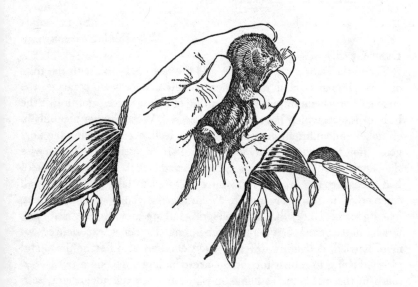

SEPTEMBER

DEAR GLADYS

Today the public schools begin, and the town is awash with the tides of small humans about to experience their first taste of bondage; the crisp cool air is vibrant with the shrilling of young voices, not unlike the hum of insects which have only lately ceased. West Chester abounds in churches and children; though I know this well, even so, seeing the next generation turn out this way every year, it is impossible to be otherwise than startled by their numbers. Several errands took me into town, so I had a chance, the first in years since I ceased to take part in this fall ceremonial, to really observe it. There are the young anxious mamas, looking scarcely older than their offspring, taking junior for the first time, much more worried than he; then the intermediate ones, experienced but more harried, delivering different aged children at different times and places, having to return for them correspondingly, and do a myriad errands in the meantime at home and abroad; then the adolescents, self-

sufficient and a little bored by it all, under way on their own steam, having been cast adrift from the support of parents.

Now that I am free of that tedious yoke, as wearing as going to school all over yourself, my heart goes out to those pretty, haggard mothers, always a bit disheveled, racing here and there, one jump behind what they have set themselves to do; they don't get to the beauty parlors as often as they could wish, their skirts hang a little askew, and they worry, worry, worry, from Johnny's first day at school, that he won't be bright, or popular, or have good manners, or get on in the world. Now, although I worried, too, at each stage, I have come to realize that it doesn't matter so passionately, and I wish that I could tell them that. Children *do* grow up, they show manners when they wish, they make the friends they need, in mere self-preservation, they get on somehow. I suppose someone tried to bring home this truth to me, too. But I had to find out for myself. And for all my detachment, I worry now about more adult questions, although with less idea of being omnipotent as a parent. In the earlier years of childhood, a mother feels she *has* to do something about it and if she just tells her offspring enough times to say Thank You, or to hang up his clothes. . . . Later, it's different. Children in their teens just look at you and smile. Politely but firmly. Yet, when all is said and done, parents never change. I remember as a girl knowing an "old man" of thirty-five who occasionally took me to the theatre. As was natural, I regarded him with a certain amount of awe, and so was filled with wonder to have his mother say to me once, "My dear, you aren't afraid of this *baby!*"

And on this special day, like a leit motif, I see our old car again. We have had other old cars, of course, since we do pass them on, as we even treat ourselves to a new number now and then. But this one, kept longer than is our custom, for having been purchased in wartime, represents a big piece of our family life, so many, many things. All over that car too is written the years of Ned's growing up: from the moment when we brought it, shining new, to the door of the Westtown School Infirmary, where he was convalescing from the whooping cough. While that car was still in our possession, he had discarded this childish name for the more manly Ned. By that time, he had learned to drive, behind its wheel, and was well launched into the stormy waters of adolescence. Whose waves still jiggle our family barque from time to time.

The old car was a station wagon. Is, I should say, for it still runs and has not entirely fallen to pieces. During our tenure of it, we replaced almost every part. And I find that even now, I know it so well, every scratch and dent mean something. The first time I saw it in other hands, I had a distinct sense of loss. Someone else is riding in *our* car, I cried inwardly, like Goldilocks of the Three Bears. I wanted to put my hand out and touch its battered fender. At the same time I was irritated with myself for being maudlin. After all, you can't keep *all* the cars you ever owned, any more than you wish to collect endless pairs of wornout shoes. Still . . . While I hesitated, standing there, the present owners returned, and piled noisily into the car, unseeing. There was a plain, wholesome-looking woman, wearing blue jeans, and a pack of children all ages. They also had an undistinguished dog, and a lot of bundles and books. They laughed a lot, and as they drove away, I heard the mother-woman say, "Oh, *dear,* I forgot the laundry! We'll have to go back!"

Feeling strangely empty, almost like a ghost, I still stood there. It was just as though I had seen myself go by, a self which was more familiar than my present one. For I had just come from the hairdresser, and I was perfectly neat, and I had nothing further to do. Walking back to our irreproachable sedan, I got in it sadly, and drove home.

BARBARA DEAR:

What you write about the beginning of school takes me back to the days when Connie was little. She was a small, grave-eyed child with a fluff of shining curls, she was rather like a drawing in pastels. Being a faculty baby, she had been much with academic adults, and not enough with children. How my heart ached when she disappeared into the maw of the big sprawling school, smoothing her blue smocked dress and bending her head timidly. Into the mass of whooping children, she vanished.

She was too clean, I knew at once. Her vocabulary was frightening. She was utterly unable to play any rough games. She could not even climb a tree and swing by one hand! She could make up little tunes on the piano and play them softly with one finger, she could write small verses with a stub of a pencil clutched firmly in one hand, but what assets were these?

But somehow she managed, with what struggles she never said, and came the day when she skipped in from school to say rather breathlessly, "T.J. kissed me today!"

"Who is T.J.?" I asked.

"You know, Mama, the one that wears the lavender up-top," she said. Mama felt better.

All of the Psychology students wanted to use Connie for their intelligence tests, two or three eager wind-blown girls would swoop off with her, and I feel sure no child ever was more tested than she was. They always brought her back to announce that her I.Q. was beyond measuring, even though she did say a plumber must be a man who fixed the piano!

Later, when she went to camp, came the sewing-on of nametapes. One of my darkest hours was when I realized that each sock of a pair had to have its own name whipped on. And woe to the hapless mother who chose the wrong shade of blue for the middy tie!

Later still was the day when the train bore her away to Ann Arbor, to a new world, which I could not share. Great excitements I would not know of, new ideas I had no traffic with, friends I might never meet—maybe even tears I could not find a clean hankie for—these terrified me. She looked so small and slim on the big platform, the Red Cap flung her shiny suitcase up, the conductor called ALL A**BOARRD— and it was indeed all aboard. The click of her new slippers on the steps, the farewell wave, and she vanished again. Stumbling away with my released tears, I knew how dreadfully vulnerable a parent is. Of course I couldn't go with her, that was not the thing. Not for me to unpack, make

up her bed in the dormitory, look at the registration sheets, and carry her to the best restaurant for a nourishing steak. No, I had to stop crying and tell myself it was wonderful that she could go to a fine University.

At least, I told myself, she had the right clothes. The budget bent permanently, but a Virginia friend came up to shop with her, and the simple little velveteens and smart soft suits and taffeta evening dresses were just right. When I left home for Wellesley, I had not one single correct item for the Freshman in college, and I knew what that meant! The kind of raiment suitable in Appleton, Wisconsin, was just peculiar, the prints, the navy crepe, the dressmaker-made evening dress—they were all terribly wrong.

But Connie went off in a blaze of Lord and Taylor's best and this was about all the security I could offer her.

I may say, however, to you as the mother of a son, that nothing compares with getting the young male off to prep school. Jill and I did our best with Don. "I wouldn't be caught dead in THAT," was his most frequent remark. The expensive raincoat he was to lose next week, and the glorious flannels that were to be spotted and stained for four years, and never, never cleaned—the sport jackets that would have the pockets ripped by too many shells being stored in them—all this and more, we went through with. His best shirts always came home for the summer decorated with ink and a mysterious brown stain. His shoes never had any soles to speak of. His slacks shortened on him every week so his long legs looked dreadfully like a heron's as he stood telling us all we didn't know.

As for his underwear and pajamas—I decided after his first round at school that the boys used them for polishing floors for inspection.

Don went to school near enough for us to be the burden bearers when he departed. Loading four suitcases, tennis rackets, guns, boots, blankets and the deer head in the car was quite a chore. We always had to bring it all back at Christmas, including the deer. By then he added a large portly desk chair and a fancy lamp to the collection. Some of our best pictures, too, to hang by the deer and the school banner.

Sometimes I think parents only exist to transport things to and from school.

One of my darkest memories is the loading that went on when Jill's daughter graduated from college. It was broiling hot, as Commencement always is. We were stuffed in our girdles, perspiring madly, our fancy sheer dresses hung limp and discouraged. But we had to climb up and down a dormitory stair from the first to the top floor, carrying 150 coat hangers, wastebaskets, odd parcels of nobody knew what. When the car was finally loaded, we could get in, but we couldn't see anything at all out of any window. So equipped, we had to drive from Ohio to New York. The coat hangers kept leaping about, which added nothing to our comfort.

Another of my thinking times is when I see our neighbor's daughter striding down the country road to get picked up by the bus at the corner. She grows so fast—only yesterday her mamma had to lead her by the hand and now, she goes alone. I feel a little gloomy when I think that our Regional School was all ready to be built when the towns began to bicker and the whole thing fell through. Now each town has to build its own school, at a great cost, and the children who skip down the road have to suffer for our perverseness. Our state, Barbara, was once the leading state in education, but times have sadly changed. Many of our schools are so poor that a college-minded student might as well pack up and go to a private school. This is not good.

I believe thoroughly in public school, for the democratic merging of bankers' and yardmen's children. It is part of America, very special. But when the public school no longer prepares a student for college, one relies on a private school to din in the necessary Latin and Math. We need a whole going-over of our education in this country, and a new approach to elementary and High School education.

I am so glad I grew up in a town where the public school had a top rating. The millionaire's children, the white-collar children, and the mill hand's children, all learned together, had fun together, grew into Americans. It was wonderful. Not a single child in my town was "sent away" until college age.

DEAR GLADYS

Today I've been leafing through the piles of notebooks, dating back to my earliest writing days, tracking down a bit I wanted to use. I was amazed at my diligence in writing down trivia; it's a kind of literary freezer. I think, I'll just put in that little bit of spring description; it might come in handy sometime. Well, Somerset Maugham did the same thing. But I do wish that in those first entries I had written a bit more legibly; not only faded with time, they are scribbled in the tiniest script. I remember quite well why this was so; I was apologetic about these initial attempts at writing, for I was a painter then, and never thought that they would come to anything. It would have been unthinkable if any but myself had ever read them! To this day, when I'm unsure of a sentence, I scribble it indistinguishably at first, trying it out.

I keep this collection in an old sea chest, along with my considerable store of unsold manuscripts and rejection slips. And mournfully I often muse, looking at them all, Does writing ever pay off? Think of all I've sacrificed for it, like a heathen worshipper before his Moloch! I'm never neat, or rested, or well-groomed, or charming (a person always in a hurry cannot have charm). I don't do anything well that women should excel in. I'm not endlessly sympathetic, a soft cushion the family can sink into on returning from a day of cares, as women without other purposes are. Yet I'd be lost without writing; it's a thirst, a disease, a mania, at once a slave-driver and a refuge.

But I was at the same time struck at the change which has come from year to year in the goals I have set myself. At first, just to be able to put words together and have them make sense was intoxicating, like riding a bike with no hands. Then, any idea or discovery which seemed fresh to me was seized upon and put down as important, no matter whether it was crude, ugly or revolting, like the harsh bright pictures a child draws, upon first looking at the world objectively. But that is not enough now—it is too easy, and after all, what is the use of it? Although, of course, there are those who go on doing sophisticated primitives all their lives.

I wanted to do sensational romantic novels, too, full of the raw stuff of life, and earthy details. For I have my earthy side. To lean upon Somerset Maugham again, every person is composed of myriad selves, any one of which may be unpredictably dominant at any time. This is not a very original thought; I've had it myself long before reading his corroboration, but it's comforting to be backed up. Well, after the publication of my first novel, which was as full of purple passages as a Christmas cake of raisins, I was stunned at the consequences. The nice old ladies

I knew exclaimed in horror, "Can that be *my* Barbara Webster!" And when a party was given for me while in the brief glare of the limelight, my earthy self must not have been in control, for I heard later that people who met me for the first time were considerably disappointed not to find me very dashing at all.

But now what I'm interested in is a big uplifting idea which will carry me away, and on which I can use all I've learned about writing, and which, finished, will bring all who read hope and encouragement to continue. What this idea may be is still hidden from me. It may never come. Do you remember what Katherine Mansfield said about the need for purifying herself before she could hope to write as she wanted to? I'm not sure whether these two things have anything to do with each other. If she is right, I and my wonderful idea may never meet. But I go on hoping. Any day, dawning fresh, may be the day.

B

STILLMEADOW

DEAR BARBARA:

So this is a thinking month for you too! There is something about the soft September days that sets me reflecting. For one thing the richness of summer is still with us here, until the black frost which may be around the 21st and may defer its lethal blade until the first of October. The bounty of the garden is precious, because we suddenly know that every ripe glowing tomato picked today may be the last. We get a little intoxicated with the amounts of peppers and squash and new potatoes and red cabbage and cauliflower—Jill brings in great basketfuls of everything. And a pail or two of Mexican zinnias and a few late roses, very perfect and delicate.

This extravagance of our New England gives me thoughts of how much I would like to share with hungry people all over the world. I am so conscious when we have so much that many have not. Our stony intractable soil, our frequent and heavy rains, our cool temperatures most of the time and our broiling Julys—all this means we can grow great crops with just a little hard work. And once you heave out the boulders, the remaining earth is friable and fertile. A little lime, some compost— and the garden will bear on and on!

Much of our forty acres is woodland and rocky pasture, in fact the Farm Bureau man tactfully said we should call it wild-life refuge. Nevertheless we not only raise most of our own vegetables but George harvests a goodly crop of corn, potatoes, tomatoes, and hay on our upper fields. With intensive farming, our land would yield much more. And maybe someday there will be a community collection of surplus crops all over our land which will not be dumped, or ploughed under, but shipped from central stations to wherever they are needed.

The woods are so green and the country roads are bordered with chicory and goldenrod. Do you notice how color follows the season? In spring we have the blues—violets, Scilla, hyacinth, then on to lilacs. In summer we have predominantly the pinks, roses and sweet rocket, and the magenta of phlox. By September we have moved into the rich goldenrod, the marigolds, the zinnias. You cannot pursue this too far without argument, for we do have all colors at all seasons, but I think the color spectrum varies with the change of the season. The Autumn colors are richest and most dramatic, the spring colors most pure and delicate.

Mexican-colored zinnias in a copper bowl are heartwarming. Russet azaleamums in an old, blue sugar bowl are nice too. And comes the morning when the first swamp maple catches fire, a branch of that is most beautiful in a stoneware jug. There is always that feeling—enjoy this all you may—and I do.

We planted all the daffodils and narcissus on the farther bank of the pond, and as I float idly, I often think Nature does better planting than we do, her colors are blended, her textures just right, and she creates beauty with no regard to fertilizing or weeding or special seeds. She walks in beauty like Byron's lady.

The last swim is a melancholy joy. Around Labor Day the pond really begins to get numbing cold. I jump in, catch my breath, sputter, swim a fast circle, and pop out to sit on the terrace and develop some circulation again.

Don't you envy those brave souls who break the ice and swim? Or are they pure exhibitionists? One never knows.

GLADYS

SUGARBRIDGE

DEAR G

Once in a while comes a day when, waking up in the morning full of energy, I still feel too restless to sit down at my typewriter. Then it is that I am apt to look about the house speculatively, and plunge into some phase of cleaning, usually highly unnecessary, or a job no one else would think of doing. Quite often, I find, non-domestic women do this, as though they found it important to assert their ownership and closeness to their homes, if only on these rare occasions. Writers like you and me (although you are not really un-domestic), women who have office jobs, and are away from home all day. I myself sometimes find that, with my hands occupied, my mind is unhampered and free to move.

It is also the best way to learn to know a house intimately. With ours, to scrub its white walls, freckled from the summer damp, is to speculate about their construction, and to guess who the mason could have been. For their surface, so pitted with little holes, and whorls, and roughened with unevenness of plane, marks it unmistakably as the original plaster, and narrows down the identity of the workman to one of the early inhabitants. I incline myself to an eighteenth-century shoemaker, whose name is on the records as having lived here then, and some of whose shoe-lasts we found in the barn when we came, at the bottom of a fascinating dump of old iron undisturbed I'm sure, for over a hundred years. Whoever that mason was, I wish we had him back today when a wall has to be replastered, for the old walls have a loveliness of texture —I suppose it's the refraction of light on their variation in surface—which makes a modern smooth-plastered wall totally uninteresting.

The wide boards of the living-room are of oak taken from these same acres long ago; refinished from the gray spatter paint job which we found on them, they took on, with each successive waxing, the rich fluidity of molasses. Upstairs the same wide boards, although of butter-yellow poplar, a much softer wood, are held together with great square steel nails, so cold to the touch of bare feet, that I often think I must have stepped upon a piece of ice. I have a special friendly personal feeling toward all our floors, which would not be so, I think, had I not upon occasion waxed them myself. The old battened doors, too, still bearing the mark of adze and hand plane, through the white paint; I love to run my hand over the grain of the wood, familiarizing myself with every inch.

Like all amateurs, I am proud of my cleaning efforts, and when they coincide with my cleaning woman's day, have sometimes invited her to admire. One time which I especially remember, she shook her head disapprovingly, as she viewed the shining white walls, which when she came in the morning had been blackish with damp. "That's man's work, Ma'am," she said.

"Oh, I don't mind," I answered gaily. "I do like to scrub sometimes. It makes me feel I've really accomplished something. Just see how different the room looks!"

Alverta, Clinton's wife, is an exquisitely perfect performer at all the domestic arts, and, a trait which is much more unusual, mercifully uncritical of those who, like myself, are not.

Though she is a gentle, kindly soul, still her woman's pride would not allow me too much to plume myself upon my achievement, with its implied reproach to herself. "Just see how tired you get if you have to work like that all day!" she observed.

Rebuked, I saw what she meant. I did this dilettante cleaning for an hour, or at any rate, only as long as I wished to. But she, before she had learned to put up defenses against too demanding employers, had often no doubt cause to know the truth of what she said.

I don't think I sound very restful to live with, somehow. And indeed, I suppose I am not. I like to think that this is an occupational development; there *are* so unendingly many things to be done around a place in the country! Ed is contemplative, let us say. (Never indolent!) He sits and smokes—or sips—by the hour, like a yogi meditating. Although something good usually comes out of it, stories, or poems, it is not possible to have two yogis in the same household; nothing would get done in the material way. So I do my thinking while on the move. But sometimes Ed gazes at me, and says, for I always manage to remain within hailing distance, though I may be deep in any one of my daily dozen, "I wish you would come and sit down a minute!"

Yes, I should be happier, believing that my activity is merely a necessary acquired characteristic. *Dolce far niente* has such a lovely, languishing sound, as well as a connotation of grace and poise which I could wish for myself. But I fear the truth goes deeper. The women of my family, on one side at least, are filled with a driving energy which never lets them rest. If they are happy, it is a constructive force, and many are their good works and accomplishments; if not, this energy becomes destructive, and then—beware of them! Luckily, I am in the former class—but still, shall we say, not restful.

Someone in my family told Ed this story, before we were married. I wonder that he had the courage to continue. It was about me. As a very young child, visiting a country place my grandfather had in Missouri (the men of this family were said to have made money at law, and lost it at farming) I was standing beside a window with my nurse, watching some men working outside. The day was hot, and presently they sat down in the shade of a tree to rest, but remained too long to suit me. I am said to have leaned out the window and called commandingly, "Up! At it!"

This has become a household word with us, and to subdue me, when I become too demanding of myself or others, Ed has only to say significantly, "*At* it!" and I am deflated.

B

GOOD MORNING!

In contrast to your frenzied and, I suspect, somewhat exaggerated account of your activity, we are going to have a no-work day! Lunch is packed and we shall drive over the winding country roads and look at the turning leaves. Our favorite picnic spot is by a dark amber trout stream with deep pine woods on one bank, and tawny harvested fields on the other. Since we can't build a fire during this season, I opened a hoarded can of Gloucester lobster for lobster salad sandwiches. With hot coffee and apples and cheese, we shall fare very well.

I can't think of a better present to anyone than a no-work day. Tomorrow we can begin again on the million chores of life in the country, but today we are idle as butterflies at dusk.

The villages in the valley look especially lovely as summer turns slowly to Fall. The church spires are more shining, the old white houses have a secure happy look. The late flowers glow against picket fences and gray rails. Occasional branches of pure flame burn against the summer green, exciting but sad.

We can drive to Litchfield and admire the stately elegance of the great houses there, or go up in the hills and pass the farmhouses and red barns opulent with sweet hay. Or follow the river road and watch the mysterious fall of roaring water in the deep chasm near Roxbury Falls. There is all the variety in our part of the country which any one would wish for. There are the blue deep lakes, with a few sailboats still spreading petal-sails.

And the roadside stands! Everything from new-laid brown eggs to evergreen snugged in burlap for Fall planting. The golden honey, the currant jelly, the baskets of fresh apples, the red and golden ears of corn, and the piled up richness of pumpkins and squash. Our nearest stand has gone elegant, too, with a line of frozen foods which are very special. We stop and poke in the freezer and bring up deviled crabs, chicken pies, tiny canapés of shrimp, or lobster thermidor. Fearfully expensive, but so good, and after a day of adventuring I always think a nice reward is a deviled crab fixed by somebody else!

Daphne goes with us on this or any day. It is impossible to depart without an Irish. She simply glues herself to Jill and that's that. Once on the way, however, she will sit in the car on command to "Stay" while we wander into Mr. Read's antique shop or visit with Grey Fox.

Grey Fox is one of my favorite friends. He is a real, authentic Indian Chief. I mean just that. He *could* be authentic and yet not seem real. He is a tall and easy-walking man, straight as a knife-blade and darkly

handsome. And it seems strange that he runs an antique Trading Post. But he loves old pine furniture, early chests, hobnail glass—and has a fine hand with the sanding and refinishing job.

He also knows the best herbs for common ailments, and we respect his advice highly.

As a side issue, he goes to country fairs and Indian pow-wows in full regalia, and when we stop to visit with him in the hot little tent at the fair, his eyes have such a curious wise and witty look. The fringes, the bead headband, the striking dark face would make a fine portrait of the true American people we so demolished. "This play-acting," his eyes seem to say, "you and I know it isn't the real thing."

He is both proud and gentle. And he has a way of looking at a person as if he saw right through to the inner being.

In the early troubled days, our valley was one in which the Indians and the white people got along together well. I am glad to think that in the dreadful history of our relationship with the Indians, at least here all was quiet and well.

And now we can comfortably visit with Grey Fox, with a little less guilt hanging in the back of our minds.

We can stop in and buy one chipped moss rose saucer, and have a fine visit on any bright day.

So here we go appreciating Autumn again

GLADYS

SUGARBRIDGE

DEAR G,

Your talk of Autumn reminded me that Ed came back from his early morning walk with a ruddy countenance, and a beautiful fall bouquet which he handed me proudly. For one who usually has to be forced to look at a flower, it was indeed a miracle.

> "A primrose by the river's brim,
> A yellow primrose was to him,
> And it was nothing more . . ."

All summer long, I am imploring him to come with me to inspect my particular pets among the flowers: the mertensia, a glade of cerulean beauty in earliest spring, the spotted lungwort, so like it, although smaller; the hardy amaryllis, which shoots up amazingly, a tall bare stalk, and almost while you watch bursts into a sheaf of breath-taking pink blossoms; or the fleece bush, a rarity whose mist of white bloom turns to pink, later to carmine in the fall, another treasure I owe to Viola and Mrs. F. "It's only a few steps," I plead. "You mustn't miss it. *Do* come!" So he follows me then, a faint indulgent smile upon his face, and, "H'm, yes, it's very pretty," he says, his mind all the time on something else. Although Ed admits that zinnias are the only flower that he can identify, yet he can go out and pick this nosegay which the most esoteric floraphile might plume himself upon.

"How effective," I murmur, my head on one side, jealously trying to assess the bewitching quality he has given his arrangement. Edged with cinnamon fern, lacy and sylvan, a-swirl with wild asters, star-white and lavender and pink, spiked with orange bittersweet, weighed down with clusters of green chokecherry, it has everything.

It reminded me of a passage in a Balzac novel, *Le Lys dans la Vallée*, about which I am enthusiastic at the moment: a lover wins his lady by his flower arrangements, which speak his heart; they are rather on the lavish side. I read it to Ed, but he shook his head.

"Mine is more austere," he said.

"But much more fitting to Autumn," I reminded him, "and to our years."

208

I kept it on the kitchen window sill for a long long time where I could often see it, until it finally withered away.

Saw the announcement of your new story in the LHJ. Must get. And, since selling a story brings up at once to a writer's mind the lovely look of a check in the mail, I suppose there may be a mild orgy of spending at Stillmeadow, unless Jill takes a firm stand. Or perhaps already has been, with the interval between payment and publication being what it sometimes is. Oft has it happened to me that by the time the piece came out, the check had taken wings.

I disapprove of our common extravagance, and admire as well as envy a certain prudence. Yet frugality is not a popular virtue today. No one boasts of it, as they do of their prodigality. "Yes, I overdrew my bank balance for the second time this month," you may hear someone say with a sort of pride. It does sound dashing. But you have to discover the economical streak in your friends yourself, usually; some chance happening reveals it: someone did not buy the expensive hat which was so madly becoming, but another one not nearly so nice.

My misfortune is that I don't love money for itself, only for what it can buy. This was also said of Daniel Webster, who is a distant ancestor, and it seems to make his austere personality more human, I think. See? It's an almost instinctive reaction. Sometimes I wonder if he had a wide gap between first and second fingers. I have; it's said to be the mark of our besetting sin. A nurse of mine once told me that, and I can remember how she held up my childish hand to show me. I had hoped to outgrow it, but, alas!

Perhaps we might wind up in the same poorhouse; that would be a help. And after all, how much more attractive *la Cigale* of La Fontaine's table always seemed than the stingy ant!

I was glad to hear of Grey Fox. How is he, anyway? I often think of him, but always forget to ask when I see you. I still wish we had bought that Windsor chair, the last time we were there. But, as you probably remember, Ed was feeling poor. A very different matter from *being* poor, and far more of an obstacle to buying anything. When we *are* poor, and no mistake, we have been known to commit shocking extravagances, out of mere bravado. In fact, most of our possessions have been bought that way—a beautiful piece of furniture, an elegant fur for me—no doubt if we hadn't acquired them thus, however unwisely, we never might have had anything at all. And then, too, extravagances serve a

specific purpose with us, that of a shock, a spur. To have spent a lot of money when you shouldn't have—that frightens us badly, and we urge ourselves sharply on to write a story or do something to pay for it.

But to *feel* poor, ah, that's another matter. It's really an apprehension of the future, resulting from a lowness of spirits, and has little to do with your financial condition. Just have to sit tight, and ride it out.

STILLMEADOW

BARBARA DEAR:

Yes, I think when you feel poor, you should squander your money! Jill has such patience with me regarding finances, one minute I talk lavishly about building on a room so we can have a piano for the few times we have a musician visiting us, and the next minute I am worrying about investing in three extra pair of socks. The truth is, I have never become en rapport with money. When I get a fat check for something I have written, I view it as a present, dropped from the blue. Let's spend it, say I happily. I never relate it in any way to work on my part. But if the check doesn't come in, I can see Jill and me in the poorhouse creaking around on a diet of porridge and salt pork, unable to crochet, for we cannot crochet, and doomed to die in misery. After we have gone in for some horrendous extravagance, I often wake in the night and think of the drab walls of the poorhouse (beige, no doubt). But the arrival of a twenty dollar check for the serial rights in Australia of some story I cannot even remember, whips me to an orgy of spending again.

Jill, being Scotch, executive, practical, finds this difficult. She tries to hold me down when I want a greenhouse, to encourage me when I think we should live on beans, and that takes some doing!

It is a lost cause. Money in my hand just asks to be spent, and money just coming in eventually is no money at all, as far as I am concerned. No doubt, without Jill as a balance wheel, I should be bankrupt in a few months.

Or making a precarious living selling home-baked beans in little brown crocks. I don't actually, even in my darkest moments, feel anybody starves if they can cook, for people always want to eat, and many people like to eat easy, as I say.

On the rare occasions when Father got to be TOO MUCH for Mama, she always said she would just start a tearoom. I know she would have been excessively prosperous, for her way with food was something "Gourmet" never dreamed of, and she never had truffles or Oregano or saffron either. She had a gas stove and a skillet and a fireless cooker which you packed with straw or something to keep the heat in, and a soapstone griddle, and what she did with them is a memory on a good many people's lives. "Run a restaurant," said Father, throwing down his napkin.

But it never came to that. Father would come round, when he was really threatened, and we rocked along, in spite of Father's having bought three Oriental rugs for a mint of money when I needed a new dress for the Football dance.

We are up to our eyebrows in dog shows. Jonquil finally made her Companion Dog Excellent, just as we despaired of her ever bringing in the dumbbell. "Something just clicked," says Jill dreamily.

"Maybe you just hypnotized her," say I.

"Lady, I was in no state to hypnotize anything," says Jill, "I was just about to collapse."

Going to dog shows, we get up at dawn, do the chores, hunt for the leashes, pack the show kit, drive anywhere from thirty to three hundred miles. We try to go only to shows that we can make in four hours, so we can reasonably expect to get home. We get rained on, we get baked in an oven-hot sun, we freeze as the sleet falls. Obedience always puts the show to bed. Breed people load their station wagons and tool off while we are still waiting for Open A. Afterward we drive home, dirty, tired, and too full of black coffee drunk from weak paper cups. The pale boiled frankfurters on dry rolls have not done us any good either.

Or if I leave packed a really good lunch, we have been too nervous to eat at all that day.

We get home very late, and first wait on the dogs, then sink down to a plate of canned chili.

And Jill says, "Now I think we had better enter for Springfield and Pawling—and how do you feel about Boston?"

The other side of the picture is the people who go through all this with you. I like them. They are bankers, lawyers, factory workers, housewives, clerks, they are descendants of the early pioneers and they are still working on the American accent. They are, some of them, writers, some are top engineers in aircraft companies.

And they are all friends on an equal basis. The dog, and how the handler manages the dog, that is the measure of man or woman in Obedience. To me it is the most truly American group I have ever been under the hot sun with, or driven through the bitter sleet to meet at the ringside.

When the man with the top Doberman has to go on the day shift and miss a show, everyone is sad. When the eminent lawyer needs a lift, the filing clerk goes out of the way to pick him up. For Albany or Framingham, a car starts out with four or five assorted owners and a cocker, a Dane, two wire hairs, and a Dachshund. Everybody gives advice, discusses for miles and miles why Perigord does not come BACK over

the jump, or Annette follows her handler right out on the Long Stay.

Possibly the reason our closest friends are Obedience friends is that sharing a few hardships makes a sound foundation. I believe this may be the basis of the best friendship anyway.

I remember Danny Peters, on a day when my dog had been absolutely terrible in the ring. I staggered out, at the sharp edge of weeping. There stood Danny with an ice-cold Coke. "Take it easy," he said, "she'll do it yet!"

And the time Daphne took off after a pheasant and could not even be caught for an hour, George Recor wandered over to Jill, and said, "My own dog did that once—she's going to be a fine worker when she steadies down. I know how you feel."

And finally, I shall tell you, as an Obedience amateur, that nothing, but nothing makes a better dog, a happier dog than an educated dog. And nothing makes better companionship for you and your dog than to work together. We began with reservations and with our most difficult cocker. For, said Jill, if Melody can be trained, anybody can. True, it took eight weeks to persuade her to sit on command. But we have never had a better dog since. It is hard for our dogs to go to the kennel when it is their turn, they naturally feel if five can stay in the house and sleep cozily on beds and sofas, why not ten? But Melody can be ensconced on my blue pillow and Jill can call her to go to the kennel for the night. She goes. She goes lingeringly and with head bent, but she goes. And Jonquil, who never paid any mind to what anybody said, will pop in when the oilman comes and opens the gate, will pop out when we suggest it. Will get down from the table.

Melody only got as far as the first degree, but when you have Utility dogs, like Sister and Linda, you can almost read poetry to them and have them enjoy it with you. "Time to make the bed, Sister," I say. She takes herself to the sofa. "All right now," I say, and she hops back. "Go in my room," I can say, when guests are arriving, and Sister flies in. I don't know why knowing how to pick out one object I had touched from fifteen in scent discrimination, the handiest exercise of all, brought this about, but I guess education has by-products which we cannot measure.

I won't promise that if you get Duke his C.D. all will be perfect. That's like expecting a grammar school graduate to quote Catullus. But a C.D. is better than no education, I can promise you that.

Now Jill says can we get Teddy and Tiki ready for Saw Mill River Show? Better get at it, says she.

Good training to you,
GLADYS

SUGARBRIDGE

Just a short, slightly hysterical note, to say that Duke took a first at Devon, one of our big swank dog shows.

Poor lamb, he collapsed, as usual, before entering the ring, but once in put on a wonderful performance. Ed says that lots of prize fighters are like that; they practically have to be carried from the dressing-room; but when the gong sounds they're okay.

I don't know how this fits Duke, except that he did try to take a huge mastiff apart. Fortunately, they were separated before anything serious happened.

So, now we have a blue ribbon on the mantelpiece.

How nice!

B

P.S. Ed says, No more dog shows! He claims his clavicle is torn loose from his sternum. I didn't even know they were attached. He can still walk, so I don't understand why he is complaining.

B

213

SPECIAL TO SUGARBRIDGE:

Who ever asked you what you find to do in the country? People still ask us that. If you live in the country a day is like a quick breath. My only fear is that it makes time go so fast we shall be old any minute and never know how we got to be there!

If I could stretch the days like a very fine rubber band, I would pull them out and out—and out!

I wonder sometimes if the people who built Stillmeadow ever were dissatisfied. They had no radio, no phone (not that ours ever works), no record player. No car. They could not climb in and whisk away to look at a special sunset from the New Milford hill, for that would be a day's journey. They certainly had no dog shows to take up all the time there is. No movies—and we can go to Newtown to see a special movie any time we wish to. They had no weekend visitors. They had no electricity. I often look at the great fireplace and imagine that first home-maker doing all of the cooking on it. We do stews and steaks and soups, but we do not also bake bread and make cakes by means of it.

But they had the same blessings of the sun coming over the apple orchard, the moon pure and pearl-like over the garden, and the same garden too. They had the glory of the changing seasons, the quick excitement of spring, the tender fullness of summer, and the glowing fires of Autumn. They had the hard winter days, and the sudden promise of the February thaw. They had their land, and the wondrous security that when they planted, they would harvest.

They had, also, some things we lack. They had a sure faith in the rightness of things. If a man was good and labored justly, he would be rewarded. They had no fears of taxes bourgeoning, of hydrogen bombs—how fast we move when it is obsolete to talk of atom bombs. No big industries threatened them with flooding their homesteads—as we are now threatened by an adjacent water company. Maybe they had a teen-age problem, but they probably didn't realize it. Children grew up and helped run the farm, and married and brought their spouses home and everybody planted and hoed and lived together without any understanding that it made problems.

I do not mean to say, Barbara, that I do not respect and love my freezer, my coffeemaker, my toaster, my dish washer, for I love any and all of the gadgets that make modern life feasible. I know the value of an electric light bulb for I used to spend my summers washing oil lamp chimneys when I was young and we had a cottage up North in Wisconsin. There we had no icebox, no bathroom, and we were quite happy lugging milk and eggs from the flowing spring. I admire every modern aid to living.

But as I walk down to the pond on a September evening, I often think of that first woman who made this her home, and wonder whether she wasn't pretty happy. Rather nice to think she didn't even hear about Lexington and Concord until it was all over, whereas I would be there, blow by blow, via NBC or CBS. In a way they were very lucky.

I have noticed, when visiting Sugarbridge, that you never have the radio on. Ed, bustling around at break of day, gets a weather report, and that is that. I have to admit that I am a radio addict. I turn it on, and feel like skipping when a Viennese waltz is played. Times when I feel very sorrowful, I turn on WQXR and hear the best in music without having to change the record myself. I even like the Polka hour on our local station, the Polkas are so dancy.

The same to you,

G

OCTOBER

HELLO NEIGHBOR:

I like that word. Has nothing to do with proximity, it's a state of mind. I have a neighbor in Woodland, Washington, whom I have never even met and we are the best of neighbors. Lois's children and house and "the boss" and the adorable and wild Siamese and the dog are as familiar to me as if they lived right down the road.

I also have a Greek neighbor who lives in Cyprus and she writes about the flowering almond and the sea and her children and their dogs, and it is fine to have the friendship.

The glory of October in New England is getting highly publicized. Cars go by on the main highways from every state in the Union and photographers are around every corner. I have an overpowering desire to stop and lean out of the car and say—Have you been on the New Milford road? Don't miss it!

You stand at the edge of the world. The land falls away below like an

216

ocean headland. Far down in the valley a white, white farmhouse and a luxuriously red barn and a great silo stand. Beyond, the hills break in dark blue lines against the sky. It is always beautiful, in October it is blazing with splendor from the ancient sugar maples. The pure garnet of oaks is there, too, and the tawny squares of harvested fields. The sky is immense over all this, a wider sky than any I know.

I somehow always thought that farm was a dream, so far away, so isolated by the greatness of the hills. But when the Boyers were here from Orlando, Fred, who is a map man, got out a map and said he felt there was a road somewhere—and found it, and we rocketed down a very spidery dusty little road, past woods and wild thickets and old tumbled-down sheds, and around a curve there was the farm! It was very exciting, and so, I may say, was getting back up the road!

The turn-out for this breath-taking view is named, with a neat placard. Lillinonah. I someday shall find out who Lillinonah was. But the name is so singing, perhaps I should leave it at that.

Our own road is blazing with red and gold. My favorite tree is a maple that has bright gold leaves with rosy pink edges. It gives its own light, even on a dark day.

The swamp is cinnamon and copper and blazing red. The purple stalks of the wild blackberries are frosted over with a delicate film of white. The black alder has her red red berries. There are not enough words meaning various kinds of red, are there? There's the blue-red of an American Beauty rose, and the yellow red of salvia, and the purple red of a cranberry bog in winter and the pinky red of some climbing roses—and a lot of others. But nothing really describes the color of the swamp maple down in our own swamp, it is a color of its own. So I shall tell you it is red. And that it burns in the heart.

The air is as exciting as young love now. I almost wear my lungs out trying to get it all in. It is full of sun and cool secret places in the woods and burning brush and dark-running brooks. It makes me feel nothing is impossible, everything is there, just waiting for a hand to reach for it.

When the blizzards come, I shall not only get what I can out of being snug and toasty by the fire, reading by candlelight when the "electric" is off, but I shall tell myself, as always, that without our special climate, no October.

One of the first school poems I learned was about "October's bright blue weather" by Helen Hunt Jackson I think, and it has seldom been better said. It is bright blue, the weather itself.

Blankets on the line for a last sun and wind freshening, curtains making patterns against the pines as they whip out. Rugs in the yard, with dogs pulling at them every few minutes. Teddy, no, stop it!

G

SUGARBRIDGE

DEAR G

The only time I am really out of patience with Nature is after a storm. An Autumn rain, which has on the landscape the effect of a weeping fit upon an aging person. Only a child can cry naturally and attractively. And the earth in Autumn is no longer young, although carrying it off well, with ruddy colors and ripe fruits. But it takes only a wind and rainstorm to strip away these subterfuges. Afterward the ground is littered with branches, twigs, leaves, bark, dead flowers. Everything has suddenly grown sere and yellow. The appearance of a rag of blue sky and a watery sun can only emphasize the destruction. Nowhere can the eye rest that it does not meet untidiness. I am disgusted with the mess, the more so that it is I who must clear it away, sweep the roof free of branches, drag off the larger boughs, rake the lawn.

In April, it is different. One expects sudden tantrums of Nature. There are no leaves then, nor flowers, only the promise of them, and that, to our ungrateful minds, is so much more entrancing than the reality, and its decline.

B

DEAR BARBARA:

On such a golden day as this, Jill and I drove to Steepletop, the home of Edna St. Vincent Millay and her most-wonderful husband. The "Journal" was doing over their kitchen, and they were both excited, Edna because she could now wash dishes and look out of the big new window at her birds; Eugen because there would be room for a freezer where he could "put down" the fresh peas, tender beans, and the elegant dishes he cooked.

Eugen did the cooking. In his travels around the world, he had collected marvelous recipes, and he was famous for his menus. Edna, however, did the clean-up jobs as well as small carpentry work about the house. She was expert and neat, her tools filed, her nails sorted, her work bench in order. Those small strong hands that transcribed the swift beauty of her mind were wise in the ways of hammer, saw and chisel.

We drove with difficulty up the winding rutted mountain road. The way to Parnassus, I thought, must always be steep. At last we came on the house, steadfast and old and generously proportioned, white against the dark green of the woods that climbed into the sky.

Late afternoon light slanted on the worn steps, the air was cool and still. I went up the steps thinking of her lines:

"My sky is black with small birds bearing South," and as I looked at the great door, I thought, "Autumn is no less on me, that a rose, Hugs the brown bough, and sighs before it goes."

This day Eugen and Edna were at their Maine island. The house was, nevertheless, full of their presence. I have never been in a house that so evoked the owner. Miss Millay's small, intensely lovely face seemed to look up from the loved grand piano, music was her second

219

passion. Did you know she might have been a concert pianist except that her hands were too small to stretch for the octaves?

I went out, and took the path to the pool, where the tall Arbor Vitae stood dark in the low light. The rustic gate had broken its hinges and hung loosely. A merry snack-and-drink bar made of hand-hewn logs stood just beyond, with an antique pricked-metal lantern to light wayfarers. But spiders had woven their webs across the lantern, the stool leaned against the counter, there was nobody there. Only a very lovely small white marble statue presided over this quiet place. The pale purity of stone was tarnished.

I do not know why the scene was so much like an ancient Greek garden, but it was, as if Miss Millay's profound love of the great Greek literature has somehow shaped the long narrow pool and passed itself into the planting, the narrow paths, the still statue. The afternoon light was softer, more tranquil; here was the secret haunt of beauty, I thought. Yet the air of sadness was so great that I cried. It was forlorn, lost, lovely, so incredibly still.

I could have had no prescience that the time was so short before Eugen would die, and Edna follow him. But the hour is one I shall not forget.

After Eugen died, Miss Millay lived at Steepletop alone, working and studying and reading her loved Greek. She was gallant, she was brave, now and then a cry burst from her. "He does not come up the hill any more," she said.

220

They had lived together for many years, they had endured many sorrows, had their share of the world's troubles, and yet, in the end, his last words to her were, "It was lovely while it lasted." What better tribute could a life have?

Steepletop is a fit resting place, with the wide sky so near and the wooded slopes so deep around it. In Miss Millay's grave lie the leaves she gathered at the grave of Keats and the grave of Shelley, together with a sheaf of the bachelor buttons she and Eugen loved so much.

I tried to put some of my feeling when she left into a small personal note to her.

> Under the mountain sky
> Her ashes lie:
> The channeled splendor gone,
> The song laid by.
>
> Where Keats and Shelley sleep
> She plucked two leaves to keep.
> Now let them fall on her
> Who climbed their summits steep.
>
> Comfort it is she stands
> In the immortal lands
> With April in her eyes,
> And laurel in her hands.

On such a day as this, I left her garden and the dark pool with the leaves drifting on the polished quiet surface. I wonder if it be tended now. Fortunately the garden of the mind is more permanent, and I think of her own words again, "I shall die, but that is all I shall do for death!"

SUGARBRIDGE

GLADYS, how privileged you were to have had that private glimpse of a shy poet, an enchanting personality! Miss Millay had lived so retired the last years that few people knew anything of what sort of life she led. But she could not have had a more tender admirer to report upon it. I can see her so clearly, and it is very touching as you evoke the picture. I could have stood hearing much, much more.

B

DEAR GLADYS

Did you ever catch an animal unawares? It's very enlightening. I don't mean merely at rest, or asleep, but at some time when they feel themselves unobserved, and are engaged as they would not be if they thought they were being watched.

One morning, as I was about to open the door from our kitchen into a sort of garden-room where the tools of country living collect, I happened to glance through the upper glass panes first. In through the doorway open to the outside there stepped gaily a little black and white skunk. His eyes were very bright, and his coat as shiny; he gave off a fine feeling of vitality and alertness. I got the impression that he was smiling while he ambled about this place I considered my own, as though it were *his* own. Utterly off guard, he bit a piece out of a paper carton and spit it out, he tried the lid to the garbage pail, unsuccessfully; he considered a stray hickory nut and discarded it. I watched hypnotized, not daring to breathe. Finally he turned and scuttled out again, and at last I opened the door. There was no trace of noxious odor, and no dissertation upon the more desirable qualities of skunks could have convinced me as this brief experience had done that they are really rather amusing little fellows.

The other glimpse I had was of our own Duke, no wild animal, and, one would think, as well known to me as the palm of my right hand.

I have often wondered in times past, just how he looked when he was being consciously naughty in our absence. Then one day I *saw* him do something which convinced me that if anything I was underestimating him.

Well, I was in the kitchen again where I could see out the door into the aforementioned garden-room, but could not be seen from there. Now we have known for some time that Duke is able to open all our doors, but we never could discover how he did it. They are fitted with the original hardware, big square iron locks with a detachable key (enormous) rather like the handle on an old-fashioned coffee mill; it serves both as latch, and key, being wound round and round, to lock, and then removed; or as a latch, its round handle end must be pressed down, hard. We could not see how Duke could do this with his nose, but only knew that he did come in and out, mysteriously, at will, and sometimes much to our inconvenience.

This time, I heard him outside, then he began to fumble with the lock. I thought, Now I'll peek, and see how he does it and was about to go and peer over the valance, when to my astonishment, through the glass I saw his head rise. *For one second Duke stood upright,* six feet tall, and the door opened. He came in on four feet. Seeing me, a sheepish expression chased across his face. I knew his secret now. He went into the dining room quickly and curled up before the fire, forestalling explanations. *He stands up and presses the knob down with his forepaw,* I thought, awed. For a moment I'd had the uncanny impression that he was really a Man Dog.

And yesterday morning, as we drove down the lane to early church, there were two wild mallards swimming in our pool, stopping over on the way South—a drake with a brilliant green head, his proud neck upright with its necklace of white, steaming arrogantly across the quiet water, followed by his drab little hen, meek and tractable. I thought, Here it is, the eternal relationship of male and female. Ed said (all unconscious of my secret thought) that we should put up a sign for passing ducks and geese, reading, "SUGARBRIDGE H₂O—TEL."

BARBARA

STILLMEADOW

BARBARA MY DEAR ONE:

There is one dreadful thing about this month. Just to keep it from being Heaven. That is I have to get some clothes. I know how you feel about shopping, but you are not as badly off as I am for you can wear anything and it fits. I face the fact in Autumn that I must have some garb other than blue jeans and red moccasins and a soft sweat shirt.

I make myself as miserable as possible by combining a trip to the dentist with my shopping bout. Connie says, "But Mama, all you do is go in and the girl brings out something and you say, 'Fine, I'll take that.'"

There is no sense to this for I love to see a woman smartly dressed, I can enjoy it no end. I see everything, as Don said the first time we took him to the circus. I note the matching earrings and the cut of the little casual suit. When I have lunch in town with Bernice, I am always secretly examining her pocketbook, her gloves, and her quiet gray dress.

But it happens to me that I always have a brown hat the time I buy a gray suit. I cannot co-ordinate, even if I read about being well-dressed in the helpful women's magazines. I may even start with a dim plan. But after ten minutes, I buy whatever seems to fit my odd figure and dash home, exhausted.

Then, too, I am afraid of salesladies. If they are simpatico (a word we should add to our language) we have a fine visit about children and dogs and the war and aching feet from long hours, etc. But if my saleslady is very polished and superior, I creep into a shell. I note that her nail polish matches her lipstick. I note the size nine figure she has.

I note her eyeing me and thinking how much I can spend. And all I wish to do is fly out of the store.

Some women shop just for fun, I have a friend who took me with her once. While I stood around, waiting to go home, she studied the entire gamut of fashion. She didn't buy anything but she and the saleslady spoke the same language; it was a game.

This touches on another of my troubles. I cannot ever go in anywhere and not buy something. This makes it very difficult in antique shops for if we are looking for Leeds or milk glass or a pine bedside table and they have none, I will come out lugging some moss rose saucers, an odd tea-cup. Or even a pine rocker. "And just where do you plan to put it?" asks Jill sensibly. "Oh, we'll move things around," I say vaguely. It always seems so discourteous to go into a place and poke around and then go out emptyhanded.

But the only time I am really ashamed of my sex, I add, is when I hear how some women talk to clerks and salesmen.

I do think one of the best things ever said, in or out of the Bible, is "Be ye kind to one another."

Connie says the world is divided into two kinds of people, the giving people and the taking people. Sometimes that seems awfully true! We have friends decidedly in the latter category. It's best not to think it out, but to get pleasure out of giving whatever it be. Reminds me of the moment after we had known Steve and Olive for several years, and I said, "I never knew anything like it, they do more for us than we ever can do for them!" It was an astonishing thing. We thought it over for a little while, and Jill added, "They never want to be thanked either!"

On the other hand, we all know people who are so charming and interesting, they have a glitter like costume jewelry and they just love to have you do things for them. But they never feel any urge to undertake the responsibilities of friendship, and I think there are some. Friendship, like all precious things, involves a caring-for the other half of the relation-ship. Enough to do things, if need be, that aren't even fun.

You can pretty well sum up a man or woman by how good a job they do at being friends.

And what can give you a more secure feeling than to KNOW that if the house burned down, you lost every nickel you have, you got an in-curable disease, and you even lost your mind on account of it, there are those few who would still sit it out with you? This is a wonderfully comforting idea.

Have you tried pressing leaves with a hot iron and wax? I have, it doesn't work. Shellacking is no good either. I decide it's best to bring in a sheaf of golden and garnet and russet leaves and put them in a tall container and look hard at them just as long as they are fresh. We are always trying to make things permanent that can't be permanent, that is all there is to it.

But the memory of a flaring branch against the old stone fireplace, that needs no wax, no fixing. It is there, tucked in the small hidden place in the mind, to take out and cherish when the snow drives down with the North wind.

GLADYS

SUGARBRIDGE

Oh, yes—shopping. . . . A chore and a bore. Oh, maybe, sometime when you just feel in the mood, and have a fistful of beautiful green money. But, like everything else on this earth, it's too much a matter of chance to suit me. One day, no matter how diligent or determined you may be, you find nothing that you would take home as a gift, the hem comes out of your skirt, and you lose your purse. Some other time, with as little reason, fortune smiles upon you; all the salesladies call you "dear," and in the twinkling of an eyelash, you have found a dream dress for far less than you had expected to pay. I am a fatalist about this; there is not a thing you can do. The only shopping tour predestined to success was that one undertaken with Ed, in the very early days of our acquaintance, when I was trying to impress him with my utter difference from all other women. We were out to buy me a riding habit, and I coolly took the first one offered me, without trying it on. The special providence watching over rash shoppers must have been on duty that day. I still have that riding habit, and it still fits.

Usually, I have a lot of sales resistance. I want what I want, but there I am in trouble right away. Only when you have unlimited money, or none at all, can you afford in this country to indulge yourself in individualism. If I wish to wear green, I may be told, with variations of expression ranging from surprise to scorn, that there is no green at all this year, the color is gray. Now it seems to me dull and humiliating to have to take what everyone else is wearing, just because the high priests of style decree so. Women are the captives of big business, I'm afraid, always being needled into something new. And advertising is its tool.

How can the average female be impervious to that constant insidious whisper? Sometimes I think that if all the money and mental power spent on this, to me, most loathed of businesses, huckstering, were diverted to some critical need of today, such as furthering brotherly love among men, we might be living in a very different world. I became early inimical to advertising.

Poor, poor women! They buy gadgets to make their lives more convenient, so that they may have leisure to go out and buy more gadgets! A squirrel on a treadmill has a sinecure by comparison.

On the rebound, perhaps, it's so peaceful to be contented with what you have. When I have no money at all to spend, I most nearly approach serenity. I need not bother about what I'll wear to the party. It will have to be the same thing I've been appearing in for the last months or maybe years. I may contrive some way to make it look different, but that will be good for me. Ingenuity, if not exercised, tends to die out.

It's only in states like Maine, with a low per capita wealth, that the inhabitants have that peace of mind which is today looked upon as belonging to the past. They keep their Model-T Fords running, nor do they yearn after a yearly change of radios and refrigerators, as the rest of the country is made to do. The way these small villages come to life after the summer folk have left, reverting to salt pork and cracker-barrel conversation, hunting and fishing, and church sociables, shows how little they really need the dollars that resort-keeping brings them. They have something in their rugged existence which satisfies them, and is not dependent upon modern business methods.

Though I am much in sympathy with their way of life, I must go on living in Chester County for the things I love about it, its color, its earthiness, its sense of the past. And, in a more limited way, there exists the same feeling about living here, in a kind of undercurrent. The qualities which have made it resistant to change over the last two hundred years have not died out. We have a good many Model-T Fords around here, too, and they still run.

B

HELLO SUGARBRIDGE:

Do you make lists? We have them all around, and the only trouble is we never find the right list when we need it. We have a magnetic bulletin board too, and it has that recipe for shrimp creole pegged on, and some long-ago paid bills.

Now and then I pay the bills over again. The refrigerator people were very nice, they sent back the second check.

But alas, we get two copies every month of one of our least-favorite magazines. We figured, with great thought, that we might change the address on one—but how also to change the name? No use. I learned about magazine circulation departments with the old "Literary Digest," which I had three years after I stopped subscribing!

We also this year were the startled possessors of three licenses for the DeSoto. Lost the paper once, paid again—they couldn't manage to just make out another paper—then they sent another because the second had a wrong figure for the motor number. The most thoroughly licensed car in all Connecticut, I dare say.

GLADYS

SUGARBRIDGE

I suppose I make lists as assiduously as anyone, and use them as little. When a lack develops in household commodities, I write it down at once, not trusting my sketchy memory: I even remember to take this document with me when I go to town. But once there, I find I never glance at it. The mere writing-down serves to fix the necessities in my mind, I guess. The one time I remember using a list was almost fatal: I was standing in a closely packed line, waiting to have my purchases checked up, and thought, just for a change, I'd look and see if I had everything. When I took out my slip of paper, I stared at it unbelievingly. Right between the humdrum items was printed in bold black letters, LOVE. And down at the bottom, below the milk, the bread, the sugar, it went off again into Loves. . . . LOVE, LOVE. . . . The women standing before and behind me could not help noticing. I thought they glanced

227

at me very suspiciously, No wonder! Where would you buy LOVE at the A & P?

"What a thing for you to do!" I said to Ed, when I returned. "I was terribly embarrassed. Those women must have thought I was crazy."

But he remained un-contrite. "We've been needing some LOVE around here lately," he said.

And notes! We are a family of note-writers. We leave them for each other on the wheel of a parked car, we leave explanatory notes when one has gone away somewhere in the absence of the others; there are ex-hortatory notes, notes of contrition when we have quarreled and parted in a rage. I came home last week to find one affixed to the kitchen table, scribbled on a paper towel,

"Have gone to view the countryside on Horse (since I can't draw one today)—avec Pooch! I SHALL RETURN!
DOUGLAS MACSHENTON"
I put this away with the one which said, "Honeydew, Honey!" (I kept forgetting to cut a luscious melon which had been languishing away in the refrigerator over a week.)

Placing it in my collection, my eye lights upon another:

"Breakfast was dull without you. Please be a little glad to see me when I come home this evening.

E

P.S. Half my grapefruit is in the refrigerator, and all my heart."

How could I have been otherwise than melted by that? I wonder. Ed's notes have the quality of being more like him than he is himself. Under-neath this is a strange one,

"Do you remember the girl who looked in the window of the publishing house, and saw the moody young man . . . ?"

Of course I remember, I think to myself, but à propos of what was this written? Were we at odds, then, to hark back to beginnings? But it eludes me; I can't place it. Lost somewhere in the past, and I think, half con-sciously, Some day . . . perhaps when we are very old, and nothing mat-ters much any more, we'll go over these souvenirs together, laugh a little at our youthful folly, and have total recall. I Know My Love? Well, per-haps, if anyone ever does.

HERE WE ARE:

And a cold crisp night with the stars like pieplates in the sky. I would rather stand in the doorway while five dogs race out, and in, than contemplate what is beyond those stars and whether we shall ever travel to them, with men signing off their lives to take a ninety-year journey to some star which may not have a reception committee on it anyway. Better, it seems to me, to rake the leaves and prune and mulch things—but I am not a fine adventurer at heart. When we plan to go away for a little while and Jill makes lists and on the last list there is "Say goodbye to the dogs," I quail then and there. When we do go, I rush to the car and turn my face away. She says the goodbyes. Those noses, and knowing sorrowful eyes make me ready to unpack right off and just stay.

I do not think, Barbara, that we are all victims of circumstance. We make our own. If we love a garden, we tend it. If we love dogs or cats, we accept a responsibility. (I was a frightful nuisance when Connie was a baby because I would not whip around and put her to sleep on the lower piece of somebody's living-room table.) I like to read about the free and untrammeled couples who take a small boat round the world with two small children, but I always think the children would be happier and better off in one house, dry and getting to know other children their own age. But I expect if you are a true adventurer, you disregard everything but the adventure itself.

Otherwise, you would be putting the glad bulbs away and lugging in firewood for the winter nights.

There is ruthlessness about these fabulous sailors of the sea in a sailboat. And the mountain climbers who court the abysses in the unclimbed mountains. And the men who penetrate the jungles. But as Mama always said comfortably when such things came up, "It takes all kinds of people to make a world!"

Mama never criticized anybody, she felt everyone had a right to his or her own course. This is probably why so many students came to ask her what they should do. Mama had never heard of Psychiatry, but she listened and poured hot tea for them and nodded her head. It usually worked very well. When they had told her all, they went off and got married to the man with three children or to the girl with a very difficult background, or they put in for a career. Or took that job in the library.

After she died, many people wrote me how she had helped them. Mama never made any point of it, never mentioned it except to tell me someone was coming to see her and I better take books back to the library. Mama had a very small education, what would amount now to High

School, she never followed the latest in books, she just had an understanding heart. She never even learned to spell and this was a trial to Father who was so erudite. But she could find her way around in somebody's heart over a teacup.

Sometimes I think what a superb Dean of Women or President of a Women's College she would have made.

Then I am glad she was just my mother.

Selfish—

ME

SUGARBRIDGE

DEAR GLADYS

We've had one or two rather half-hearted frosts, yet there is little left in the garden but broccoli and raspberries. (The surrounding tall weeds don't seem so disgraceful now, for behind them the last berry crop had a chance to ripen.) Now is the time when Ed comes into his own; he haunts the garden, tenderly collecting: one tomato, like a forgotten sun, hanging on the frost-burnt vine, a solitary lima bean pod, blanched and brittle, a single zinnia glowing bravely in the withered flower row. He says this vista means to him all the things he cherishes most: "the last love, a note of the hunting horn, sweet on the threadbare wind, the dregs of sherry in the bottle, the final flight of grackle, blowing above the ravished cornfield." The prose in quotes is his: I cannot write so pretty.

I know we agreed about "Exploration of Space" by Clark. Wonderful! But I've come on a few others I think you would like—perhaps not to be mentioned in the same breath, since they are space fiction. But perfect bed reading, nonetheless. You'll get them on your bedside table if you come to see us soon, if not I'll send them, as they are Bantam books. By a pulp writer, Ray Bradbury, and if all of them are like him, I'll certainly have to revise my opinion of the pulps, for his stories are little gems, written with warmth and tenderness. In itself an achievement. Could *you* make space fiction appealing? I'm sure *I* could not. "The Martian Chronicles" is one. Discovered by Ned, on a train trip, it has come to be our family favorite. Then there is "Illustrated Man," and "Green Hills of Earth." I thirst for more, and am glad Mr. Bradbury *is* a prolific pulp writer.

B

Last year the three boys who run the Southbury Food Market began something fine. They gave a prize to the schoolchildren who did the best decoration on the store windows for Hallowe'en. Instead of the windows being soaped and marred, bright-colored witches rode red brooms on one window, a very yellow pumpkin in a field was on another, and a nice lurid graveyard with a clock set at midnight was on the third.

It worked so well and everybody had so much fun over it that they have established it as custom. Now the garage and the General store have decorations too, and at Christmas another contest begins.

Such fun to drive down for the groceries and see an earnest little six-year-old boy smearing jade green busily on the glass. He sticks his tongue out in the effort to concentrate, he doesn't even know when anybody watches him. An older girl draws in a very authentic witch—two middle-sized boys argue over blue versus red. The school art teacher picks out the students who have done the best work and they can display their talents to the public.

Since there are three big show windows, and First, Second and Third prizes, everybody gets a prize too!

When I was growing up, Hallowe'en was almost my top holiday, next to Christmas. We always had a big Hallowe'en party with everything from a wash tub filled with water and red bobbing apples to spiderwebs of string leading all over the house, down cellar, up attic with prizes at the end. Mama decorated the whole house with orange and green cats and witches and garlands, and it was all very gay.

I used to think it was very nice to be popular with the gang, but looking back, I can see Mama had a lot to do with it! She didn't even murmur when one of the boys ate most of a green apple pie she was going to have for supper!

GLADYS

SUGARBRIDGE

Boo!

Hallowe'en still keeps its flavor for me. I could make a pumpkin lantern, only for myself, even now, although I seldom do. In West Chester, there is a long-standing tradition of a Hallowe'en parade, which does take the small fry's mind off undue mischief, and is in itself quite a spectacle. Prizes are offered for the best costumes, which as you may imagine are fearsome and wonderful. Large crowds gather on the sidewalks to watch the route of ghosts, demons, sprites and hobgoblins wind its way through the town, and before anyone knows it this tense evening has passed.

But out in the country things are different, and mischief, or worse reigns supreme. The aggressors are not children, however. In fact we hardly ever see any children on that especial childish fiesta; the distances are too great for them to walk. Only, very occasionally, a solemn little group of small girls, dressed in their mother's long skirts come over from some neighboring farms to display themselves and be presented with pennies and candy. No, the depredations I speak of are committed by those old enough to know better, grown boys, and in some cases, men. They carry off and destroy signs (we've lost three), take down fences, letting out the stock, and this year, started several fires. I think they can't be very bright, but that is no excuse, to my mind. We were awakened at midnight on Hallowe'en by a neighbor calling to say that there was a fire on our land. Still half asleep, we leaped into clothes, and then into the car, and drove around looking for it. The whole sky was lit up by the flames, and we soon located it on a hill behind our barn. Quite a crowd had gathered, and several good souls who lived around had brought their shovels and were beating it out. I had thoughtfully snatched a broom in my flight, but that didn't turn out to be much help. While we were waiting for the fire engines which arrived shortly after, we heard that several fields of fodder had been burned in the vicinity. We all agreed that the fun had gone far enough.

A tendency toward destruction is disturbing. It must go deeper than mere ignorance or irresponsibility.

After returning from town, and entering the house as is our custom by the kitchen door, I did not at first see what had been left for us on the bench by the front door. It was only next morning, going out to look at the thermometer (30 degrees at seven a.m.) that I saw, resting there, an overflowing basket of hickory nuts, with a slip of cardboard affixed: "Happy Hallowe'en, from your friend. K.C.K." On the card was scribbled a grinning pumpkin face. This seemed an unexpectedly frivolous thing for Miss K to do, but it was very pleasant, I thought. Later, I heard from Mr. D that he had gathered the nuts, from a secret and particular tree he knew of, bearing much larger and sweeter nuts than were ordinarily to be found. They did look extra large and plump; I couldn't resist cracking a few at once, just to see; it *was* true they were extraordinarily good. Mr. D, I mused, must know everything about this countryside; someone should be appointed to take down his reminiscences and garnered facts while he still remembers. . . .

B

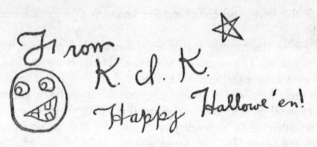

From
K. d. K.
Happy Hallowe'en!

DEAR BARBARA:

Our friend and house-helper, who was raised in Scotland in a one-room family apartment, tells me she only was allowed to walk to the graveyard on Sunday. Nowhere else, no Sunday School paper, only the Bible and a walk to the graveyard. She says she didn't mind, some of the gravestones were very funny if you read them!

It set me thinking about the changing times and the new theories of child-upbringing. Also about my tombstone, if any. Have decided mine should say simply, "She was never bored." I think I have never been. Whether this is a good epitaph, I would not know. It might seem dull never to be bored. But when I used to attend the most boring club meetings at one time in my life, I sat with my hands under my knees and got simply fascinated thinking about all the women who were speaking. What were they like as little girls? How did they feel about their husbands? Did they really love their children? I could almost get a fever at such affairs, just on my own thoughts. When I was teaching at Columbia I had a few students nobody could bother with. They just were not material. But I always loved thinking of whether they spoke in clichés at home, or whether then they said something different. I had fun by myself wondering. Ever since, I have been intolerant about people saying they were bored by people or groups or things. Because I think maybe, just maybe, if you think enough about anybody, they are not boring at all. Maybe the boredom lies in the beholder just as beauty lies in the eye of the beholder.

And how true it is about beauty. Those you love look as you love them. Time may etch a few deepening lines, hair may go gray, but you never see it. If you love someone, they are forever fair and forever young. This is nice.

As for beauty being in the eye of the beholder, truer word was never spoken. It is true of everything. It is what looks out of our own eyes that makes loveliness. When I was growing up, there was a really fiercely homely woman in our town. To me she was dazzling. For she saw everything lovely and fine that was around her, her quick mind illuminated many things for me in my young ignorance. She was not a teacher, just a family friend, but I have carried the imprint of her loveliness all my life. I could spend an hour with her, and be lightened. This was really beauty.

Take dogs. My Little Sister is no breed champion. But when I look at her, she leaves nothing to be desired. And once at the Spaniel Specialty Show we came out with two women with a very ratty little dog, looking suspiciously like a mongrel. As we got in the elevator at the Roosevelt, one gathered him in her arms and said, "Never mind darling, WE KNOW you were the most beautiful of all!" He was, to them.

One of my best moments, on this account, was when I met a very dear friend whom I had not seen for fifteen or twenty years. "Why, you haven't changed at all," he said happily.

I sighed, but it was a happy sigh. I knew very well I was no longer a size sixteen, my hair was darker, I wore glasses. My pink and white complexion was now a freckled and sunburned country woman's. But I still looked the same to this one! For he meant it. What a moment, to feel the essential you was there and could be visible, no matter what time had done to the outer person!

By the way, have you ever noticed how people look like their dogs? I haven't as yet been able to see just how small you resemble an oversized Great Dane, but it must be you do. Or you are the exception. We can almost say what dog a person has at a show just by looking at the face of the person. Nothing is funnier than to see a Dachshund at one end of a leash and at the other a human Dachshund. I know I am a cocker, cockers tend to be plump and over-loving and yet have a bright eye for what may come. I am also a cocker as to the excitements of life. A cocker tail thrashes so madly—and no tail at all, just a whiff of tail gyrating around. Jill is a problem, however: she is en rapport with the Irish and built rangily, but she is much more practical than any Irish we ever had. She has the Celtic depressions that Maeve introduced us to, but is not always flying around barking at nothing. She is possibly more like the dog she once yearned for and didn't get, an Old English Sheepdog, steady and with all paws on the ground, and able to manage flighty things like sheep with no trouble at all. However, we never got the Sheepdog and she and the Irish are an awful lot alike at moments as they lope off across the field looking for something.

The cockers align themselves according to temperament. The odd ones, by and large, think *I* am their first mama, the solid citizens turn to Jill. Tiki has a conflict, he was in my lap most of the time when small, but now he admires and adores Jill. She has more on the ball, he says, although I was a fine nursery tender.

When we lost Maeve, the sun dimmed for the rest of time. Maeve, whom you saw once briefly, was a great Irish. She had "a high heart and lucky eyes," as her namesake, the legendary queen, did. She and Jill were always moving step by step like one. She was a C.D., C.D.X., U.D. and a Tracking Dog, which not only meant she had all the learning a dog could have but that she and Jill had worked together in sun, rain, snow and sleet. She was beautiful and she knew every thought we had.

Jill was never without her. I only had to look out of the window to see Maeve's waving plume and know Jill was there. All their occupations were mutual. If Jill planted, Maeve buried her velvet nose in the same trench and dug—usually what had already been snugged down. At dog shows, if Jill went off for a cup of coffee, Maeve strained at the leash, miserably watching the beloved figure vanish. It never vanished long! When Maeve had a melancholy Celtic fit and leaned her head on the sofa back and gloomed, Jill got discouraged about everything. When they went to the dump, Maeve supervised the disposal of the interminable rubbish we seem to collect. As they took off for the postoffice, I always thought Maeve was licking the stamps for the envelopes as Jill drove.

Jill could always think of the most rational reasons why Maeve should go with her on any excursion. They were long-drawn-out, sober, explanatory. I always listened very gravely too, and then said, "Well, I do think you ought to take her."

If she made any mistakes, we knew it was all our fault. Even when she ate up Henry Kistner's new felt hat, it was because we had left it so nicely available!

Alas, the days will soon grow shorter. Practically this means the dogs are put up earlier, ourselves tucked in with books or odd household chores that are not too dreadful to do in the dark. Do you ever think how light decrees our living routine in the country? In the city, so much is by neon now, but here in our little valley we tend to snug in when the sky darkens.

The first people who had our little house must have gone to bed very early, the firelight and candlelight, or the whale oil lamps would never encourage one to late hours!

GLADYS

SUGARBRIDGE

DEAR G:
When Indian Summer brings its hazy days to Chester County, *our* Indians return; the hill behind the house blooms with phantom tepees, and the smoke of campfires rises to mingle with the blue misty distance;

down at the spring, the braves sit, whetting their quartz arrowheads. An old old man in West Chester brought us the tale, and now they live in our minds; even in their incorporeal state, these vanished Lenni Lenapes have become as much a part of our place as its hills and stream.

"Ever find any Indian arrowheads on your place?" he asked us, a stout parrot-faced old fellow, as he sharpened our lawnmower. "Those Lennis used to camp at your spring, on their way back from summers at the seashore."

We knew that a big Indian trail ran near us, at Whitford, and that a winter camping ground was located there, too. But it was news that they had stopped at our little spring.

"They were all loaded up with the fish they'd dried over the summer," the old man went on, busy with his files and grinders. "Liked your spring because it was cold. That vein of quartz 't down your road was what they needed for their arrowheads."

I knew the old man had quite a reputation locally as a geologist, and I was glad to learn, from the horse's mouth, so to speak, just why it was almost impossible to have post holes dug along the road. It was this vein of quartz, too, which had almost defeated the utilities company last summer which chose to lay a gas line down our road, in spite of warnings we gave. In time, all shall be revealed, I thought, if you can only wait.

But our habitual procrastination defeated us. We intended to have the old man out sometime, to show us where we would be likely to find arrowheads, which, he affirmed, he had done often. But we let the time go by, and before we got around to it, the old man died, one winter, and with him, his store of legend.

B

NOVEMBER

The hunting horn blows again!

DEAR GLADYS:

It's time for November's task—posting the land, for small game season opens next week. I've never heard you speak about doing this, and perhaps you don't have hordes of hunters, as seem to swarm out this way. Shooting is a great pastime hereabouts, and come nine o'clock on opening day, they surge in all directions toward the country like an army, armed with red-marked garments, licenses, dogs, and, naturally, guns—although I've heard something about how it is more sporting to bring down your game with bow and arrow. This onrush on opening day always seems ominous to me, and I await the first shot with apprehension. I feel as though I were the land, lying helpless, to be beaten over, and torn up. But I have in my mind too a magnificent picture by Pieter Brueghel, one of my very favorites of all pictures, called "The Winter Hunt." It shows the armed hunters, in hose and jerkins, starting out with their dogs through a bleak landscape, and when I think of this, I reflect that basi-

cally hunting has not changed since then even though our hunters pour
out of an old Ford, with numbers sewn on their backs; the relation between the hare and the hound still remains.

When we first came here, the hunters would have shot the windows
out of our house, if we had not checked them. The place had been
allowed to run wild for years, and had developed into a fine game preserve, with pheasants squawking from every tree and cover. Now, with
more of the land in cultivation, there are fewer pheasants, and this is a
blessing in disguise, for our acres are not much temptation to their pur-
suers.

Ed is a good shot, with Army medals to prove it, but no hunter. The
only pheasant we've eaten in years was one which friends, permitted to
shoot here, had winged, and lost in the underbrush. Our lady Dane,
beloved Draga, brought it to us in her mouth after they had gone, and,
finders keepers, we roasted it thankfully.

Ed wrote a poem, since become famous. It was published in the "New
Yorker," and has been taken up by all the Chapters of the S.P.C.A. and

other societies of animal lovers. Myself, I think this poem would spoil even the most hardened hunter's pleasure in his sport.

> "The rabbit, running down the dawn,
> Before the evening will be gone,
> Leaving the measure of its leap
> Marked by a broken, bloody heap.
>
> The pheasant's iridescent arc
> That fired the morning with its spark,
> Will lie beneath the sun at noon
> As cold and lifeless as the moon.
>
> The squirrel that bore the acorn cup
> To fill his wintry granary up,
> Still holds the Grail he cannot see
> Below the sanctuary tree.
>
> Now, with the gift of day near spent,
> The hunter sits in tired content,
> And warm and peaceful in the sun,
> He cleans the murder from his gun."

Its lines have a wonderful sonorous roll to them, as we discovered when we heard Claude Rains read it aloud. It made quite an impression on him and for some time after he went around muttering to himself, "And wiped the murder from his gun. . . ."

To kill, or not to kill, is one of the questions of our time. Among the lower animals, it serves to keep the balance of Nature, but more is expected of men, further along the way of evolution. (Even after the last war!) Pity is thought to be an attribute of man alone. Although Konrad Lorenz claims in "King Solomon's Ring" that a wolf is unable to kill in cold blood when a rival bares its neck to him.

It seems to me an anomaly that we refrain from killing with our own hands, those of us who have this conviction, yet eat unthinkingly the meat which is unobtrusively slaughtered for us. No doubt it is in consideration of principle rather than health measures that most vegetarians get that way. I myself could easily exclude meat from my diet; the difficulty for me would lie in fitting such a regimen into life with other people. And then the inevitable quibblings that result: is butter, are milk and eggs animal food? You know, as well as I, that all cooking worth the name would be impossible without this priceless trio. I remember a story Ed told me about a witty doctor he used to lunch with at a literary club they both belonged to. The doctor was a vegetarian, and someone said, "How come?" when they saw him eating shad roe one day. He replied he believed in birth control, too.

I think if I became a vegetarian, I would carry this sort of questioning even further, asking myself whether plants were pained by being plucked? If so, are we not as wrong in doing violence to them as to animals, for they are only slightly lower in the scale of life? In "Book of the Winter" compiled by Edith Sitwell, there is a marvelous line quoted, to the effect that an animal is just a plant without a stem. I have been thinking along these lines for years, so it was most amazing to me to come across a story called "The Sound Machine" by Roald Dahl, about a contraption so delicate that it was able to record the "throatless inhuman shriek, sharp and short, very clear and cold" of a rose, being severed by the shears. This, as one of the considerations of everyday life, is going a bit far, I feel.

I only know that I do not like to kill, myself—I could not bring my hand to pull the trigger against a downy rabbit, as much as I could wish him removed from our vegetable garden. I even wish that I could be a Spartan, and steel myself against swatting insects in the summer. (I do escort spiders out on a piece of Kleenex, but wasps are not very cooperative.) For I still remember a day when, walking in the Wisconsin woods as a child, with some other children, and an older boy with a gun, we saw a little chipmunk run across our path, a pretty bright striped creature. Sensing destruction among us, as wild things can, it turned and ran up a tiny tree no higher than our waists, pitifully climbing to the very top. Though we all begged him not to, the boy with the gun shot it, hanging there defenseless, and it is something which I can never forget.

P.S. Many confabs among the neighbors about our deer family which has grown so tame over the summer. Marshall Grover reports that there is a man living over the hill from us who says he intends to shoot one of them if possible. This has a familiar ominous ring to me. Does it hark back to the story of Baldur, the Norse god of youth? As I remember from the mythology taught me in childhood, he was threatened by death, and all the animals and plants on earth were canvassed and asked if they would be loyal, refusing to act against him. All agreed except the mistletoe, and it was with a sprig of this plant that the wicked Loki did him in. I suppose there always has to be somebody like that, animal or vegetable. We'll just have to wait and see.

Love
BARBARA

STILLMEADOW

DEAR BARBARA:

I am emotionally a vegetarian too. That's why we gave up chickens. I just did not want to eat them after they had been around with us, being fed and watered and waited on. As for hunting, I can't see how anyone can bear to bring a film over the bright eyes of a wild free animal.

Our land is posted, but we still hear shots very close to the barn on a crisp Fall morning.

And we often see a smart sedan drive down the main road with a limp deer lashed to the fenders, the delicate hooves quiet forever, the bright gaze gone. I wonder how murder can be sport, and yet my own father, who would nurse a small broken-winged bird, would rush out at the first dawn of hunting season and try his best to get his quota!

I come of a long line of expert hunters and fishers. On Father's side they were all tops. So I must inherit my lack of the joy of this particular sport from Mama, who always shut her eyes at a football game when the ball was passed and the scrimmage began.

I spent the best hours of today sitting in the doctor's office admiring the growth of his wife's giant fern. Ferns must just love the sterile air of a doctor's office, I thought, shivering slightly. I could see the fronds begin to grow as I sat there, and wave toward me, encroaching on my aches and pains—any minute the fern would TAKE ME OVER.

"There's nothing the matter with you except you have flu," says Dr. Ghiselin briskly. Mrs. Ghiselin boils things up and the penicillin goes in—all very tidy. This is the new kind—isn't it strange there are styles in ailments too? Improved short version, so I am up today puttering.

Puttering is a fine exercise if you are in the mood for it, but if I once start puttering when there is too much I should be doing, I get "all nerved up" as George says his mother is when a calf gets loose.

But a day spent fixing the mending box, polishing Sister's silver loving-cups, hunting up fresh clean candles, and refilling all the salts and peppers can be pleasant.

Washing the milk glass is a bigger job, a backaching one, but it is rewarding. The pure translucent glass is beautiful and almost every piece has a special memory in it. I would never want a collection of anything all at once in a clump, would you? I like to collect hours and occasions with the pieces.

We began our milk glass collection a long time ago, with one piece. When we got the second, it was a celebration! The blackberry egg cups were our first important find, and then one day we located eight lacy edge plates all alike. Then we looked for more lacy edge—and this is the way collectors do, I imagine.

The one thing I hold against Thoreau, by the way, is that time he had a very nice stone on his table, and he threw it away because it was a thing to dust—he was a thoroughly emancipated man, no doubt of it.

My favorite of his writing is the walking trip to Cape Cod. I can just see him striding along the great beaches, thinking his profound thoughts. And stopping to eat a sea clam to find out whether it was *really* inedible. Being a naturalist and philosopher, he was perfectly happy just to pick a handful of wild berries for a meal as he hiked around. How tiresome he would think me wanting to build a small fire and toast something!

Well, my dear, the season is drawing to an end. There is a feeling at dusk, a prescience of short and shorter days and pale pure dawns. I hope the squirrels have all their nuts tucked safely in. And the tiny fawn-colored deer mice are settled down to housekeeping in some burrow or thicket and not already making apartment houses out of the bureau drawers in the storage house.

I have not talked myself into a mood for winter yet. Summer's lease seems to have shorter and shorter a date and Autumn is nothing more than a comma in the sentence of the year. It would be nice to pack away a whole day or two and bring it out in January.

Even a pocketbook full of moments would be pleasant. Out of November I would save a moment when the haze is deepening and the shadows slant and a little unborn moon floats over the bare branches. The big exciting orange-red full moon is wonderful, but the delicate sickle is ever lovelier.

I would save George's cows moving slowly down the lane, their tails making a special flick now and then, their heads turned toward the barn. Old Shep nips at their heels if they change their mind about the direction and the puppies roll along in a wavering course. George walks to the barn with that swinging gait farmers have, he stoops just a little, for he carries many burdens.

I would tuck in the face of Especially Me looking earnestly at me through the window and waiting to see how fast I will let him in. Sticks and odd bits of leaves are in his golden fur, his ears are muddy, he has had a nice day. Teddy, I say, dry your paws before you jump on the couch, and he doesn't. He jumps and leans his head on the back of the sofa—and gives me a look of love.

Simple things make up my treasures most of the time. There are many in the country.

One of my favorite sayings is that of Countess Aurélie in the "Madwoman of Chaillot": "There's nothing wrong with the world that a sensible woman could not fix in an afternoon!"

Possibly if we all saw to it that everyone had enough of the simple things—it's a thought anyway.

My best,
G

SUGARBRIDGE

My Poor Dear G,

What! penicillin again? I do feel for you. Not only because I'm sad that you are sick, but also because penicillin gives me the shudders. Do you know that it was first manufactured in West Chester? Still is, and the odor of the stuff in the mass is the most nauseating of smells (I'm glad for your sake that the taking of it is scentless). The plant is right across the street from the postoffice, and many a time, I have to shroud my nose in a handkerchief, and make a quick dash to the letter box.

Our bedroom is the perfect spot to be sick. All windows, it provides a variety of views, and a great flood of light, so that you never feel shut in, even if you are. From the head of my bed I can see, framed by the bare inky branches of the maples, the emerald glint of our pool with

the stream flowing into it, and beyond, the naked brown backs of the hills rising, changing color each hour of the day. At my foot, without raising my head there is visible the tips of the little wood I planted years ago; Scotch pines they were, and now they have grown into a respectable thicket inhabited by rabbits, foxes, and who knows what wild life. There is always something going on there, and while I intended it primarily as a windbreak for my flower garden, I am not by any means displeased with the by-products.

Any day you may see an assortment of our winter birds perched on these green tips, juncos, titmice, and greatest of treats, a cardinal so ruby bright it hurts the eye. Above the wood, the steep slope of hills mounts, obscuring the sky, a giant beech tree a-top. This is a view which I never tire of, and it is restful just to lie there, looking out. But we pay for our hills, and are often hard put to it to find one flat spot on all our acres. The terraces we've leveled off! I feel for the ancient Peruvians; we would have had much in common, if we had ever met. At a dinner party not long ago, I made the acquaintance of an archeologist whose preferred excavation spot was Peru; he wondered at my immediate grasp of the inhabitants' problems. We haven't yet undertaken to build a temple to the sun in tiers, but you never can tell.

The lowest moment of any illness is the first day up. You feel too weak to take any pleasure in your new freedom, yet would find it stupid to go back to bed. The house looks drab and untidy. (What has everyone been doing since you were sick, anyway?) There you pay up for your idleness, and with interest. Lately I came across a delicious line in Trollope: "With the delightful privilege of a convalescent, he was allowed in these days to get up just when getting up would be more comfortable than lying in bed, and that time did not usually come till eleven o'clock was past."

When I have been ill, I always resolve to bear more patiently with the whims of invalids. No Florence Nightingale, I, alas. I do all right for two days or so; a flower on the trays, delicate food, books, entertainment, sympathy. But after that, I wear thin. I urge them to get well, to be up and around. This is wrong, I tell myself; I must remember the gloomy climate of the sick, and how it changes everything. I must learn to accept crabbedness as its result.

But once recovered, in the returning exhilaration of well-being, I feel myself forgetting, and know there is really no meeting ground between the sick and the sound.

Ed is a very unusual patient. He dotes upon being sick, claiming that a degree or so of fever is the perfect temperature for creative effort. Last year when he had the virus, he wrote a poem, "Country Sickbed," which, when sold, paid the doctor bills, and in addition, bought a couple of bottles of Scotch.

B

DEAR BARBARA:

This is a dreaming day. I believe it is Indian Summer, but it may not be. Nobody has ever cleared up for me the exact time of Indian Summer.

The soft pale haze over the woods, and the still look of the harvested fields, and the drift of fallen leaves on the lawn—and the way the sun feels—tender—all of it is lovely, lovely.

And then the feeling that winter will walk in any day makes every moment more precious.

Yours,
G

DEAR B:

Do you ever hear the commercial about taking a coffee break? I am having one right now. In the middle of house-cleaning—the worst part of it, my closet. The state of my closet is chaotic. Sometimes I look wistfully at the magazine illustrations of modern closets as big as ball-rooms. In 1690, closets were just little left-over corners in the house, cubby-holes. Mine is pint-size, but Jill's is like a pencil box.

I always decide, at the point of having everything out and knowing it will never, never go back in, that "a little wardrobe" is what I should have. A suit that turns into a dress if you reverse it and a play dress that doubles for a beach robe and/or a cocktail jacket. But I am not clever enough to work this out. And there is always the limp cotton that I think I might wear once or twice—the faded print that would be all right under a raincoat.

Every little while, we pack boxes to give away and the children view this with alarm. "Have you been giving-away again?" When you think of all the people who need things, it seems immoral to have anything around that you can do without.

Jill is banging around in the cellar, cleaning it up for the winter. It is always full of what our Finnish man used to call "yust yunk." It's my belief it wanders in in the night and settles down. We always find odd bits of iron, coffeepot tops, chipped plates, and damp cartons. Jill rides off to the dump nearly buried in the stuff. I can see Daphne's Irish flag

247

waving through one small corner of the station wagon window as they turn the corner by the mailbox.

If we had one of those rumpus rooms, it would be the same way, I know.

We are always vastly helped in our projects. Jonquil bounds to the top of the heap of my best dresses, laid out while I sort the shoes. Daphne whips up a nice bit from the cellar pile and makes off, pursued by ardent Teddy, who can't catch her, but can make the run worth the money. When the Irish runs, she skims. But Teddy, I notice through my window, is smart about taking short cuts. She runs the long way around the house, and he nips in by the terraces.

G

DEAR GLADYS,

Today, my one fan came to tea. Doesn't this amuse you? I love it. You with so many, I with only one! Of course, it's not quite that good; I tend to exaggeration; I know it. I am excepting friends and acquaintances, and the casual new people who write after the advent of each book to say they enjoyed it. By fan, I mean a faithful loyal reader of your works, who is always on the lookout for a new one, and who in between, writes to you uninterruptedly even though you may not answer.

Such a one is Mr. A, a charming gentle old fellow, who does, as a hobby, beautiful manuscribing, with as little effort as you or I would write a grocery list. He has presented us with several of Ed's poems, handsomely lettered—for he has become a fan of Ed's, as well—and will presently do "Dark Adversary" for you, which you said you'd like to have? Mr. A uses a typewriter with the most fascinatingly small type I've ever beheld, and when we get one of his letters, which are always wise and witty, one of us can be expected to exclaim, "No more twist!" Do you remember in "The Tailor of Gloucester?" by the inimitable Beatrix Potter, the mice leave a note in tiniest writing on the suit they finished for the old tailor, explaining why one buttonhole was not done?

Well, anyway, on this occasion, Mr. A had come over from his home in Germantown with some relatives who live near us, and we had an agreeable afternoon's conversation, sitting by the fire, comparing books we had read, and talking about music, and lettering, and pictures. Long after it was all over, and they had left us, and the fire died away to coals, I was still thinking how agreeable and stimulating it had been, and that we should feel honored to have such a fan. For all the books that Mr.

A reads and cherishes are just the books I admire, too, and I am proud, even in a minor way to be associated with that company.

B

HELLO TODAY:

I wonder whether I would be better off if I took today as all there is? Sort of *look your last on all things lovely, every hour,* as De la Mare does. Or is it more satisfactory to take little hopeful hops toward the future?

Of course today is the only security we have, but if we live as if we were going to live forever, a long-time effect comes into our lives. I know some people who are convinced we are done for very soon, just one more bomb to be completed, they say. Therefore, doomed as we are, there is no use looking forward. This involves not doing anything constructive—I even know a young couple who have decided against having children for that reason—no world to be born in.

It might be a psychiatrist would find out they just naturally don't want children, but at least they think that is their reason, and it's a sad one.

Now I've thought about it, I believe in living every minute to the utmost and yet dreaming ahead too. For after all, nobody would ever have a garden if they lacked faith in the seed!

Hopefully,
G

DEAR GLADYS

Now the year is drawn in, and the edges tucked up; the nuts picked, by squirrels and by me, the fields trimmed of harvest, only a few ears spilled here and there, for wild things to pick at, and scattered golden grains upon the roads; the flaming leaves fallen rosy upon the ground, a warm blanket; earth ready for a long sleep. I have visited all my favorite places; this is a hunger I have in autumn, as though I had to say farewell to them before winter shuts down. Stillmeadow is alas too far to visit thus fleetingly except by memory, and see the rocky meadows and dark cedars, the tidy white New England houses, with the house doors handsomely bedecked with ears of corn, for Thanksgiving. We have taken this custom from you, and it has become as characteristic of the season as a wreath is to Christmas. But we have no corn so spectacular as those black Mexican ears we saw that time upon your door.

249

One night last week, we had come home late, in the dark, and were scuttering around the kitchen assembling some bits of supper, when there was a loud knock upon the front door. Duke announced, with a roar, his intention of taking the intruder apart. When we had calmed him, we looked out, and there, in the moonlight, we saw the frail small figure of Mr. D. But his eyes were shining brightly, and he said, "It was such a nice night, I had to get out and take a walk. *She* was sewing away. . . . I brought you some walnuts," he pushed a large paper bag toward me. "They're from a tree nobody else knows about, a special tree."

We urged him in, but he said, hanging back, "I don't go into other people's houses much." He had on, formally, an overcoat, a suit and tie, a homburg hat. I thought of Miss K's remark, when I'd asked her whether she saw much of her neighbors. "I always remember what the Bible says," she answered. "Put not thy foot in thy neighbor's house, lest he weary of thee, and smite thee." The complete expression of a countrywoman, I'd thought to myself at the time.

We got Mr. D as far as the kitchen, and sat him down upon one of our stools. He took off his hat, but insisted upon retaining his coat. We gave him a little nip of something warming, and he solemnly proposed his usual toast, "To the Woman Who Understands."

"Well, you've got a nice house," he said suddenly, looking around.

"It looks pretty grubby right now," I objected, using Ned's favorite expression for untidiness.

He went on, unheeding. "And a wonderful husband," he shook the amber liquid around in his glass. Smiling, I thought that Ed and Mr. D did have some tastes in common. Draining the last drop, he got up. "Well, I must be on my way," he said.

"Oh, not yet!" I wanted to ask him about his prize-fighting career (Miss K had confided to me that not long ago he had subdued a thug who had set upon him on a lonely road. "But he'd been a prize fighter for years," she'd said. "That was nothing to him.") Then there was a story he'd told Ed that I wished to hear firsthand, about his having, when a young man, rescued a young girl of a wealthy family from drowning—a romantic tale; and then, I was still on the trail of those truffles. But he shook his head.

"I'll walk around a little more," he said, "and then I'd better get back. She'll be wondering where I've got to."

I knew he wanted to be out in the moonlight again. Eighty-five, and moon-struck enough to walk miles of an evening. There weren't many like him, I said to Ed, when he'd gone, even in Chester County.

B

HEIGH HO FOR THE FIRST SNOW:

So light and casual and falling with such feather-soft flakes. And a pewter sky. It's just a little note from winter so far, but we know now that the wood must be piled in the woodshed and the kindling carried in baskets, the kennel heaters cleaned and the oil tank filled. We bustle.

Storm windows too. I do dislike storm windows, but our fragile little-paned windows are no better than sieves in the winter. I think a storm window cuts the light and makes you realize you are looking through two layers; the outdoors is just that much farther removed.

Father was very peculiar about storm windows. Once he got them on, he wanted them left on and it took Mama half the summer to get them off. Finally she would say, you take them off so I can wash them. If you want them right back on, all right. Then when they were off and clean, Father lost interest.

Those new aluminum year-round windows must be wonderful!

For November reading, I have gone back to "Out of Africa," and "Pickwick Papers." Then I shall re-read Katherine Mansfield—which might seem like a fine way to get literary indigestion as it is a mixed assortment.

Then I will read Keats's letters and the letters of Millay, and after that undertake something hot off the press and contemporary. Usually I feel old books like old friends are best. Because when you go back, you add the memory of the other times you read and loved them. Beauty is a cumulative thing, I think. Don't you?

My favorite books of our day are ones like "Don Camillo and His Flock." Have you read it, and "The Little World of Don Camillo"? I nominate them for great books. Tender and real and with that rich sense of humor which has sadness on the reverse of the coin.

This is a very hard period to be a writer in, it seems to me, because it's hard to keep the importance of the individual clear when the world moves in great sweeps of disaster. And the drama of a single life is a small thing compared to the drama of millions of lives. Nevertheless, it is the business of writers to assert the value of the individual.

It takes a Hamlet to be immortal.

I would certainly never think of making a list of the world's greatest books. I admire the courage of those that do. A book is what the reader finds in it, so how can you assay them except for your own pleasure?

Music is the same highly personal affair. I am not very discriminating, I am afraid. I seem to like best what I am hearing. Whether it is a folk song—especially an old folk song with the speech and rhythms of the past —or German Lieder or the "Good Night" quartette from "Martha," I always think "this is the best." How I wish I had a really sound musical

education. I'd like to know the structure of symphonies and chorales and the shape of opera.

The sad truth is that no life is long enough for half the things one could learn. If this is amended in Heaven, you will find me speaking ten languages flawlessly, doing counterpoint, and *sewing*. Not to mention other things. Violin, not harp. I'd like to ski down the slopes of the eternal mountains, and swandive in the blue infinite seas of Heaven.

But I wonder if even in Heaven there would be time for everything? Or would I be too busy with all the cockers and the Irish who are just waiting to tell me about things?

Do you suppose there would be a small corner there where I could have a kennel? And do a little cooking?

Hopefully
G

SUGARBRIDGE

DEAR GLADYS

I envy you your early winters. I have a childish love of snow. Yet our Indian Summer is agreeable, too, and those mild brooding days of November, when all Nature seems hardly to breathe, waiting, waiting. It might snow then, but it doesn't. Of course there has been a distinct change in the cycle of seasons even in my lifetime. As far as that goes, the last five years have been markedly warmer. When we first came to this place, roughly ten years ago, we had a succession of cold snowy winters, plenty of skiing and sleighing, and terrible driving. But of late winters, only a few token flurries.

There was an ominous article in "Life" some time ago—did you see it?—developing a theory of constantly increasing heat, and the probable effect on the earth, with the ice caps melting, and temperatures gradually rising. Just to read it gave you the sensation of being slowly broiled on a gridiron. Also, the article ran on cheerfully, higher temperatures affect the brain unfavorably. In southern climates, the rate of suicide is higher, as it is during the summer months in temperate zones. This is probably true; I know I felt near to it sometimes last summer during the heat wave.

It suddenly came to me the other day how much our thoughts, our feelings and desires, are conditioned by the temperature.

Comes an unseasonally mild spell in March; the thermometer may go up to sixty degrees; the knee-deeps begin to pipe, the crocus bloom, all the birds you could wish to hear start to sing. Insensibly, I find, I adjust myself to spring thoughts, spring preoccupations. I may get out a pair of jeans. Horrors! The belt has grown too tight. That means a course of salad lunches, coffee and grapefruit breakfasts. We've been having too many puddings and cakes during the wintry weather. This mild ethereal time makes all that seem most unnecessary. For inherent in spring is the need to mortify the flesh, and purify the spirit. Lent, I'm sure, was a health measure, as well as a spiritual effort, to thin the mediaeval blood after a winter of salt meat. But my sensations go further—I want to put behind me the winter way of thinking, the drawing-in, the gathering by the fireside, the cozy bed beckoning. How stuffy that all seems now, with the outdoors calling, fresh and fragrant.

But if perchance on the morrow, we wake up to find ourselves buried under ten inches of snow, the picture changes. One look out at the bleak landscape, and we are back again in that wintry state of mind. Build up the fire with huge logs, against the dreariness outside; bake the pudding, the richer the better! And how unutterably enticing bed will be, with a good book, the fine needle-like tinkle of sleet against the pane.

Thanksgiving is subtly altered in our house by having Ed's birthday occur the same week, so that we celebrate each of these great days together, and now I cannot think of either apart. There have had to be concessions on each side; the birthday dinner is naturally always turkey and cranberry sauce; on the other hand, mince and pumpkin pie have had to give ground to lemon meringue, the birthday man's favorite, and since he dislikes cake, we decorate the pie with lighted candles. I suppose this would seem odd to anyone else, but to us slightly wacky ones, it is all right, a touch of fantasy superimposed upon tradition; indeed, in our family we have become quite fond of this arrangement. As for me, I think it is ideal for Ed's birthday to come at a time when I can publicly give thanks for him, which I do privately most days of the year, excepting the ones when we have disagreed, and I feel he is impossible to live with. So when Ned asks the blessing on Thanksgiving Day (which is always his duty, and he invariably chooses the shortest possible one), I am grateful for my Sagittarian.

But I'm afraid that materially, he suffers from the immediate incidence of Christmas. I tend to exhaust all my ideas for presents upon the birthday and often large is the pile of vari-colored packages, upon the Thanksgiving dinner table. But then at Christmas, comes a dearth. I am uninspired, and fall back upon the banalities of socks and shirts. Not that he cares. Although Ed is always suitably pleased by whatever is given him, he would be just as happy with nothing at all, having reached the comfortable state of being above THINGS. Although not so much as he, I have been becoming that way, too, I think, for a long time. One of my clearest feelings from childhood is that sense of anti-climax after all the Christmas presents were opened. There has to be something *more*; I felt, even then, something more satisfying.

BARBARA

STILLMEADOW

HAPPY THANKSGIVING:

I always remember a friend of mine who spent Thanksgiving in France shortly after or during the war, and her efforts to explain what Thanksgiving meant to Americans were prodigious. In the end, they decided it was a church holiday, but also meant roasting something, which they did. With a group of French country people, she said grace and carved a real turkey, and everyone agreed it was a fine holiday; Americans were quite right to observe it.

If I weren't so frightened of shipping breakables, I would send you a jar of our own cranberry sauce for your own table. But knowing my luck, someone would drop an elephant on it, and you would simply scoop up pieces of broken glass.

Our wild cranberries are pale and rosy, much larger than the commercial and very delicate in flavor. We only have them when Jill gets the jump on George, who hays the lower meadow in season. One year, when we had to go to New York, Jill laid blankets and rag rugs over the whole end of the bog to save our crop. Those peering around the rug edges froze into little wilted nibs, the rest were fine.

I read that the cranberry was the Craneberry and whether cranes ate it or not, I shall probably never know. It's a fine sturdy berry anyway,

polished and sound. I used to sort the berries when Mama made her orange and cranberry relish and the smooth fall of the berries in the stoneware bowl was a fine thing.

Faith Baldwin gave us a real cranberry picker, but we use it as a rack for magazines. Once we were on Cape Cod when they were picking in the bogs. It was incredibly beautiful, the Portuguese do most of the picking and they bend and sway with a rhythm not Anglo-Saxon at all. They wear brilliant blue and red shirts and their voices come soft and persuasive in the bright air. The cranberry crates are stacked at the edge of the bog, the lines are like etchings. Clare Leighton did the cranberry pickers for her New England plates, and I wish I could describe them as well as she does with her etching tools.

We get ready for Thanksgiving with a deal of baking and stuffing. It is so easy now we can pop the turkey in the freezer, slide the pumpkin pies in. How fast we forget the days when we had no freezer and everything had to be done right at the hour. I always think of Mama, with the iceman bringing fifty pounds of river ice every other day and how she managed. She did, but she was a gifted cook.

Mama could turn out a Thanksgiving dinner for fifteen and only be a little flushed. I do well if, with Jill's help, we thaw what we have fixed last week for the occasion. Jill does all the stuffing, the basting, and I do the gravy. She says gravy always lumps for her. I say her stuffing is better and more savory than any.

The children turn up at odd hours, and we always feel glad when the last chick is under the roof. Jill's son and daughter and their partners in life usually drive in, plus one cat. Connie comes ahead, on the train.

It is quite an experience meeting our local train. It puffs in laboriously as if every breath were the last it would draw.

Commuting men climb off, their wives greet them with not too much excitement. A few New York shoppers slide down, lugging large cartons. My heart sinks—Connie is not there.

Then, far down the platform I see a slim hurrying figure, and the world shines again. She travels with a small suitcase, a basket, a paper sack, and a long-playing record under the least busy arm.

And she has always just made the train!

How time does come back, in waves like water on a deep beach. I instantly see her going off for the first time to camp. Leggy and untidy, and nervous. Going off and coming back, brown and assured and with her glasses tied on with a string. I see her starting for the University, pale and shy. Coming back, a college girl, quite poised and secure. (I think the hardest thing for a mother is not to go along when protocol demands she stay home!)

If the train is two minutes late, I have time to see myself in retrospect coming back from my Eastern college. My stomach tight, my eyes out of focus. I have a new hat. Papa won't like it. My beau will be there, his hair like wheat in the light of the train. Standing apart, because we cannot be serious.

Then my mother, brown eyes shining with tears, hair falling softly down under her strong hair net.

As I fly down the platform to meet my child, I wonder if it could possibly be as important to her to see me as it is to me to see her. No, the world has changed. Children are on their own now, they do not feel quite the same as Mama and I felt.

Nevertheless, I am thankful I had my mother just as she was, and, this makes Thanksgiving better. For I feel it is a long heritage of family tradition, and we should endeavor to maintain the feeling of family unity, even in these independent days.

When the turkey, breathing of rich crusty goodness and redolent of sage, and the fluffy mashed potatoes, and the whipped turnip—which two of our children will not eat—go on the table and we sit down and I ask the grace, I always begin by thanking God that the family is together.

If all families could be together, and all fed by a staunch dinner, the world would be in better state. It is the time, Barbara, to remember the cold starving days of the first Americans, and to be glad they persevered.

You are probably rolling pastry and adding a dash of this and that to your own turkey stuffing. I can see the fire in your deep fireplace and in my mind I walk around the stretched length of Duke. He is quite a lot of dog. I am sure you are talking as you mash the potatoes. You are a talking cook; I am not. I have to think when I cook.

A Happy Thanksgiving to you all,
GLADYS

SUGARBRIDGE

DEAR GLADYS,

This is a Postscript Letter—all the things I meant to tell you which for one reason or another never were written. I hate to have them lost, so I send them, like a bouquet of forget-me-nots.

P.S. This I remember because just now I came upon a drawing Ed made last summer of a hummingbird in the hand! It flew in one day through the open door of the studio, a green living flame. Yet Ed had no difficulty in catching it, and, quiescent, it lay in his palm, giving forth a low musical note when its breast was stroked. I should have said "she,"

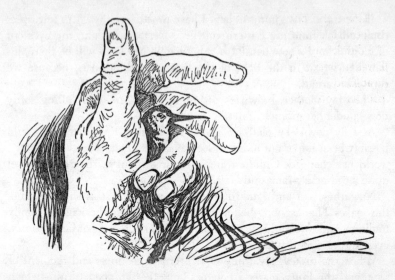

because Viola later told me it must have been a female, with a green breast; a male would have had a ruby waistcoat. She posed quite contentedly while Ed made a drawing of her, and then, escorted to the open door, she darted away again into the sunlight, none the worse for her strange adventure.

P.S. As I came over the hill one evening, West Chester-bound, at my customary rate of speed, an even fifty m.p.h., something burst upon me, large, round, pale orange, effulgent. It was the hunter's moon, bland and beaming.

P.S. Ed was carrying the scarecrows down from the corn field the other day, accompanied of course by Duke. Midway down the hill, he stopped to shift the load, tilted one scarecrow downwards. Suddenly a grisly thing happened. A little mouse ran out of the scarecrow's head (stuffed with straw, and no doubt, a cozy nest). The mouse landed, and stayed a moment immobilized. Duke and the mouse stared at each other, hypnotized. Then it turned and zipped swiftly into the underbrush. Too late, Duke came to life, and flew in pursuit. Ed, a little shaken, continued on to the barn, with his zombie freight.

P.S. Then there was the blacksnake. The snake Ed wrote the poem about. The poem no magazine will buy because readers do not like snakes. One warm morning in spring Ed shouted for me, and when I came on the double, there he was with his arm wound 'round by a big blacksnake. I barely bit a scream in two. I don't like snakes, either. Or I didn't.

"Come and put your hand on it," he ordered. "I want you to see it isn't cold or slimy."

I didn't want to. But when I laid two fingers on its black scaly surface, I was surprised. "Why, it's warm," I said. "And dry." But its eyes, in the head held in Ed's fingers, glared wickedly at me, and its tongue flickered back and forth. Here is the poem that gave editors the jitters:

"Today, at dawn I found you, still
And black, beside a daffodil.

With forked stick from apple tree
I caught your curving ebony;

To lift, with gentle hand around,
Your length of midnight from the ground.

And when you knew I meant no harm,
You coiled dark bracelets on my arm;

Not slimy-chill, as old wives told,
But warm and quiet in my hold.

Linked for a magic moment's span
Were mystic Tree and snake and man,

Held in the Garden's dream of peace,
Before I gave you your release;

To watch your fabled body pass
Like liquid coal through emerald grass."

Love
B

DECEMBER

DEAR G,

Here is December upon us already! To me, it comes with a sense of doom, and let's confess it, a certain admixture of annoyance. Why, Thanksgiving is barely over, and cleared away, the turkey used up, and everyone just about recovered from the parties! And now it's beginning again, and I have no Christmas shopping done. Tell me the truth; you have yours all handsomely wrapped, and laid away! I know it. You're that kind of person, always on time, neat, and ready. It's what I'd like to be. . . .

December began very mild and open, and I did a good deal of riding. It acts as the most soothing of balms upon me, to get off into the open peaceful fields, after giddy days and gay nights. No matter how peevish and oppressed by my wrongs I may be on starting out, after an hour or so, alone with Chief on the country lanes, with Duke galumphing on ahead, I am at peace with God and man, and so overflowing with good will that I wish everyone something so tonic as riding is for me.

So subtly the time stole away. I thought, it's too early to do the wreaths; I always make my own. There's so much growing around here in the way of evergreens, and we have ground pine, too, or creeping cedar, or whatever you want to call it, anyway, good to make into ropes for twining. It's fun to do this, and not too hard, but it takes time. It seemed too early to bake cookies, as well, another pleasant seasonal duty; they'd get stale, or else eaten up by over-zealous tasters. So I went on my dilatory way. But it needed only one stone tossed into the still pool to agitate it with violent ripples. I met a member of my family who was in despair over what to give another member. "What *can* you give him? He has *everything!*"

All at once, I realized I had nothing for anybody, and suddenly, there was everything to be done. I thought yearningly of that ingenious article I had read last summer in "Woman's Day," (A&P) about things to make for Christmas; they all looked possible, and any one I should have welcomed myself. But alas, I didn't, and now I must pay the penalty, and plunge into the maelstrom of Christmas-crowded shops. But some time (this I vow each year), I'm going off alone, or with anyone who wishes to come, well before the season starts, and spend it far off, as it should be, a quiet, holy mystic time.

Although you mightn't think it, from my Scrooge-like mutterings, I really love Christmas, albeit in my own way. The truth is, I haven't the stamina most women possess, to stick out a long stretch of preparations. I want to stop for a while, to read, listen to music, go for a ride, maybe do some writing. There was a great to-do made about Christmas in my childhood home, and although my brother and I were never allowed to decorate the tree ourselves, it was always a splendid one, since my father took a deep interest in trimming it, and always brought back ornaments from whatever city his legal business took him to. We had odd little Mexican demons, fur-clad; gay gimcracks from New Orleans, even some Indian trimmings, if I remember aright. Each year's tree was different, and each one still lives in my memory.

Well, not to keep you in suspense, My Christmas spirit descended upon me at last. However delayed, I can now hardly wait for the great day.

P.S. One of our deer family was killed—the buck. I suppose we all knew it must be so. After all, it was hunting season, and if a man wants to kill a tame deer by the side of a road, it is his privilege. Out for a ride last week, Chief and I came upon the widowed doe and her fawns up in our rye field; before we knew it, we were in the midst of flying white tails—and Chief was flying, but upwards, and it was only luck that I came down in the saddle and not in the rye.

BARBARA

STILLMEADOW

HELLO TO YOU-ALL:

One of the nicest phrases I learned when I lived in Virginia. It's controversial, for the highly literate of my friends always explained that they did NOT mean you-all as a single person at all. It means, they said, all of you, a nicely inclusive term for whoever is around. But I noticed when I met them on the street, they said, "Good mawnin, how ah you-all?"

It is somehow pleasanter than an abrupt YOU. Although I un-learned it when I came to New England, I always liked it. Southern speech has a gentleness, a grace, that we miss in our clipped Yankee talk. When I say happily to Mr. Bennett—what a wonderful day, he is just as apt to cock a weather-wise eye at the sky and say, "Could be worse." Or simply, "Seems fine." A Virginian would carry on for five minutes about the same weather.

However, the heart underneath beats as warmly. It is the Yankee who will dig you out of a snowdrift, shrug his shoulders and say, "Neighbors, got to help." He does not bother to commiserate at all, he just digs!

Prejudice is a strange thing. The Southerner often thinks the Northerner lacks manners, and lives mostly on raw meat. My first close Virginia friend asked me quite seriously whether I *liked* raw chopped beef. She heard it was a delicacy up North. The Northerner often, on the other hand, thinks the Southerner is light and shallow.

Neither is true.

The East thinks the far West is a rootless place, the West thinks we are a little stodgy.

But anywhere you live, the people are the same basically, it just takes time to get through the outer differences.

Ways of speech fascinate me. A "run" in the South is a "crick" in the Middle West and a "brook" here. A "croker sack" is the kind of mesh bag oranges come in up North. Once I was at a party with the famous novelist Jim Boyd and he asked for "a little branch water" with his whiskey. His hostess was flustered. "Just turn on the faucet," he said. So a brook or clear running water was a "branch" to him.

Our names are interesting in this part of the country. I like Fawn Brook. One can see the first little dappled fawn putting a delicate velvet nose in that un-named brook and some farmer or hunter saying, I saw him—down there—Fawn Brook.

Fern Brook is sweet too, so cool and shadowy sounding. And Kiss'n Brook sounds delightful.

Then we have Dark Lantern Hill, which I think could not be bettered. Kettletown Road of course commemorates the buying of the land from the Indians for one kettle. Poverty Hollow offers endless possibilities, and Tory Road, in Woodbury has its own history of persecuted King's men. On the borderline between Connecticut and Massachusetts is Chop Mist Hill, a strange and wondrous name.

The speech in our valley is special. George tells me on a frosty morning that "a rat has been grouching around all night in the barn." This word includes grinding of corn, the crouch of the rat in the dusty corners, the whole feeling of the situation. "There's a rat grouching around in the kennel," says Jill, since that time.

We have one unsavory neighbor, as most people do. When he chopped down a stand of trees in our back woods, George came in to say "that man—he's nothing but a bandit!"

I had always associated bandits with the bad West in the early days. I felt quite excited at the idea we were living next door to one!

When things go wrong in our neighborhood, the thing we now say

is "she was all nerved up." This describes so well, that particular state of mind.

The first snow affects us deeply. It is as if all the struggle to save the vegetables, get in the flowers, rake the leaves, put the border to bed, fix the kennel heaters, stack the kindling neatly in the woodshed—and wash the bathroom mats a last time to be hung in wind and Autumnal sun—all this is done, it is over.

There is a sudden strange quiet as the first flakes whirl so lazily down. The sky is no deeper than the edge of the pond, it is flat. The wet frozen fields look darker suddenly. Those first round stellar shapes come so easily, they even melt on the warm windowpane.

But we hurry to the village to lay in supplies, just in case the big storm should come early. And everyone else is there too, talking in loud cheerful voices, snapping the dampness from hatbrims and scarves. How warm and gay the market seems with the colored boxes of candy near the door, the bright tropical fruits in their racks. Joe's wife at the check-out counter is prettier than ever with her bright eyes and dark hair. Joe and George and Louis, the three brothers, whisk about with extra energy. Their very aprons are starchy with vigor. Never mind winter, they seem to say, we are in it together.

Joe, who has a beautiful voice, sings sweetly as he lugs groceries to the damp snowy cars. "Do not forsake me, Oh my darling—" he sings. Louis cuts a very fine choice chop to hearten a body on a cold day. George gives everyone a gay smile, his green-gray eyes shining. He piles sweet, golden-pink onions in bags.

Somehow the onset of winter has lost its darkness.

264

We of the valley may be in for winter, but we are all together, and we are all neighbors.

"Guess the wooly caterpillars are right," says George. "Don't forget if you ever need anything—any time—give us a ring."

Indeed we feel very rich as we slide back toward home. We are not two lone women way out in the country at all. We are surrounded by good folk who are with us as the cold closes in, for any need that may arise.

Often, in the kind of country life we live, we do not see our neighbors socially for days or weeks at a time. But we know they are there. The phone may ring, it is the Thomsons up the road asking if our current is off and can Phil do any errands when he goes to work.

Or Cliff drops over, his hunting cap dripping, his shoes snowy. He has put in a full day's work somewhere but he just thought he would "stop by" to see if the plumbing was all right and the pump working.

"Just don't worry about anything," he always says as he goes out, bending to get his tall self through our old low doorway, "just don't worry about a THING."

Well, we don't. We bask in the blessing of living with such people, and as the snow thickens, we feel perfectly secure and ready to face the long cold days again.

The first snow-deep twilight is so still, the world is a pale shadow beyond the meadow. The dogs drip on the hearth, the apple logs burn with their clean flame.

"Maybe I'll get time now," says Jill, shaking the snow from her mittens, "to do over your pine Windsor chair."

Love to all,
GLADYS

SUGARBRIDGE
"The bells of St. Agnes"

GLADYS DEAR

Woke this morning to the sound of metallic pounding. Now what . . . ? I wondered drowsily. Then I knew. The blacksmith had come, at dawn as usual, and was shoeing Chief. While the sound continued, clink-clank, clink-clank, I thought about the scene down at the barn; in the early chill, the forge glowing red, the white-hot horseshoe hissing as it was plunged into the water tub; the old blacksmith (he's one of the last in the countryside) bent over Chief's hoof, resting on his leathery apron, his face, no less leathery, intent on trimming, hammering, nailing, a big cud of tobacco bulging out his jaw. I didn't know at the moment whether I should arise, as is always my aim, and go down to talk to him, for varied and salty are the stories he has in stock. I contented myself for a while in remembering my favorite of last year's telling: having spent some time in the hospital with a back injury as the result of an accident with a skittish mare, the old man was told, on being discharged, that he would have to buy a surgical girdle. Now there is no more rugged individual than my blacksmith, and he saw no sense in paying out a lot of money for one of those newfangled contraptions. "So I goes up, and looks around among me wife's things," he told me. "And finds an old corset." He cut it down, he told me with glee, and that childish, seamy smile I am fond of, and it fitted him "perfect."

Little did we realize when we acquired Chief that we also got Mr. R too, in an indissoluble bond. Horses have to be shod, and blacksmiths are the ones to do it. Although I have heard that up in the Amish country, Lancaster and thereabouts, the horses which draw those sedate black buggies are never shod, and develop a hardness to their hoofs which make it unnecessary. Such a thrifty habit is in keeping with that admirable race, but Chief is no Amish horse, sober, careful and patient. He is wild and unpredictable, and he needs his shoes, so we are committed to Mr. R, and the ever-rising cost of steel and iron. It is surely better to have him, in our case, than not to have him, as we found out when he was in the hospital last winter, and Chief went many months unshod. For I knew better than to employ his rival. All would have been over between us then, most certainly. So I did little riding over that time, and when I began again, sparks flew between me and my steed, and it was many a day before I could be reasonably sure of coming back alive.

I spoke of Mr. R's rival, and I believe there is but one other blacksmith serving our countryside, for they are a vanishing race. Young men are not interested in entering the trade, Mr. R tells me ruefully; the veterinary courses are no longer including it. He is unable to get an assistant for what he is able to afford to pay from his intake, and he is an old man, unable to cover as much ground as he used to. That is the crux of the matter; there simply isn't enough money in it. Blacksmithing is one of the few primitive trades which operates unchanged by any new wonder process; I suppose it was never worth anyone's while to try to improve it.

But while blacksmiths, mobile in their vans, still do exist, the village smithy has passed forever, and I doubt if anywhere around there is one in use. It is not hard to see why. The other day a neighbor called me to say that she'd found a strange horse grazing in her field; did I know whose it might be? Well, it wasn't mine; I could see his red flank from the window, as he grazed beyond the vegetable garden. But it might be one of Frank McKean's, I told her; or perhaps belong to the new family that lived now on the Flick farm, and kept horses. As I hung up I realized suddenly that in all this valley, there are only three horse owners.

But nuisance or not, I'd regret never to have seen a white-hot shoe pounded on the anvil, heard the hiss of it when plunged in water. I should have been the loser never to have known Mr. R, stern individualist, man of his own mind. "And a mighty smith was he. . . ." But smiths are only mortal, like the rest of us, and when the last of them is gathered to his fathers, I suppose we will have to give him a Viking funeral, and entomb all the remaining horses with him.

BARBARA

STILLMEADOW

NOEL, NOEL:

The Yule log is big and sturdy, a last gracious gift from a big dead maple. The family is all here, the house bulges. The smell of pine and buttered popcorn, of mince pies and bayberry candles is all through the house, and most pleasant.

Last year we simply could not locate the Christmas tree stand, but this year we found three! Nice feeling to have extras. Connie came early and we did the tree, the old traditional angels came out, and the colored balls and the icicles, and the lights in the usual dreadful tangle. I thought I had them all straightened out when I put them away last year, but between times, they knotted themselves into a labyrinthine confusion. We wound and unwound, started over again, freed one circuit and the other two were worse than before.

Our lights are the old-fashioned kind, so that after we get them all on the tree, there is always one dead bulb. And it is always, always the last one you try.

Do you always think of all the other Christmas trees in your life when you trim the current one? I do. I remember my mother, pink-cheeked and with her brown eyes shining while Father lugged in a tree bigger than the room. He went to the woods and cut down the tallest and fattest. Then he would cut it down, muttering, "Confound this thing." I jumped up and down getting underfoot. I just couldn't wait to see again my little pink wax angel with the frilly wings. There she was, only a little battered by time.

We do the tree in blue and silver with just a few pinky rose balls for accent, and Connie made an extra tinsel leash for one silver angel and hung her down in a bald spot between branches so the tree was perfectly

267

balanced. We have not the heart to cut one of our five hundred Christmas trees planted according to George Bennett's stern command, so we bought a sturdy balsam. Spicy and green, it looks and smells delightful.

Roast goose for Christmas dinner, nothing left but a bone or two. I feel better when a ham is in reserve for the next meal, a flitch (lovely, lovely word that) of Canadian bacon. This time Burton sent us a huge package of bacon from a special place in Michigan. And we had Irish bacon from Don and Anne. None too much, for the children can eat a pound at breakfast, settled down with a dozen eggs and half a loaf of toasted bread. The Michigan bacon has a different flavor—I wonder if the little man who does it could use sassafras for smoking?

We keep those big spicy crisp apples from Pennsylvania in a bowl and the cheese board filled with Swiss Colony Cheese, so nobody has to suffer hunger very long.

We open our presents Christmas morning, with ceremony. Don is the grand master and hands out each package with a special remark. There is always the fine moment when we find that I have three identical Edith Piaf records and Don and Anne have two sets of glasses.

I am always amazed at the thoughtful gifts the children choose now they are grown up. The special small things that mean they consider what we really like.

On Christmas afternoon, we drink eggnog and listen to the records. My prize this year is a complete concert by my favorite tenor and good friend Glenn. With that and the Madame Schumanns' record of a Bach song, I could face anything.

We always give the house a present, too, for the house is a very important and real personality. This year it was some stainless steel flatware. A silver fork is a fine thing, but dip it once into scrambled eggs and you know what happens.

Most of the neighboring villages have Christmas contests for decorations, and it is pleasant to drive over the night roads and see the colored lights, the feathery pine swatches, the reindeer and Santa Clauses. I like the simple ones best although I do admire the perseverence of anyone who climbs up on the roof and establishes a complete set of Donner and Blitzen and Prancer and Dancer plus Santa and the sleigh!

We usually give a buffet supper during Christmas week; one year we had so many people that I could not get from the kitchen to the family room with a fresh hot casserole of baked beans! This year we felt puckish from having bad virus colds, and decided we had better forego the party, so we had a small buffet for ten or so. It is so much easier to have ten than forty, I decided, stacking the blessed dishwasher.

My favorite time is when night folds down quietly, and the hugger-

mugger is over, and the fire has fallen to embers, and the candles sputter with melting wax. And I can poke my nose out of doors and take a look at the stars while Sister and Jonquil and Teddy scrunch around.

The world rolls on her course, and Christmas comes, and we keep faith in God, in spite of any troubles we are heir to. Christmas is gay and bright, but Christmas is also renewing our belief that the Christ Child was not born in vain.

God rest you merry, Barbara,

GLADYS

SUGARBRIDGE

Aftermath

DEAR G

Christmas came with a rush, somehow was coped with, and went by like a rocket. There is a poem of Victor Hugo's which I had to learn in French, for my childish sins, and recite before school every morning for quite a while. It describes the approach, and disappearance of a troop of Djinns, quite marvelously expressing speed and noise by the meter, and the length of lines. Thinking back on both, Christmas was just like that.

Afterwards, it all telescoped into a composite memory of the most shining moments (luckily). The scarecrow we dressed up as Santa in my red shirt, a cotton beard, and white fur cap of mine, and put in Ned's room to surprise him on his return home; the midnight carol service we always go to—those ancient lovely songs hold the very essence of Christmas for me; the splendid spruce tree that Ned brought us all the way from Maine on top of his car, one of the handsomest Christmas trees we've ever had, bedecked with ornaments old and new; the old familiar Yuletide joy of seeing someone you love open your present which is for once just the right thing, you hope; the almost equal bliss of being given a thoughtful gift yourself; Ned's presents, this year, almost uncannily well chosen: a Hathaway shirt for Ed (Ned goes to Colby College near the home of Hathaway, prized by men above all other shirts), a Thoreau for me, one I'd never read: "The Maine Woods," and a Hans Kindler record, almost unobtainable now, and one of my favorites, since he was a friend. Then Christmas dinner, a perfect one this year: I cannot remember anything but goose, and just that whatever went with it was right. After, the blessed release of having my part of Christmas over; now I could begin to enjoy it. Then: a little gathering at the home of friends: on Christmas, I always have a childish delight in seeing what others received.

Before it is all quite gone, I am savoring much that went by so fast it could hardly be recorded. Though you certainly know by this time I am no ardent shopper, I still am not insensible to the color and drama of the streets at Christmas time. Particularly West Chester. Any little town is fun at that time of the year, but this one serves such a large rural area that the type of shoppers is amazingly varied. People of every age, nationality, shape, size and dress can be seen passing in and out of the five- and ten-cent store, if you wait long enough. I won't go so far as to rival the claim of the Café de la Paix in Paris that you'll see someone you know go by even if you are foreign to West Chester, but I'll stand by my original contention. The lights this year were prettier than any I've known; they gave the town the look of a carnival, and reflected rosily upon the faces of the Christmas shoppers, with their armloads of bundles. During the last days before Christmas, there was that feeling in the air, too; a sense of release from workaday routine: Christmas is coming; we're not going to care for the time being about fear of war, worries of subsistence, age, death, unhappiness or poverty!

STILLMEADOW

Dear B

While you burn the greens, Barabara, picture me madly sweeping up pine needles—they sink in the cracks between these old wide floorboards, and they CLING! Weeks afterward, I shall find a drift of balsam when I run the cleaner, and Jill will cry despairingly, Will we never get them all?

Jill chops up the tree and makes fine fires of it. The standard will sit on the well house for weeks, until we finally get around to putting it back somewhere where we can't find it next time.

Thinking it all over, I sat down yesterday with a cup of coffee and a basket of Christmas cards to re-read. What I think is that Christmas is too commercial by far in these days. In my childhood, Christmas giving was simpler and more personal. Mama made things for weeks ahead, delicate hand-stitched linens, knitted bedjackets or baby bootees. I made pen-wipers. Mama baked little fruit cakes, made plum puddings. And we packed the gifts in baskets tied with holly and ribbon and carried them around Christmas Eve. Nothing was expensive except of time. But everything was a true gift, something of the self that made it.

The excitement with which I carried the baskets around cannot be equaled today by the delivery of an expensive gadget.

I know one never can turn back the hands of time, but I sometimes think of those simpler and more innocent times. Boughten things were

271

never quite as special then as things made for the receiver by the giver. Wouldn't it be strange if we got back to something of that?

The blue shadows on the slopes are dazzling as we drive to the village for the daily give-and-take of the country store. It is a pure blue, I think cobalt, but I am no painter. The trees are charcoal against it, and the iced brook is almost silver, but underlaid with amber from the stony bottom. Mr. and Mrs. Woodpecker are so busy on the suet, and the chickadee almost sat on my shoulder when I carried the peanut butter jar out tonight. Some of the ground-feeding juncos have risen to the peanut butter feeder, ground birds or no. And the woodpeckers, who cannot perch on the tiny swaying perches, brace themselves on the trunk of the great sugar maple and stretch their necks until they too can have a snack. Good, they say, whacking their bills around.

The chickadees understand what I say to them, this I now know. Just a minute, I am bringing it, I say. Dee dee dee, say they, popping their sweet small heads around the tree trunk. Here it is, I tell them. Hurry up, say they—dee dee DEE.

The bluejays come early in the morning and act very important, walking like senators somehow. The sparrows have no routine, they just go on eating all day long.

We feel very smug having the pileated woodpeckers which are wood dwellers. Their proud heads are dramatic to look at. They come less often than the other birds, emerging just for a special dinner.

The brown creeper is new this year, a rather nervous little creature running up and down the trunk of the maple endlessly.

In season Faith Baldwin has mourning doves; we never see them. Since she lives not too far away, I deduce, in my limited fashion, that birds stay in a limited territory while they are there at all. She also has wood thrushes, which we never have had.

The whippoorwills have gone from us. We used to hear them in tranquil summer nights, we heard them all night long until we could not sleep. They were maddening birds. The mournful imperative sound was lost and lonely, although very romantic at first. If you hear a whippoorwill whippoorwilling endlessly all night long, you go mad. But now they are gone, I rather miss them. I suppose extra cultivation and new farmhouses going up made them move away—but where are they gone, I wonder?

I always knew we were coming into summer when that sad whippoorwill sounded from the swamp.

This is a shy bird, I have never seen one, in spite of being over-intimate with them for so long.

I did, however, last summer see a pair of bobwhites, which are also shy birds.

They strutted around with an air of sound and businesslike competence, plump and self-satisfied. Mister went ahead, Missus followed snapping up the better tidbits he had not seen. They talked to each other in an undertone. They were so near a house and they doubted the project. But they did like the hand-out, they admitted as they skipped into the brush.

Birds are fearfully time-consuming. I find myself bemused, watching to see whether the nuthatches will displace the sparrows on the feeder, whether the five earnest chickadees will cover the dining table sufficiently to protect it. Now and then a gray squirrel whisks down the great trunk of the sugar maple, thinks it over, and whisks back. I would be glad to feed him separately, but I do not want him to take the provender of my small ones.

We had a small unexpected fire on the stove yesterday, beef fat igniting while Jill turned her back. Our cleaning woman was disturbed when she came this morning, and insisted on climbing up and washing the ceiling. Tons of soot came off, tons of dirt, and the ceiling emerged pale and wan, but undeniably streaked. Trouble was she had to use steel wool pads, treated ones, to get the worst off and that made more trouble.

When you once get involved with paint, you are in difficulty. Jill decided to "touch up" a door which too many paws have batted at, and finds herself repainting a whole room, including walls. Or if she wants to do over a spot on the ancient black oak floor which some unhouse-broken puppy has used overmuch, she finds herself redoing the whole floor of the whole downstairs. She sighs, gets out the waxer and says, "One thing leads to another."

GLADYS

SUGARBRIDGE
"God bless us, every one . . ."

DEAR G,

I must tell about the Christmas visit to Miss K's house. "Heartwarming" is one of the expressions that is currently overworked. But it does say what I mean here, although if I had the time and patience I'm sure I could find something better.

Well, anyway, Ned and I went down on foot Christmas morning since the lane was impassable from remnants of a recent snow, and the usual mud. To take our customary offerings of cake and a bottle of sherry. Although I know Miss K, from her remarks, does very well on the wood-burning stove for their daily living, I think she hasn't the time, or perhaps facilities, to make a cake upon it; so I buy a very decorated one from the local baker; we always select for Mr. D a really good sherry, Amontillado, or Sandeman.

At the top of the last hill before we descended, I could see smoke rising from their chimney below, a plume of hope. Ah, they're there all right, I thought gladly (I hadn't seen them for some time). They're warm, and presumably well. Before we approached the door, we could see a little Christmas tree glowing in the window, by the light of lamps and candles. Miss K, her face flushed from the heat of the stove (there was little doubt about their being warm enough!) and we were ushered in to a scene of great activity. They accepted our gifts with pleasure, graciously; (this is one of their most admirable traits, their acceptance of whatever is given them) and began to to tell us about their Christmas dinner, which both of them were engaged in cooking, with a good deal of excitement, and some flurry. It sounded, and smelled, most savory, but as I realized it would take the undivided attention of both of them, I knew we must soon take our leave. Miss K pressed upon me some of her special turkey stuffing in a glass. I took away with me too, the feeling of their house, which stayed warm with me afterwards, a real Christmas-y feeling such as children have, and only a few favored grown-ups, of exhilarated living in the moment. As we departed, Mr. D said to Ned, fixing him with a dim old eye, "I pray every night that you'll graduate, my boy!"

Ned gave me a quick stricken look, before he ducked his head in acknowledgment. "Did he think I was that bad off?" he muttered to me as we regained the road.

Looking at his sleek crew-cut blond head, with the brown eyes enormous in the thin serious face, I wondered what Ned's reactions were to the visit. Patience with Mother's curious notions, I guessed; politeness to two old people with whom he could have little common ground. To my great surprise, as we trudged along, he burst out, "You know, I *like* that house! That great big fireplace and the Dutch oven. Built up against the hill that way, with the woods at the top, and the little stream beside it. . . ." He paused, thinking. "I could buy it, I guess, if they ever give it up. I'd like to fix it up, and live in it."

Dear me, I thought apprehensively, have I bequeathed my passion for odd nests, and out-of-the-way spots to this defenseless child? I said, "I know Miss K and Mr. D would be glad to move out of it if they could find another small country house in better repair."

He glanced at me reproachfully. But *you* are the one who loves old

274

houses, no matter what their condition, his eyes said, and solitude, yet now . . .

"Well, dear," I said, "the house has some nice features, and it is a pretty spot. But when you need a place to live, we'll find you one." Still, I knew what he had seen in it, for often, from childhood on, I'd had the same impulse . . . a tiny place, but your very own, to do with as you liked, far from the eyes of man. But there was something more here, too. Back there, his mind, like a sensitive plate, had received an impression of fiery independence and self-sufficiency, of determination and delight in simple things—all very attractive to the young.

I walked the rest of the way home, thoughtful and well pleased.

BARBARA

STILLMEADOW

GREETINGS FROM THE NORTH POLE,

or near it! driving lines of snow and sleet, the birds have tucked in under the pine branches, the dogs are snugged down on the hearth. Only poor Jill is out filling kennel heaters and doing last chores.

This sleety snow is very beautiful to watch, the angle of falling is so oblique. The straight tall perpendicular of the pines emphasizes the fall of the snow slantwise across it. It has, furthermore, a lonely look, as if the world were only snow and pines.

One solitary brave chickadee breasts the storm and clings precariously to the feeder, taking large gulps of peanut butter. Those delicate little feet must be cold, how can they help it? But when I open the door to visit with him, he cocks his head and says cheerily, "Chick a dee-dee DEE." He can manage.

I am minded of Smiley Burnette, the confirmed Californian. Says Smiley, "Why do you live where you fight the weather over half the time? Waste of energy."

But even Smiley wouldn't want every single soul in the United States to move to California. No room.

Imagine all of us who endure harsh winters packing up and loading cars and trailers and station wagons and moving to the land of sunshine and oranges? Sort of a Grapes of Wrath idea. No, Barbara, I guess we stay put where fate set our feet in the first place. We have winter, but we also have spring. We have cool running brooks, and deep blue lakes, and green, green woods. We have a lot, when you add it all up.

This is the time when we try to use the odds and ends in the freezer. The next two months should see the level lowered so we can restock come spring. We never come out even, does anybody? Days we eat squash, squash and squash. Days we have stew noon, stew at night.

But we are always running out of spinach which I love, dressed with lemon butter. It just goes with everything, according to me. Jill says, "I suppose you want some more rabbit food for dinner?"

Night comes sudden and soon. We follow the light, when it fails, I begin to think warmly of supper, and a good book savored by the fire. I tend to get up when the first fire of sun invades my window, and that is not early for it takes the sun quite a while to get around to me. If I do get up to let the dogs out very early, I am dazzled by the beauty of the winter morning sky, the pale and perfect glow, the still and cold beauty. I stand, shivering in my pajamas, waiting for the dogs, and my "forehead is lifted" as the colored woman said, seeing the purity and loveliness of the world at dawn.

We shall be shoveling in the morning. While I have been visiting with you, the flakes have grown bigger and fall with great purpose. The ground, which was icy and bare, is feathered over with white.

But Mr. Campo, who services all our electric units, has come in briskly to see why the refrigerator thaws everything in the freeze section and freezes everything in the lower part. It is a schizophrenic, I think, but he feels he can solve it. Sleet and snow make no difference to the servicemen, they are my heroes. They drive miles over impossible and impassable roads, they are always cheerful, and they are on time. Without them, where would the modern country dweller be?

Hoping you need none right now,
Me

Sugarbridge
"Christmas gambol"
(Sir Walter Scott, of all people)

Dear Gladys

It was suddenly surprising fun to go to parties this holiday season. Ned, as a little boy, used to say to us, wondering and rather reproachful, "The other children say to me, 'We never see your parents at parties.'" We were amused at this, and secretly a little worried. Was this going to make him feel different from his fellows? We'd always put him first when we could. But we couldn't have done much about this, even if

277

we'd tried. A business job in the city, as well as careers for both parents, topped off with the difficulties of a country home, left no trickle of time over for a social life. As it turned out, our son went blithely on his way through a very social period during which time our house was so crammed with teen-agers that often neighbors down the road thought traffic had been re-routed this way because of some accident. Now, I must add, Ned is in a getting-away-from-it-all stage, and sighs with relief on returning from some large rout to which he has been forced to go. "Gosh! I'm glad I don't have to do that every night!" he says, just like us. Perhaps this similarity frightened us momentarily into amending our ways.

In any case, our little fling was a revelation to us. How gay and care-free, how charming these people seemed! Those I'd known only slightly became suddenly dear to me, in the short space of an evening. What had I been missing all this time? I had for the moment a wonderful warm sense of being part of it all. Would this feeling last, if I continued in the giddy round? I cannot tell, because of course I didn't. Life took care of that.

But on a certain night, after one of these evenings of revelry, having fallen exhausted into bed, I awoke suddenly, my heart pounding from too many cigarettes, too little sleep, too much talking, the most over-stimulating of all. Then I heard Duke rise up, from his bed in the hall, shake himself with a sound like a pistol shot, and begin to pace restlessly. This heralds a not-unusual midnight quandary. If he continues to walk the floor, I know I must arise, and take him out. If on the contrary, he returns to his bed, makes a couple of turns, and lets himself down with a resounding thud, it means I can safely go back to sleep again. I listened tensely to learn my fate, but no reassuring thump. Instead, he came in and nosed me, so I got up, not too unwillingly this time, since I began to feel restless myself. Downstairs, I put on fur-lined boots, and my storm coat with the hood. It was just three o'clock in the morning. We put our noses out the door. The air was very cold, like dry ice. But what a glory! It made me gasp. The night was very still and deep and quiet, almost holy, in a strange way, lit with innumerable stars. We crunched forward over the frozen ground, and then I stopped and stared. There were stars above, but what was this? Stars beneath our feet, too; frost stars, I saw, bending down, so big and glowing and iridescent, as I had never even imagined before. The ground was alive with them, each blade and twig boasted its own private jewel. I stood still, drinking it in. The stillness and the brilliance were as grateful as water to a parched throat.

We walked then, Duke and I, down to the barn to see how Chief did. This is always my first thought on a cold night. But we found him quite cozy, and drowsily surprised to see us. He started up out of a nest of straw, arranged to his own taste, his blanket as usual awry. When we left, after I'd straightened it for him, he sank back with a relieved sigh. I resolved never again to worry about creatures that sleep outside without much protection in winter. There must be a wondrous vitality, a secret underlying strength that comes up from the earth, however frozen, and sustains them—all the furry things in their lairs, the birds tucked away in their nests. I'd like it myself, I thought, if I were hardy enough. How stuffy indoors is going to seem after this!

When we came back to the house, I simply could not go in. Walking in this world of wonder was a never-ending delight. So up the lane we went, and when we reached the orchard, we took the hill path, and mounted it. Always the frost stars flamed underfoot, and over us, Aldebaran and Orion, and all the company of heaven shed their glory. From the top of the hill, we could see away in all directions; the great bare slopes, faintly brown, lay naked under the brilliant skies which lit them up clear as day. The silence was complete, with no sign of life at all, not even a rabbit scuttering through the bushes. Only, far, far away, a light from a distant barn gleamed.

The big dog walked along docilely beside me, not straining at his leash as he usually does in the open. Every moment I became more myself. I could feel my ego flowing back like a warm tide, building *my* world up around me again, my projects and occupations, my thoughts and beliefs. Too much talking dissipates a personality, I thought, and realized then that unconsciously I had always known this; you tear off a little bit of yourself for each person.

It was curiously like a dream, this walk; only we did not float, as you do in dreams. We continued to crunch over the hard ground, and came finally home down the slope behind the house, having traversed the length of our land, to drink hot milk, well peppered, with a big lump of butter in it, sitting in the kitchen at four a.m.

Well, it's almost time to ring out the old, ring in the new. This was a good enough year, with its own triumphs and failures. There'll be another along soon, presenting its unwritten slate. That is our hope. I like to think that there is always another chance with anything that really matters; you may lose your looks, or your lover, or a friend, but not your faith in ultimate good, or your courage. There's always another year to try in, another book to write—and, who knows?—another life. Although we do not know why or how, the manner or the purpose.

BARBARA

DEAR BARBARA:

A steady deep snow has piled drifts along the picket fence, the old windowpanes are silver, the hemlocks are bowed with a burden of glory. The birds are deep in the pines, the trees quiver with them.

I think I can see the bird of time sitting on the snowy well house, wings folded, head bent. Reluctant to go into the new tomorrow, he stays a moment, one wise and wary eye on this old white farmhouse, one closed against the falling snow.

As I sweep the snow from the doorsill, I think if we could gather up all the happy hours of a year and distill them, we would have Heaven. If we added the dreary and sad times, we would no doubt, have a good foretaste of a lower region.

The bright and the dark are so inseparable.

Every life, I think, has a burden of sorrow, and every life has also the delicate excitement of happiness. Cherishing the golden hours and forgetting the black ones probably make for the happy person, the fulfilled life.

As the old year vanishes into the land that no one can ever visit again, I can see the New Year coming with a pale pure fire into the old darkness of the night sky.

I always hope I can meet the tomorrows with more strength, more courage and more love than I have ever met the past with.

The snow has stopped, the stars are shining.

GLADYS

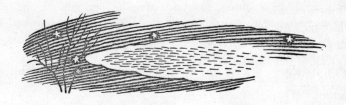

SUGARBRIDGE
The Studio

DEAR GLADYS (*friend*)
and
BARBARA (*wife*)

It's almost epoch-making that a male should have the last word—especially with *two* women.

Since I have undertaken to be companion, husband, editorial-consultant, amanuensis, filing-clerk, as well as illustrator, in this collaboration, there should be—if Justice still exists—some reward besides a harp and a halo.

And because letters still flow between Stillmeadow and Sugarbridge and this book has to end somewhere I seem to be Atropos, the third Fate who snips the cord.

So I have the chance to make a few observations of my own about living in Chester County, Pennsylvania and Southbury Township, Connecticut.

I am an urban man, or was until marriage. The city streets were my environment and I doubt if I knew a maple tree from a sycamore—or a rose from a phlox.

When Barbara informed me—shortly after we'd been joined in holy matrimony—that from this day hence I not only had to love, honor and obey, but also live in the country, I was, to put it mildly, appalled.

But year by year the call of the city became fainter, and now I know that never again could I exist in one, even though it would be in a penthouse overlooking Rittenhouse Square.

But during this time I have reached other conclusions; one being that no man can live in the country unless accompanied by a woman with a passionate love of the land.

I do not mean that a solitary male might not be able to survive, but it would not be long before he was lost in honeysuckle, bunch grass, weeds and sumac, as well as being over-run by field mice, rabbits and tent caterpillars.

For when I should be mowing the lawn, I am off searching for snakes; the orchard would stay forever unpruned because I admire the manner in which the slender sucker limbs spring out of the gnarled boughs. The weeds would take over the garden while I merely sat in the sun, basking in the little court back of the studio.

Only a resolute woman can successfully oppose the green onslaught of Nature. I'm sure that every feminine country dweller has in her veins some of the blood of that wonderful female, Mrs. Daniel Boone.

And I'm consoled for approaching age, by remembering the story of how, when Boone was eighty and so crippled by rheumatism as to be unable to walk without crutches, that Rebecca Boone—herself nearing the four-score mark—went with him on his last bear hunt, carrying his Kentucky rifle, powder horn and bullet pouch.

When they met the bear, she propped Daniel against a tree, loaded the rifle, and held his crutches while he shot the poor beast.

You, Gladys, will carry my paintbox; you, Barbara, my easel, so I can envision myself going on a last hunt—not for bear, since I'm not a killing man—but to make a drawing, perhaps of some small ancient farmhouse, hidden in the folded hills.

As ever,
Ed